PELICAN BOOKS

THE WEAPONS CULTURE

Dr. Lapp's association with the nuclear community goes back to 1943, when he was an associate physicist with the Manhattan Project. Since then he has served with the Argonne Laboratory in Chicago, as consulting scientist at the Bikini Bomb Tests in 1946, adviser to the War Department General Staff, executive director of the Research and Development Board, head of the nuclear physics branch of the Office of Naval Research, and since 1950, as consulting physicist of the Nuclear Science Service.

THE WEAPONS CULTURE

Ralph E. Lapp

PENGUIN BOOKS INC
BALTIMORE MARYLAND

Penguin Books Inc
7110 Ambassador Road
Baltimore, Maryland 21207

First published by W. W. Norton & Co. 1968
Published in Pelican Books 1969
Copyrighted © 1968 by W. W. Norton & Co.
Introduction to the Pelican Edition
Copyrighted © 1969 by Ralph E. Lapp

SBN 14 021138 1

Printed in The United States of America
by Kingsport Press.

to

H. J. Muller

who through the wings of the fruit fly
perceived the nature of man.

Contents

Introduction for
the Pelican Edition

At the moment when General Eisenhower died, I was sitting in the hearing room of the U.S. Senate Foreign Relations Committee. An investigation into the Nixon Administration's proposed Safeguard anti-ballistic missile program was under way. When a television man informed the committee of General Eisenhower's death, Senator J. W. Fulbright concluded the day's hearing by noting Eisenhower's great contributions.

Senator Fulbright recalled Eisenhower's Farewell Address and his warning about the danger of a "military-industrial complex." "Time has confirmed his judgment in a most dramatic way," observed the chairman of the Foreign Relations Committee. He added: "I hope we will take his advice more seriously in the future." To those who listened to the sessions of the committee's inquiry into the Safeguard system, it was clear that Senator Fulbright regarded the U.S. decision to build up its ballistic defenses as a turning point in the strategic arms race—an intersection from which there might be no road back.

Eisenhower's death came a little over eight years after he gave his Farewell Address. In turning over the power of the Presidency to the youthful John F. Kennedy, Eisenhower gave profoundly good advice on arms policy. The tragedy of President Kennedy is that from his inaugural day he set forth on the old path of military power—"arms beyond doubt"—a policy that could serve to instill doubt. It proved to be a blank check to the powerful interests formed by the fusion of military, industrial and political components of the American arms establishment.

The eight years of the Kennedy-Johnson era saw the United States spend over $500 billion on its armaments. In 1969 when President Nixon took office he chose for his Secretary of Defense Melvin Laird, a man having a well advertised view on the arms race. In a word it amounted to "superiority." To be sure, President Nixon's first press conference featured the concept of "nuclear sufficiency" but this rhetoric permitted a wide range of interpretation. The Nixon Administration inherited an ABM system known as Sentinel which was beginning to be deployed as a "thin" defense for U.S. cities. Work had already begun in the metropolitan area of Chicago, Boston and other cities when public opposition forced the White House to interrupt construction.

Following a high level review of the overall problem of ballistic-missile defense, President Nixon announced the Safeguard system. This emerged as a phased system, politically sculpted to quiet opposition in the cities and designed primarily to protect part of the U.S. Minuteman force of intercontinental missiles. That the U.S. deterrent force was in need of being shored up came as a surprise to students of U.S. defense policy. Defense Secretary Robert S. McNamara had made a fetish of long-range planning and had programmed strategic forces on a 5-year budget, allowing for contingencies to meet "greater than expected threats."

Defense Secretary Laird proceeded to justify the necessity for defense of U.S. missile sites on the basis of the future threat of a single Soviet weapons system—the SS-9 missile. He disclosed that this heavyweight intercontinental weapon was a liquid-fueled missile, capable of carrying a 20-to-25-megaton warhead. This would be a hydrogen weapon having almost two thousand times the power of the Hiroshima A-bomb. (U.S. estimates rate the power of this 1945 bomb at 13 to 14 kilotons or 0.013 to 0.014 megatons.) Mr. Laird made the assertion that the Soviets would have 500 of these supermissiles by 1976. Most surprisingly, the new Defense Secretary maintained that the SS-9 was a first-strike weapon. Thus were enemy intent and capability specified for a single weapons system— a rather unorthodox overture in arms policy.

Possibly the new men at the top of the Pentagon's hierarchy were depending on the American people to respond to a megaton scare and rush to the support of the Safeguard program. Surely the Defense Department could count on strong support from the U.S. Senate Armed Services Committee. But in shifting the basis of an ABM program to defense of Minuteman missiles, the Pentagon invited public scrutiny of nuclear policy. For one thing, the history of its justification of ABM systems was one of ambiguity and debatable validity. At first the Sentinel system had been geared to the threat of Chinese nuclear irrationality—that sometime in the seventies Red China would possess ICBMs and might launch a reckless attack on the United States. When the timetable for Red China's missiles lengthened, due to the political turbulence of Chairman Mao's latter days, the Pentagon's Red China case weakened.

Senator Richard B. Russell, veteran chairman of the Armed Services Committee, summed up his attitude on the Sentinel in an interview published in *Atlanta* magazine in 1968.

Q. Senator Russell, this so-called 'thin' system is just a foot in the door to beginning construction on the full or heavy ABM system, isn't it?

A. It's a base for a system throughout the whole nation. I didn't deceive anybody. When we brought it up they tried to dress it up as being designed to protect us from China. But I stated very frankly on the floor of the Senate that I consider it the foundation of a complete antimissile system that would save at least eighty million Americans against any atomic attack, however drastic.

In other words, Senator Russell viewed the Sentinel system as the beginning of a "thick" anti-Soviet defense. His candor in speaking of Pentagon deception raises profoundly disturbing questions about the management of U.S. defense policy. Here we sense something deeply hostile to a democracy—the confluence of forces within the defense power structure to promote weapons systems on a false base.

Perhaps the most disturbing aspect of the Sentinel system was that it could be interpreted by Soviet planners as the foundation of a "thick" nationwide defense that could deny the destructive potential of a Soviet second-strike. Should the United States erect such a stout ballistic shield, the Soviets would have no choice but to respond by increasing the strength of their deterrent forces. Only in this way could they be sure of maintaining the balance of what Winston Churchill called "mutual terror."

President Nixon acknowledged the provocative nature of a "thick" city ABM defense but his Safeguard system still contained many seeds for suspicion on the part of the Soviets. Phase I of Safeguard would deploy ABM defenses around 200 Minuteman missiles at the Montana Malmstrom base and about 150 Minutemen near Grand Forks, North Dakota. Phase II would extend light ABM coverage across the nation, but no city except Washington D.C. (the National Command Authority) would be specifically defended. The total system would cost up to $7 billion with coverage extended to Alaska and Hawaii. Thus it was not a "sharply cut back" system as claimed by its proponents.

Many defense experts were puzzled by Secretary Laird's evaluation of the Soviet threat to U.S. security because they remembered that Secretary McNamara had made quite a different evaluation early in 1968. Mr. McNamara stated:

"I want, however, to make one point patently clear; our current numerical superiority over the Soviet Union in reliable, accurate, and effective warheads is both greater than we had originally planned, and is in fact more than we require.

Moreover, in the larger equation of security, our 'superiority' is of limited significance—since even our current superiority, or indeed with any numerical superiority realistically attainable, the blunt, inescapable fact remains that the Soviet Union could still—with its present forces—effectively destroy the United States, even after absorbing the full weight of an American first strike."

Clearly, Mr. McNamara pictured a situation in which neither the United States nor the Soviet Union could possess a true first-strike capability. Each side would retain the power of retaliatory devastation and this prospect would be the basis for keeping the nuclear peace. Mr. McNamara's successor, Secretary Clark Clifford, agreed with this viewpoint and his "posture statement" of January 15, 1969 expressed confidence in the adequacy of U.S. deterrent forces. Yet within two months, Secretary Laird summoned forth a terrifying view of an emerging Soviet "first-strike capability." Had there been any basic change in the intelligence about the SS-9? This weapons system had been known to U.S. officials for over 4 years and had been orbitally detected in deployment in 1966. On March 20, 1969 the SS-9 was described as capable of carrying a 25 megaton warhead and as "a very dangerous weapon in terms of attacking the Minuteman sites of our missile force." It was asserted that it gave the Soviets a "low-risk, first-strike capability."

On March 20, 1969 the SS-9 was singled out as the primary threat to Minuteman. Yet testimony that day disclosed that the Soviet deployment of this missile amounted to 200 SS-9s and that Mr. Laird said the intelligence community projected a total of 500 by 1976. Even if every one of these 500 SS-9s could be launched successfully and even if every one scored a bull's eye strike—a military impossibility considering the fallibility of modern weapons systems—only half the U.S. ICBM force could be destroyed. This would be far from a "low risk" as is evident from inspection of data disclosed by Mr. McNamara a year earlier. He projected the following statistics resulting from a hypothetical U.S. retaliatory attack on Soviet cities:

| Number of warheads | Soviet Fatalities | | Industrial Destruction |
(1 megaton)	Millions	Percent	Percent of Capacity
100	37	15	59
200	52	21	72
400	74	30	76
800	96	39	77
1200	109	44	77
1600	116	47	77

Testifying before the Congress, Mr. McNamara stressed the fact that the 400 warhead figure represented "unacceptable losses" to the Soviet Union. Here it should be added that his figures under-estimate total damage since they refer to "prompt deaths", that is, mortality resulting from primary weapons effects producing lethality in 24 hours. No account is made for secondary weapons effects or for deaths due to lack of food, shelter or medical aid.

Soviet planners must have a damage table very similar to Mr. McNamara's. Whatever first strike reckoning they may have made—assuming a first strike to be their intent—they must always keep uppermost in their minds the ultimate calculus of deterence, namely, the damage expected by return fire. Only if the return fire or second strike is so weak that the resulting damage imposes "acceptable" damage on the Soviet homeland can a first strike be labeled "low risk." Just what may constitute "acceptable" return fire is subject to much uncertainty, but a limit might be estimated as 150 city-strikes corresponding to 40 or more million deaths and six-tenths destruction of industrial capacity. If we accept such a value then we can make estimates of how effective a Soviet first strike must be. Since we are talking about the future we need to project U.S. retaliatory force-loadings or warheads to some time in the seventies. By 1975 the U.S. diversified deterrent can add up to a force-loading of 10,000 warheads.

The U.S. deterrent forces comprise nuclear explosives deliverable via a variety of air-space corridors. In the case of the Minuteman force the trajectory is a high ballistic arc over the Arctic. Shorter range missiles based in Europe have less lofty trajectories. The ocean-based deterrent force consists of SLBMs, submarine-launched ballistic missiles of the Polaris and Poseidon class. In addition to these ballistic modes of delivery, there is also the B-52 bomber, as well as shorter range aircraft based in Europe and on aircraft carriers. The diversity and geographic spread of this deterrent deployment make it impossible for Soviet strategies to target the complete system in a synchronized blitz. There is, for example, no feasible way to stage a first strike that would impose a wave of warheads on all U.S. launchers or air bases at the same time. Yet when Defense Secretary Laird pinned his case for ABM defense of Minuteman on the SS-9 weapons system, he apparently assumed that the rest of the U.S. strike forces were somehow neutralized. He so boxed himself in on this assumption that he was later forced to make mysterious references to future weapons against submarines.

But even if we assume that Soviet planners could forget about all except Minuteman ICBMs, thus duplicating Mr. Laird's case for ABM defense, their problem would still be formidable. For example, military planners are schooled always to making maximum assumptions about the enemy. In this case, the worst to be conceived of by the Soviet planners is that the U.S. Minutemen would not ride out a first strike, that is staying in their protective silos. Rather, they would be launched on radar intelligence of a massive first strike aimed at them. In such a case, Soviet warheads would be targeted on empty holes, and retaliation to an "unacceptable" degree would be on its way even before SS-9 warheads impacted in the missile fields.

All of these considerations were well known to Defense Secretary McNamara. They account for his confidence that the Soviets would not be tempted to a suicidal first strike at the sites of U.S. strategic power. Why then did Secretary Laird go overboard in his assessment of the SS-9? It soon became clear that he had in mind the threat of multiple warheads carried by the heavyweight ICBM. He proceeded to define a threat-potential in which the SS-9 could carry 4 or 5 individually targeted warheads, that is the MIRV or Multiple, Independently targetable, Reentry Vehicles. Thus if all SS-9s built to date were retrofitted with MIRVs and all future SS-9s also equipped with five warheads, the Soviet Union could have a total of 2,500 MIRVs by 1976.

It might at first appear that such a MIRV force would constitute a sure-fire, knock-out capability when directed at 1,000 Minuteman silos. It's a mathematical possibility but far from a militarily-attractive proposition if we consider a number of technical and targeting difficulties. First, it's important to bear in mind that the split-up of a single 25-megaton warhead into 5 MIRVs does not produce five 5-megaton warheads. Former Deputy Defense Director Paul Nitze pointed out in Senate testimony that a single warhead rated at 10 megatons would split up into ten 0.05 megaton MIRVs. Here the total yield of the ten MIRVs would be 0.5 megatons so that the split-up means a 20-fold reduction in total explosiveness for the weapon package. Making very liberal estimates of Soviet nuclear capability, we may credit the Soviet Union with the development of five 1-megaton MIRVs for the SS-9.

We must now inquire into the statistics of silo-killing, using 1-megaton warheads of the MIRV type. Numbers are all-important in the deadliest of all games—deterrence—and they are ultrasignificant for an enemy calculating a first strike. Everything depends upon how reliable the MIRV system becomes in the mid-1970s when a 2500 MIRV warhead force becomes a technical possibility. How many of the SS-9s can be safely committed to a first strike? Some, of course, have to be reserved for follow-up strikes and for intimidation of cities. Let's assume a first-strike commitment of 400 SS-9s with a throw capacity of 2,000 MIRVs, each 1-megaton in power.

Let's assume further that 80 percent of these are successfully launched. That's a potential of 1,600 warheads available for MIRVing.

Now we have to put ourselves in the shoes of Soviet planners and see how they may look upon the MIRVing operation. After all, MIRVing takes place when the final rocket stage has boosted the MIRV package to a velocity capable of tossing it over a 5,000 mile range. The MIRVing process aims warhead number 1 at its pre-assigned target and the vectoring vehicle then dispatches it with a velocity increment sufficient to reach the geographic coordinates of the missile silo. Then magnetic-taped instructions reorient the vectoring device and add an additional velocity increment so that warhead number 2 is targeted on its assigned silo, and so forth until all five MIRVs have been dispatched. This is high technology, to say the least, and Soviet planners, or we in their shoes, have to appraise the chances that the mechanism will work and how accurately the warheads will be dispatched. Let's assume 80 percent success in MIRVing, so that 1,280 warheads proceed along their intended trajectories.

At this point we need to worry about the 20-percent MIRV failures as well as the 20-percent SS-9 launch aborts. Presumably—for reasons that will become apparent—each MIRV would be targeted on a separate silo and an SS-9 malfunction would leave five silos inadequately targeted. Providing missile redundancy is a very difficult matter for MIRVed vehicles since the taped program for each set of silos would be different. Furthermore, whereas the failure of a single-warhead ICBM to reach its target can be observed, there is less time to monitor the MIRV sequence and to be sure that the Minuteman fields are properly targeted. These MIRVing uncertainties degrade the coverage of the Minuteman fields.

Now we come to the biggest dilemma of all for Soviet planning—the accuracy of the MIRV warheads. Listed below are the number of warheads of 1-megaton power that have to be allocated to each silo to produce a 95 percent probability of knocking out the missile site:

Accuracy	1.0	0.75	0.50	0.25	n. miles
Number of warheads	25	13	7	2	

Obviously the Soviet planners have an impossible problem if all they can depend on is 1-mile accuracy in the MIRV system. It would make no sense to target a silo with 25 MIRV warheads, costing 6 or 7 SS-9s at launch time, since it would be more profitable to use single-warheaded SS-9s. The choice is still in favor of single warheads for three-quarter mile accuracy and only when less than half-mile accuracy can be guaranteed does the decision shift to MIRVed systems. With quarter-mile accuracy a single SS-9 can target two silos.

No one, not even the Soviet experts at this time, can know what accuracy SS-9 MIRVs may have in the mid-1970s. Since the first strike represents a salvo or very rapid fire of SS-9s, military men may be dubious about attaining test-range accuracy under war conditions. This is a great imponderable in the calculus of deterrence especially from the U.S. point of view. A Defense Secretary must err on the side of caution. He will have to assume that the Soviets can attain missile accuracy with MIRVs somewhere between a quarter and a half mile. This means that the 1,280 MIRVed warheads in our hypothetical Soviet first-strike could knock out from 185 to 640 Minuteman silos.

Thus even under the most extreme assumptions 360 Minutemen would still be available for a retaliatory strike. Each one would be armed with a minimum of 3 MIRVs so the return fire would add up to over one thousand warheads. Of course we have confined the analysis to the Minuteman, neglecting the remainder of the deterrent force deployed at sea, on land or in the air. The conclusion seems inescapable that Defense Secretary Laird exercised precipitous judgment in his evaluation of the Soviet threat in the SS-9 weapons system. The compulsion to come up with some politically acceptable ABM system may have warped the judgment of Pentagon officials. Senator Albert Gore, who heads the disarmament subcommittee of the Foreign Relations Committee, once described the Safeguard system as one "in search of a mission." The decision to orient the ABM system originally called Sentinel to a modified version named Safeguard was yet another shift in defense policy, giving support to Senator Gore's suspicion about the system.

Whatever the justification for defending Minuteman bases with a hard-point missile defense, we may inquire how effective such an ABM defense might be. This is not an idealized situation in which one designs a defense specifically to protect a single-point target but rather one in which we must consider how a defense system originally projected for city defense can be deployed to defend the Minuteman fields in Montana and North Dakota. It's important to make the distinction between the real and ideal hard-point defense because of the transformation of Sentinel into Safeguard protection of Minuteman fields, which were not planned to be ABM-protected when they were laid out.

Under the Safeguard concept Minuteman silos would be protected by a one-two missile punch. The long-range Spartan interceptor would be alerted by Perimeter Acquisition Radar and then vectored toward the incoming warhead by Missile Site Radar.

Interception would take place at an altitude of over 100 miles in space and at a slant range of over 400 miles from the silo. Should this space burst from a 4-megaton Spartan warhead fail to kill the hostile warhead, the shorter-range Sprint comes into play by detonating a 10-kiloton explosive in the earth's atmosphere. The initial deployment of Spartans and Sprints would be limited by the $2.1 billion cost of Phase I in the Safeguard program. Land acquisition, radars and communications gear would leave only about $1.5 billion for procurement and deployment of interceptor-missiles. The Spartan carries a price tag of $3 million each and the Sprint $2 million. Allowing for ground environment, the allocated funds would buy only about 400 or so ABMs. Herein lies basis for doubt that the Safeguard System could provide much protection for the Minuteman fields.

Again let us consider the problem from the Soviet viewpoint. How many warheads would Soviet planners allocate in staging an attack on the 350 Minuteman bases in the Montana-North Dakota fields? We have already seen that each silo would have to be targeted with a minimum of 3 warheads. Therefore the total commitment would be about 1,000 warheads. Since ABMs would be deployed to protect the silos, Soviet experts would have to allow additional warheads to override these defenses. Suppose that they assume that they match one additional warhead for every Spartan and Sprint. This would mean a total of 1,400 or so warheads committed to the attack. Because the figure of 3 warheads per silo is very marginal, Soviet experts would no doubt add decoys and penetration aids to their attack. A safe assumption would be that ABMs in the Minuteman fields would look up at some two thousand hostile incoming objects.

U.S. command and control of the ABMs, some 400 in number, would have to make decisions (many of them preattack decisions programed into the fire-control systems) limiting the launch of Spartans and Sprints. Some would have to be held in reserve for successive attacks and others would have to be allocated to defense of the vulnerable radars. Assuming that each Spartan and Sprint could make one warhead-kill, the defense could achieve considerably less than 20-percent effectiveness. This would mean the Safeguard ABM defenses would provide only "thin" protection for the U.S. ICBMs. This is not surprising in that Safeguard is a modification of the Sentinel System that was designed to give "thin" defense for U.S. cities.

In the case of hardened Minuteman bases an ABM may make its intercept very close to the silo,—"right on the deck," so to speak. The hardened silo can withstand the blast of a Sprint warhead burst only 200 yards above the silo. Even if it served to trigger the 1-

megaton warhead of an incoming missile the latter could explode more than a thousand yards above the silo without incapacitating the Minuteman inside. For this reason a point defense could be devised using very short-range, relatively inexpensive missiles. However, the site plan for the Minuteman fields makes defense difficult even with ABMs tailored to hard-point defense. Minuteman silos have been located 7 or more miles from each other, so that a concentration of ABMs is hard to achieve. Furthermore, as Senator Fulbright asked a witness during the 1969 ABM investigation: "Do you really believe the Department of Defense would be interested in an inexpensive missile?"

The fortunes of the military-industrial complex, specifically those of the aerospace contractors, are deeply involved in the ABM program. No other single program offers such sales potential as that related to the production of Spartans, Sprints and the complex radars needed to alert and guide these missiles. Despite Defense Secretary Laird's well-known enthusiasm for strategic missile superiority, the authorization of more ICBMs was challenged by the sheer magnitude of the U.S. strategic strike-force of 10,000 nuclear warheads already programmed under the McNamara regime. Adding to the strategic weapon arsenal would test the temper of the U.S. Senate, especially that of the Foreign Relations Committee. This committee's 1969 ABM investigations marked a change in the tradition of the Senate. In the ordinary course of event the Defense Department, aided by powerful spokesmen on the Senate Armed Services Committee, was accustomed to see its money bills slide through Congress with little opposition. However in 1969 a number of factors merged to create a formidable confrontation between many Senators and the proponents of ever greater commitments to arms. The effect of the long war in Vietnam, the staggering cost of defense hardware such as the controversial F-111, incidents such as the *Pueblo* affair off the coast of Korea and the deepening tragedy of America's domestic dilemmas combined to bring the defense budget under a critical examination.

In this connection respected senators like Majority Leader Mike Mansfield viewed the defense problem in a new perspective. "I see no safety for this nation in bristling and burnished missiles," Senator Mansfield told his fellow senators, "whether they stand tall around deteriorating cities, or rise in the empty fields of an impoverished rural society." Stressing the importance of the Sentinel (renamed Safeguard) decision, the Montana legislator observed: "The decision for or against deployment of the Sentinel, in the present circumstances, may well determine the basic direction of public leadership for a decade or more." Not long later, Senator Allen Ellender of Louisiana, taking a strong stand against the Safeguard system, put the issue squarely in the framework of the military-industrial complex. "Some of us in Congress have become captives of the military," the Senator stated on the floor of the Senate. "We are on the verge of becoming a militaristic society."

A real test of the power of the military-industrial complex will come when aerospace sales drop off and worker lay-offs telegraph their meaning to legislators. In 1968 total aerospace sales hit a peak of $30 billion, about three-fourths of this total being accounted for by a single customer—the U.S. Government. In the same year General Dynamics and Lockheed Aircraft together had a total of over $4 billion in prime military contract awards or roughly 85 percent of their sales. Such a government-industry relationship must be described as tantamount to defense socialism. It operates within a figurative triangle bounded on two sides by the Pentagon and by industry and at the base by Congress, the funding agency. This military-industrial-political triangle sticks together by virtue of the enclosed labor force and the worker-voter.

The military-industrial complex has strong internal bonds created by the constant diffusion of industrialists into the Pentagon's hierarchy and the employment of retired military officers by industry. When David Packard was appointed Deputy Director of Defense the question of conflict of interest and influence arose but was quixotically resolved by the very size of the multimillionaire's equity in the Hewlett-Packard Company. Disposing of his 3,550,000 shares of stock, valued at over $300 million, would have broken the market. This leads one to conclude that there must be some intermediate peak of stock ownership (obviously zero shares mean no conflict) where a real conflict of interest is involved.

The diffusion of ex-generals, admirals and officers of lower rank to defense industry was recently studied by the Joint Economic Committee under Senator William Proxmire of Wisconsin. As of February 1969 it was reported that 100 contractors employed some 2,072 retired officers of the rank of colonel or Navy captain and above. Half of these individuals were employed by the following ten companies (dollar value of defense contracts for fiscal year 1968 are tabulated and appears on following page).

Illustrating the pressure relationship between such employment and the ABM issue is the fact that 9 companies involved in the Safeguard program employ 465 high ranking military officers. There is of course nothing improper in defense industry negotiating contracts to fulfill military needs. Nor, as arms advocate Senator Henry Jackson said to a convention of Associated General Contractors of America in Washington, D.C., is there anything inherently wrong in defense industry employing retired officers and utilizing their managerial talents. "Today some people talk as though the reason

Company	Ex-officers Employed	Defense Contracts
1. Lockheed Aircraft Corp.	210	$1,870 million
2. Boeing Co.	169	762 ”
3. McDonnell Douglas Corp.	141	1,101 ”
4. General Dynamics	113	2,239 ”
5. North American-Rockwell	104	669 ”
6. General Electric Co.	89	1,489 ”
7. Ling-Temco-Vought Inc.	69	758 ”
8. Westinghouse Electric Corp.	59	251 ”
9. TRW, Inc.	56	127 ”
10. Hughes Aircraft Co.	55	286 ”
	1,065	$9,552 million

for our big defense program is some treacherous plan by American generals and industrialists," he said. The degree of coordination required by the far-flung military-industrial complex to organize a massive conspiracy is too great for such a threat to be taken seriously. But growing segments of the military-industrial complex think alike so that the power of this complex is like the confluence of many small streams flooding into a mighty river.

When industrial contractors grow accustomed to depending on military contracts they become permanently unfit for the hurly-burly of the competitive marketplace. If, then, military orders go into decline there is always the possibility that such companies may seek to use undue influence to win new contract awards. In the spring of 1969, Senator Proxmire commented on influence of the military-industrial complex in a Senate speech:

"I speak today not to warn against some future danger of this influence. I assert that, whether sought or unsought, there is today unwarranted influence by the military-industrial complex resulting in excessive costs, burgeoning military budgets, and scandalous performances."

Detailing contractor failures to meet standards and specifications, defective military hardware and shocking costs, the Wisconsin Senator concluded:

"The problem of defense spending is out of control. The system is top heavy. The military-industrial complex now writes its own budgetary ticket."

The extent to which some companies depend on and plan for more defense business was explored by an enterprising Washington *Post* reporter Bernard D. Nossiter late in 1968. In a series of exclusive interviews with aerospace executives, he revealed that some of America's largest contractors have made corporate plans geared to winning more defense awards. For example, one Texas-based company, Ling-Temco-Vought (LTV) disclosed plans to double present defense sales of $530 million in LTV Aerospace by 1973. LTV Aerospace owns only 1 percent of 6.7 million square feet of office-laboratory-factory space; the rest is Government-owned. LTV's corporate relationship to the Pentagon has undergone spectacular growth in the sixties. In fiscal year 1961 LTV ranked 61st on the Pentagon's list of largest contractors with a total of $47 million in awards. LTV soared to 8th place in fiscal year 1968 with a total of $758 million in defense sales.

Something of LTV's corporate philosophy was expressed by Samuel F. Downer, financial vice-president for LTV Aerospace Corp. In an interview with Bernard Nossiter he expounded on the merits of defense sales:

> "It's basic. Its selling appeal is defense of the home. This is one of the greatest appeals the politicians have in adjusting the system. If you're the President and you need a control factor in the economy, and you need to sell this factor, you can't sell Harlem and Watts but you can sell self-preservation, a new environment. We're going to increase defense budgets as long as those bastards in Russia are ahead of us."

Mr. Downer is relying on the old formula of fear to sustain larger and larger defense budgets and he may well be right that this time-honored method of inflating the military establishment will prevail. But there are competitive fears in the land today. Harlem and Watts do demand diversion of the nation's energy and resources and so the military-industrial domination of the country is brought into contest.

The ABM issue, symbolized by the Safeguard system, is therefore more than just a technical-military problem. It brings the United States to a strategic crossroads where it must decide on the order of its national priorities. The build-up of nuclear defense forces opens up a whole new domain of weapons systems which have the potential of accelerating the arms race. Further dedication of U.S. resources to armaments may paramilitarize our society and create a garrison state in which all are prisoners.

THE WEAPONS CULTURE

J. Robert Oppenheimer: "The labors of physicists in explanation and in prophecy are not and cannot be ended; and there is no standing Joint Committee on the World's Salvation to which they can abdicate their concern."

(from speech of Feb. 2, 1956, to the American Physical Society, New York City)

Robert S. McNamara: "For technology has now circumscribed us all with a conceivable horizon of horror that could dwarf any catastrophe that has befallen man in his more than a million years on earth."

(from the Defense Secretary's address of Sept. 18, 1967, to the editors of United Press International, San Francisco)

I

THE EISENHOWER
WARNING

"In framing a government which is to be administered by
men over men, the great difficulty lies in this: you must
first enable the government to control the governed; and
in the next place oblige it to control itself."

—*The Federalist Papers*

President Dwight D. Eisenhower's Farewell Address in 1961
contained a barbed admonition: "In the councils of government
we must guard against the acquisition of unwarranted influence, whether sought or unsought, by the military-industrial
complex. The potential for the disastrous rise of misplaced
power exists and will persist."

Less well known than the "military-industrial complex" is
the fact that in his stinging indictment-prophecy, Eisenhower
added: "In holding scientific research and discovery in respect,
as we should, we must also be alert to the equal and opposite
danger that public policy could itself become the captive of a
scientific-technological elite."

President Eisenhower did not take the Congress to task for
its involvement in defense contracting, but he was well aware
of ties linking together the Pentagon and defense industry. We
may think of this as a geometrical figure—a defense-based tri-

angle—in which industry and the Congress form two sides. Within this defense triangle reside the fortunes of millions of Americans who depend on Pentagon-disbursed paychecks. The postwar rise of the arms industry, especially in the past decade, is an innovation without precedent in American history.

It is no exaggeration to say that the United States has spawned a weapons culture which has fastened an insidious grip upon the entire nation. This book inquires into the evolution of this new culture and seeks to explore its impact on our democracy. We shall be concerned with the deadliest game man has ever invented—deterring war by threat of nuclear attack.

Huge defense spending has become a fixed feature of our national budget. As the chart (Appendix X, page 202) shows rather dramatically, the military expenditures have loomed large ever since Korea. There was no letdown after Korea; instead, high priority was assigned to research and development, as the lower curve in the chart on page 202 demonstrates, and costly new weapons systems emerged. Never once has the U.S. Congress failed to fund a single major weapons system that was proposed to it and, more often than not, it has championed new arms while they were still in prospect. All in all, our nation has spent about one trillion dollars on its postwar armaments.

Our massive commitment to weapons development and deployment in time of peace is quite new to the American experience. Equally novel is the emergence of techno-military industries which depend for their existence upon winning prime military contracts for missiles, aircraft, and complex electronic equipment. An aerospace industry has undergone a heady growth primarily as a result of federal funding to a point where its single customer, the U.S. Government, becomes its captive. Pressures exerted by powerful corporations are felt in the Pentagon, in the White House, and are reflected in the Congress. Illustrative of the stakes involved in this defense industry is the fact that the Lockheed Aircraft Corporation has won a total of $10 billion in prime military contracts in the first seven years of this decade.

It is not just the formidable size of these government contracts that is impressive, it is also the fact that 88 percent of Lockheed's sales are purely military. Appendix II on page 186 lists the major U.S. defense contractors and tabulates their annual prime military-contract awards. Appendix I shows how defense-contract awards are distributed by state and pinpoints the military and civilian payrolls. Here we sense the impact of military spending on a geopolitical basis. Defense corporations employ workers who form part of a constituency that acts to perpetuate and accelerate the arms business. According to the Bureau of Labor Statistics, "The total employment generated by these expenditures, including military personnel and Defense Department civilian employees, is estimated at about 5.7 million persons in fiscal year 1965 and 7.4 million in 1967." The fact that the latter figure represents only a tenth of the total employed civilian labor force is often used as an argument against defense domination of the U.S. economy. However, it is a much greater fraction of the U.S. *manufacturing* labor force; and its geographic localization, together with the special political nature of defense contracting, makes it a highly significant sector of the national economy.

The United States has institutionalized its arms-making to a point where there is grave doubt that it can control this far-flung apparatus. The machinery of defense is lubricated by politics so that it has become a juggernaut in our modern society. Few Congressmen care to challenge defense expenditures, even if they possess the technical competence to appraise techno-military issues. "We are always afraid," Sen. Paul Douglas once remarked, "that if we vote for a reduction in a given expenditure not only will our friends in the Defense Department criticize us, but our opponents in our states and Congressional Districts back home will say: 'When you voted to cut back the appropriation, you voted to weaken the preparedness program of the United States.'" If this battle-scarred Marine, who at age 50 enlisted as a private, could express such a fear, imagine how Congressmen with no war record might feel about tilting with the Pentagon.

During the past 10 years the U.S. aerospace industry has steadily grown in military sales and in political influence. Total sales for 1967 approached \$25 billion, and 70 percent of these were paid for by the Federal Government. A total of 1,300,000 workers are employed by aerospace contractors, and about half of these employees are salaried. So far the rambunctious aircraft-missile industry has boomed, but cutbacks in military contracts could inflict serious economic hardships on Southern California and parts of Washington, Texas, and Georgia where new defense technology has its industrial base. To be sure, there have been a number of academic analyses of this problem, and these studies tend to minimize the economic impact of defense cutbacks. But it should be borne in mind that analysts, who cite the ability of the United States to deploy its defense plants to civilian markets at the end of World War II as evidence pointing to optimism for converting defense industry to peacetime products, neglect the significance of pent-up civilian demand for consumer goods. A rocket company that attempts to penetrate a civilian market already well served by existing consumer-oriented businesses has a severe conversion problem. Switching from the U.S. Government as its sole customer to the competitive marketplace means that the defense contractor must produce a line of consumer goods on a competitive basis and be able to market them. General Dynamics Corporation, for example, would not be tempted to risk producing motorcars to compete with General Motors, Ford, and Chrysler.

Given the stiff competition of companies long used to producing, selling, and servicing consumer goods, aerospace firms prefer to garner as much defense business as possible. One well-established principle of private enterprise is that of constant growth. While many aerospace firms are quaint cousins in the family of private enterprises, they too worship growth and corporate expansion of their plant. Some try to diversify, but others like Lockheed, General Dynamics, and McDonnell Douglas continue to depend on federal sales as their principal source of corporate income. This dependency has come to involve them in advocacy of arms and in promotion of increased defense spending. Herein lies a great danger: that the United States will be unable to break out of an upward spiral of armaments.

Defense industry today is turning out products that were little dreamed of a decade or two ago. To understand the origin of this new arms technology it is useful to look back to prewar days when science and the military were strangers. It is true that during World War I a shotgun marriage had brought scientists into an uneasy union with the War Department. But this soon broke up, and scientists returned to the serenity of their academic posts. The United States Government engaged in only a relatively little research and development, largely in agriculture, and had no R&D budget as such prior to World War II.

In the late 1930's Hitler's warlike intentions energized some U.S. leaders in science to leave the sanctity of the ivory tower and to think of applying the power of science to weapons of war. When a few nuclear scientists, all foreign-born, traveled to Washington, D.C., in 1939, they met with a very cool military reception to their proposal for an atomic-bomb project. The professor-physicists might have been men from another planet so far as the U.S. Army was concerned. Unabashed, but fearful of the consequences if Hitler's scientists developed an A-bomb first, Drs. Eugene P. Wigner and Leo Szilard, both from Hungary, seized the initiative via another channel. The two physicists persuaded their colleague Albert Einstein to write a letter to President Franklin D. Roosevelt, urging him to authorize work on the A-bomb. By going to the top, Wigner and Szilard succeeded in getting a go-ahead for the atomic project, and six years later the A-bomb was a reality.

America's $2 billion wartime A-project did more than birth the bomb and multiply a million-fold the explosive power that could be released from a lump of matter. It sowed the seeds of a weapons culture that blossomed forth in the postwar years. Thereafter science was never to be divorced from weaponry. Moreover, science was transformed in the process and mushroomed to unimagined size and affluence. Scientists tasted the intoxicating elixir of power, and they were profoundly changed. U.S. industry was also deeply influenced by its wartime experience with research and development. It soon linked science and technology as a vital component of weapons development and eagerly sought out federal contracts for researching and developing new weapons systems. Without the all-important additive of science, the "military-industrial complex" would be a humdrum affair devoted to tanks, guns, armor, and World War II-type vehicles.

Although the wartime atomic project and similar efforts in radar and electronics triggered the unleashing of American science, the spectacular technological developments of the past two decades have been largely reactions to Soviet threats. In this sense, U.S. research and development have been masterminded by the Cold War leaders, Joseph Stalin and Nikita Khrushchev. For example, Soviet ballistic successes and Sputnik I, which went into orbit on October 4, 1957, catapulted the United States into a crash program to develop rockets.

When President Eisenhower entered the White House, U.S. funds for research and development added up to $2 billion per year. But when he left, the R&D budget had shot up to $9 billion per year. The upward course of the R&D budget is clearly shown in the graph on page 202.

Khrushchev continued to dominate the research and development scene during the Kennedy years. Although Defense Secretary Robert S. McNamara managed to hold defense R&D budgets to a level of about $7 billion per year, space spending triggered a great surge in funds for science and technology. Much of the congressional support and national psychology underlining the civilian space effort to land men on the moon had a military basis. The great boost in federal funds for research and development could not be sustained at the rate of growth it exhibited in the early '60's. When he took office, President Lyndon B. Johnson was confronted with the necessity for bringing the rampaging R&D budget under control for the simple reason that if it continued to grow, then by 1978 it would consume all federal funds. It was at this point in time that science and technology came into collision with the competing demands of veterans' benefits, health, education, and welfare, as well as all the other slices of the national budget.

Under President Johnson, funds for science and technology tapered off and reached a plateau of $17 billion in fiscal year 1968. Khrushchev's retirement and the public disaffection with the U.S. space program were contributing factors in the leveling off of R&D funds from the federal treasury. No colorful successor to Khrushchev appeared to act as a provocative ogre in stimulating the flow of R&D money. Then, too, the United States became heavily involved in jungle fighting, where high technology was little match for the primitive mode of conflict in Vietnam.

Paralleling the spectacular federal underwriting of American research and development, and as a consequence of it, the apparatus of war was profoundly modified. Highly complex weapons systems using sophisticated microelectronics and computer control came into being, introducing a new technology quite foreign to the tradition of the Military Establishment. Generals and admirals felt uneasy in the new scheme of things, which seemed quite at odds with their classical training. Emphasis was placed on the concept of deterring war and, at the same time, the concept of victory seemed elusive in a contest where nuclear weapons could lay waste to much of civilization. Military planners were confronted with levels of destructive potential beyond the wildest dreams of strategists who were trained in pre-Hiroshima days. The military-industrial-political complex was beset with doubts that the weapons business could prosper by growing larger when so much destruction was at hand.

But if the generals and admirals were set somewhat adrift by the innovations in military technology, they could always hark back to the familiar world of men, guns, tanks, and ships. Initially the mere fact that a single B-29 bomber carrying one A-bomb could destroy a whole city presented air-power enthusiasts with a terrifying prospect. With such weapons in existence, not to mention even more powerful ones in the offing, might not force levels for bombers be severely restricted? The prospect of a small strategic bomber force worried men like Gen. Curtis LeMay of the U.S. Air Force. Air power advocates longed for the massed formations of World War II and the power that such massiveness conferred upon the Air Force.

Gradually the U.S. Air Force discovered it could escalate its force levels, especially after the Korean emergency took the lid off the defense budget. The latter had been pegged at $13 billion for 1950, but it quickly doubled and almost doubled again within a period of three years. Before Korea the Air Force had run into trouble pressing for a 70-wing air-power complex, which included 20 medium and heavy bomber groups. But afterward it raised its sights to 143 wings and unleashed a nationwide campaign of high-powered public relations to sell air power to the American people. Even radio-TV star Arthur Godfrey was pressed into service to drum up support for the huge air force.

President Eisenhower attempted to keep his defense budget within reasonable limits, but he found that powerful exponents of air power, both within industry and in Congress, skillfully built up pressure for more armaments. Although the President-General did succeed in leveling out the arms spending, he could not cut it back, and it was during his Administration that the weapons octopus grew and embraced the fortunes of millions of Americans. But it is only fair to trace the origins of this weapons build-up to the Democratic Administration that had preceded the Republicans in office. Eisenhower's defense spending did not satisfy many Democratic critics, and the Republican President was subjected to bitter attacks for allowing, first, a bomber gap, and then a missile gap, to develop. As we shall see, not even the President's miltary authority sufficed to protect him from charges of short-changing the national security.

The advent of ballistic missiles was an anathema to the U.S. Air Force. Air Force generals looked at the prospective manless vehicles as sorry substitutes for aircraft that required huge bases, constant operational missions and sky-blue glamour of heroic dimensions. In a very real sense missiles took the sex out of air power. The thought of burying Minuteman intercontinental missiles deep under the earth and stationing officers at underground consoles was abhorrent to the U.S. Air Force. There was even the chilling doubt that this inland artillery was more properly the function of the U.S. Army.

Another and deep-rooted reason why the Air Force disliked being saddled with ballistic responsibilities was the fact that the long-term implications of intercontinental missilery might eclipse the future of air power. One basis on which air enthusiasts had been able to sell the concept of huge bomber armadas was that losses near the enemy target zones would be heavy, and this attrition could be compensated by building more bombers. Since the alternative meant busy production lines, this pleased certain influential legislators. But the intercontinental ballistic missiles as compared to lumbering aircraft seemed unstoppable. If an ICBM could be made accurate in seeking its target, then a missile launch was the same as an assured hit. This kind of reckoning inevitably meant that the numbers of strategic ICBM's would be subject to rational assessment. Furthermore, ICBM's were almost cold-storage items— they could be built and stored away without the requirement for "spares" and replacements. All in all, the Air Force was unhappy about the long-range future if it converted from bombers to missiles. By the same token, legislators with an eye on defense-plant employment in their states viewed the ICBM as a dubious national investment—but a necessary one since a "gap" had to be filled.

Elsewhere in this book we shall trace the evolution of nuclear firepower, but it is sufficient at this point to interject that the combination of an ICBM and a superpowerful nuclear warhead rated at a million tons of TNT equivalent was a deadly package. Sooner or later an alert and conscientious Defense Secretary would add up these packages and then the U.S. Air Force would be in trouble. But at the time that ICBM's poked their terrifying noses over the technological horizon, Mr. Robert S. McNamara was still an automobile executive, and the Air Force

decided to follow a double track, amassing both bombers and
missiles.

In point of fact, the fundamental issue underlying the question of "how many missiles?" had been raised in 1953 by the
late J. Robert Oppenheimer. Writing in the July issue of
Foreign Affairs, the scientist who had headed up the nation's
A-bomb laboratory at Los Alamos, N. Mex., took issue with
the strategic doctrine of the U.S. Air Force. "The very least we
can say is that, looking ten years ahead," wrote the weapons
expert, "it is likely to be small comfort that the Soviet Union is
four years behind us, and small comfort that they are only half
as big as we are. The very least we can conclude is that our
twenty-thousandth bomb, useful as it may be in filling the vast
munitions pipeline of a great war, will not in any deep strategic
sense offset their two-thousandth." Dr. Oppenheimer was giving
voice to a deep concern over the nature of the arms race and
enunciating the folly of strategic superiority. This, more than
any other offense he may have committed in the eyes of defense
officials, was an assault upon strategic doctrine, and for it he
paid dearly.

Once a nation possesses the strategic power to "kill" another
nation, however the degree of this devastation may be defined,
then the addition of higher degrees of kill fails to alter the
strategic situation. Ultimately the other power achieves its own
degree of kill power or strategic sufficiency, and a state of parity
exists. The word "parity" rubs raw the nerves of Americans
who reckon strength in preatomic measure. They prefer superiority, for it connotes the ability to win in war or to prevail in
international contests of power. Superiority is translated into
outproducing an enemy in weapons—in building more and more
powerful arms. Thus America, which in the past slumbered
between periods of war, overreacted to the threat of foreign
competition and escalated its arms spending. Part of this over-
reaction—and it will remain for historians to dig out the facts,
if they can—was due to the self-interest of the military-
industrial-political complex. Once the defense plants were built
they could be abandoned only at great political risk. As Senator

Douglas so well phrased it, the Congress was not equipped to do battle with the Pentagon. Furthermore, the economic impact of defense expenditures on the various states grew greater with each passing year.

The degree of economic impact of defense spending on the various states is shown statistically in Appendix I on page 185. Here are presented the annual defense outlays for the past 10 years ending with fiscal year 1967. California, of course, heads the list with a decade total of $54.4 billion, accounting for over a fifth of the $252 billion for all states. During the past decade 15 states have done a total of more than $5 billion worth of business with the Defense Department. Ranked on a per capita basis, the states having the highest defense funds are, respectively, Connecticut, California, Washington, Utah, Kansas and Massachusetts.

During the course of a 1967 hearing on disarmament, Vermont's Sen. George D. Aiken looked at the flow of federal funds to the various states and observed, "I think we are overlooking one important phase of this whole program. That is the growing dependence of areas and states on Government orders until they get to where they are almost helpless. For example, for the state of Washington, over 50 percent of their gross national product is from Government orders." The state of Washington is far from "helpless" because it has defense facilities galore and it is well represented by its congressional delegation in keeping funds moving to support them. The U.S. Air Force and the National Aeronautics and Space Administration have awarded Boeing Company of Seattle huge contracts for military aircraft and spacecraft. The U.S. Navy provides funds for a huge complex of shore facilities and naval bases. The Atomic Energy Commission has built nuclear production facilities with a total cost of $1.2 billion along the banks of the Columbia River. This air-sea-space-atomic orientation of Washington's economy is capably managed by strong congressional support. Sen. Henry M. Jackson, Democrat from Everett, Wash., is highly placed on the Senate Armed Services Committee as well as on the Joint Committee on Atomic Energy. Senator Jackson has consistently championed increased defense spending and is regarded as a leading spokesman for the military-industrial complex. Sen. Warren G. Magnuson, Democrat of Seattle, is a prominent member of the Commerce, Appropriations, and Aeronautical and Space Sciences committees—well placed to protect the vital interests of his constituency.

Senator Aiken's observations regarding the state of Washington are equally applicable to other states where the dependence on defense is less visible. Utah, for example, might at first glance seem far removed from the clutches of the weapons culture. Yet the state of the Mormons has strong economic ties to the Pentagon, especially in the area of ballistic missiles. When Khrushchev's Sputnik added thrust to the U.S. missile program, it quite literally made deserts bloom in Utah. In the span of seven years, Utah won over $2 billion in prime military contracts. Defense plants have sprung up in the vicinity of Salt Lake City, Ogden, and Logan. Solid propellants are manufactured by Thiokol Chemical Corporation, which has built an aerospace complex in Utah amounting to an investment of almost $100 million, much of it an Air Force commitment. Hercules Powder Company built a plant at Bacchus which had a peak employment of 5,700 workers in the early 1960's. The Sperry Utah Company's $18 million factory attained a maximum labor force of 3,500, while Marquardt Corporation's work force ran about half that figure. Electronics firms like Litton Industries, Inc., built plants in Utah for making missile guidance systems. In addition to these industrial plants, the Air Force constructed defense facilities for fabrication of missiles like Minuteman. Utah's dependence on the Defense Department also includes the Tooele Army Depot with more than 3,600 workers and the Hill Air Force Base—the third-ranking base as measured by volume of air traffic. An annual payroll of $140 million keeps 17,000 workers employed at the mammoth air base. Utah also has other less important military posts, depots, training centers, test facilities, laboratories, and weapons ranges. One of every seven workers employed in Utah owes his job to defense. The ratio jumps to one in three if we consider only manufacturing employees.

Two Utah State University economists surveyed the significance of Utah's defense industry in 1965 and concluded: "The defense industry, as a whole, has proved itself to be one of the state's most stable industries. At least defense employment has not been sensitive to the 'business cycle,' which was true of those major industries of past years." That the defense-missile boost to Utah's economy should be reckoned as a stabilizing influence is indeed a commentary on our weapons culture. No one has suggested erecting a statue of Khrushchev in Salt Lake City, but nonetheless the Soviet leader brought prosperity and new affluence to the land of the Mormons.

When a state has a considerable fraction of its manufacturing labor force working on defense or other federal contracts, the danger exists that a temporary contractual arrangement will harden into a permanent feature of the economy. Here we find the cruelest expression of the weapons culture—its perpetuation for reasons other than national security. Indeed, since continued hostility is essential to maintaining a high defense budget, feedback from defense industry may act to accentuate the rift between the Cold War opponents. It is no accident that leaders of the military-industrial-political complex are often hard-line anti-Communists. Do they act out of conviction or are their views colored by a vested interest in the arms race?

What happens when the Defense Department comes to the brink of decision on the award of a weapons-system contract that must go to a single prime contractor? The question is even more acute and pertinent to the weapons culture when that contract may involve a total of $12 billion. Such a question was posed—but never fully answered—when the Pentagon faced the run-off between General Dynamics and Boeing in the award of the TFX contract. The latter is now known as the F-111 aircraft; it is a multipurpose plane originally designed to satisfy both U.S. Navy and Air Force requirements for a fighter-bomber and recently adapted in an FB-111 version as an Air Force strategic bomber.

It was generally considered that Boeing was the more technically qualified to win the TFX contract, but the decision went the other way and it has since been roundly criticized, especially by Sen. John L. McClellan (Democrat from Arkansas), chairman of the Government Operations Committee. It was alleged that the politics of defense had weighted the decision in favor of General Dynamics. Clearly, California stood to benefit handsomely from the TFX award, and that state could be pivotal in an election. But over and above this factor was the dilemma of what the Government should do with a firm, predominantly a defense contractor, when it faced financial difficulties and might suffer serious reverses if it did not win a contract for a billion-dollar defense system. The issue was politely phrased in a question put to President John F. Kennedy in a press conference held April 3, 1963:

QUESTION: Is it valid, sir, for the Government to give a defense contract to a firm in order to keep that firm as part of the production arsenal of this country? And, two, did that happen in the case of the TFX award to General Dynamics?

THE PRESIDENT: No, to the last part. In the first case, if it is a hypothetical case, I would say it would depend on the circumstances, how great the need is. Is it for particular kinds of tools which we might need in case of an emergency? I can think of cases where it would be valid. It has nothing to do with the TFX.

Despite President Kennedy's denial in the instance of the TFX award, much acrimony and skepticism still surround the issue. Indeed, there have even been allegations, unproved to date, that some contributions were made to the Democratic campaign chest in 1960 in order to influence the TFX award.

When a multibillion-dollar defense contract is involved, it is not unthinkable that corporations might make substantial political contributions, especially when relatively small lump-sum— and unaccounted—payments can be highly influential in a given state. Even if untrue in the case of TFX, the financial stakes involved in modern defense contracts are so high that they may well tempt business executives to seek a privileged position in contracting through political activity. This is all the more feasible because of the close association of personalities in the military-industrial-political complex. There is, of course, the common tie of military service and Reserve status. For example, Strom Thurmond, Republican senator from South Carolina, is a major general in the U.S. Army Reserve and a past national president of the Reserve Officers Association and Military Government Association. An outspoken member of the Senate Armed Services Committee, Thurmond generally comports himself as though he is still on active duty in the armed services. The line of congressional "friendship" to the Pentagon extends from elected legislators down to key members of committee staffs. In effect, the Department of Defense has a "built-in" lobby on Capitol Hill ready and willing to support almost any conceivable defense appropriation.

Industry, in its zeal to establish good relations with the Pentagon and to get on the inside track in contract bidding, uses the well-known "wining and dining" techniques of public relations, but this is rather superficial. More to the point is the fact that private industry locks itself into the Military Establishment by hiring large numbers of retired military officers. The possibility of a conflict of interest led the House Committee on Armed Services under Louisiana's Representative F. Edward Hébert to hold a special investigation in 1959. It was then revealed that 72 defense contractors employed 1,426 retired military officers. Of 251 flag rank and general officers employed by these companies, Lockheed and General Dynamics topped the list, each having 27 admirals and generals on its payroll. No up-to-date statistics on the industrial employment of retired officers are available because the Congress has not subsequently looked into this problem, but it is likely that the booming defense business now employs far more ex-military men than it did in 1959.

Defense funds flow not only to industry; they also go out to the nation's most respected educational institutions. In fiscal year 1966, U.S. colleges and universities received a total of

$385 million from the Pentagon; 54 of these institutions were awarded contracts in excess of $1 million each. Johns Hopkins University and the Massachusetts Institute of Technology are both to be found on the list of the Defense Department's top 100 prime contractors, with awards amounting to about $50 million apiece. Appendix VII on page 196 lists the Federal Government's payments to the leading 100 educational institutions. It should be noted that the National Aeronautics and Space Administration provided $126 million in funds; while these are presumably meant for scientific purposes, there is a military basis of support in Congress for NASA. The same is true for the $97 million of Atomic Energy Commission funds dispensed to colleges and universities. In this connection the AEC paid the University of California over $100 million in 1966 for running its Los Alamos weapons facility and an additional $169 million for operating the Lawrence Radiation Laboratory and associated facilities in the state of California. During the emergency of World War II there was a reason for having the University of California manage the affairs of atomic weapons laboratories, but a quarter century has passed and these facilities should more properly come under the administration of the Department of Defense. All in all the Federal agencies call upon the universities to handle more than $1 billion in funds each year for operation of federal contract research centers (see Appendix VI on page 195).

Since the United States has a priceless resource in its institutions of higher education, there is a great risk involved in contaminating the campus with military research. Our colleges and universities have a cherished tradition of being oases of independence where freedom of inquiry and unfettered research are practiced. But the inflow of federal funds, especially when they are tagged for secret research, can disrupt the pattern of academic life. When a professor has to keep a triple-locked file-safe in his office for classified work, he courts a conflict of interest on campus. His responsibility to the university, to his colleagues, and to his students is brought into jeopardy by dependence on funds from an interested off-campus source. The very integrity of the educational institution may be compromised by enlisting its scholars in *sub rosa* activities of the type funded by the Central Intelligence Agency, where even top university officials are kept in the dark about the nature of the work done for CIA.

Even with this brief survey we can sense the spread of the weapons culture through our society, extending to almost every phase of our life. Because this impact is not felt as a flash flood but more like the gradual rise of a swollen river, the American people are as yet only imperfectly aware of how far the infection has spread in our society. But a recent development, so to speak—a clinical manifestation of the disease—illustrates how the forces of military, industrial, political, and scientific elements are conspiring to plunge the nation into a new phase of the arms race. In July, 1967, L. Mendel Rivers, chairman of the House Armed Services Committee, released a report titled, "The Changing Strategic Military Balance—U.S.A. vs. U.S.S.R." It turns out that this is not a committee report at all, but rather a private paper which is given the committee's imprimatur. The report is actually the work of a Cold War institution called the American Security Council whose chairman, Robert W. Galvin, is chief executive officer and chairman of the board of Motorola, Inc. The American Security Council describes one of its major functions as "the mobilization of U.S. business in the continuing Cold War."

The American Security Council's task force for its comparison of U.S. and Soviet military strength included eight retired generals, six retired admirals, two professors and Dr. Edward Teller. Gen. Curtis E. LeMay, Gen. Thomas S. Power, and Gen. Albert C. Wedemeyer were three of the task-force members who illustrate the complexion of the group as being unalloyed air-power advocates and champions of the political right wing. "The stock in trade of almost all these individuals" writes Daniel Bell in *The Radical Right*: "is the argument, reinforced by references to their experiences, that negotiation or coexistence with Communists is impossible, that anyone who discusses the possibility of such negotiation is a tool of the

Communists, and that a 'tough policy'—by which, *sotto voce*, is meant a preventive war of a first strike—is the only means of forestalling an eventual Communist victory."

The overt alliance of scientific, technical, and military men under the aegis of a congressional committee to promote a step-up in the arms race is an ugly excrescence in our weapons culture. The committee report is a blatant attempt to increase U.S. armaments by preaching the gospel of a "megaton gap." It trumpets a cry for more nuclear warheads, more ballistic missiles, more strategic bombers, and pleads for a stout defense against ballistic missiles. We shall return to the issue of the "megaton gap" after examining the "bomber gap" and the "missile gap." For the moment, it is important to focus on the critical issue of ballistic-missile defense.

The U.S. Army, the service with primary responsibility for missile defense, began applying pressure for deploying an anti-ballistic-missile system (ABM) during the second term of President Eisenhower. Powerful industrial and congressional forces merged to promote the ABM system, which became known as Nike-X, the Army's project named after the winged Greek goddess of victory. Both Presidents Eisenhower and Kennedy resisted development of the Nike-X system but authorized continued research and development of ABM defenses. By 1967 about $3 billion had been expended on the development of ballistic-missile defense, and the military-industrial-political complex pulled out all stops in an effort to win approval for deploying the system. A sidelight on the issue reveals how this complex appealed to the speculative interest of many Americans. The following advertisement appeared in *The New York Times*:

ment. Some companies are benefiting from this spending now, are likely to continue benefiting even if the program remains in the R&D stage, and could profit handsomely if a full-scale program is approved.

Arthur Wiesenberger & Co., stockbrokers who paid for the ad, invited readers to mail in five dollars for a 24-page special report on nine U.S. companies apt to reap the most profits from Nike-X. Investments in defense stocks thus bring even more Americans into the embrace of the weapons culture than the number of aerospace employees.

No sooner had Defense Secretary McNamara announced that he had capitulated to the Nike-X pressure groups, by deciding to deploy a "thin" ABM defense ($5 billion), than the weapons cultists began demanding a "thick" ($40 billion) system. We shall in due course examine the merits of ballistic-missile defense, but here we stress the significance of venturing into a whole new domain of weaponry and accelerating the arms race. In pressing for greater national defense efforts, the military-industrial-political complex takes advantage of the fact that military technology is today largely incomprehensible to the average, or even not-so-average, layman. As University of Chicago's Prof. Hans J. Morgenthau observed shortly after the Nike-X decision, "The great issues of nuclear strategy, for instance, cannot even be the object of meaningful debate, whether in Congress or among the people at large, because there can be no competent judgment without meaningful knowledge. Thus the great national decisions of life and death are rendered by technological elites, and both the Congress and the people at large retain little more than the illusion of making the decisions which the theory of democracy supposes them to make." Professor Morgenthau's observation would subordinate democratic decision-making to elitist circles, and it is therefore of the greatest importance that national decisions on such matters as a $40 billion Nike-X system be made on the basis of public discussion.

The tragedy of the U.S. decision to deploy a "thin" Nike-X system is that it jeopardizes the treaty that the United States

was attempting to get with other nations in restraining the proliferation of nuclear weapons to nonnuclear powers. It was
well summed up by presidential assistant Walt W. Rostow in
remarks he made early in 1967: "We are all actively trying to
find the terms for a non-proliferation agreement; and the emergence of an anti-ballistic-missile defense for Moscow has posed
for the United States and the Soviet Union the question of
whether the nuclear arms race shall be brought under control
or go into a vast and expensive round of escalation on both
sides with respect to both offensive and defensive weapons."

If the United States is incapable of applying restraints to its
own weapons industry, then what hope is there that other
nations will be less aggressive in pursuit of national security?
As will be shown in subsequent chapters, the United States has
overreacted to foreign threats, building up military strength to
fill fictitious "gaps" and in the process creating a weapons culture that threatens to encage the nation.

I I

KENNEDY

The Bomb and Missiles

"The weapons of war must be abolished
before they abolish us."
—JOHN F. KENNEDY
U.N. Address, Sept. 25, 1961

Sen. John F. Kennedy gave little indication of being much interested in nuclear issues until he actively began his quest for the presidency. In the House of Representatives he tended to the chores of his district and occasionally spoke out on defense issues; for example, backing the 70-group Air Force. His contact with scientists was not notable, although he was named a member of the Visiting Committee to the Department of Astronomy at Harvard. Despite a lack of contact with the scientific community, Kennedy was to become its hero and was to associate himself with the affairs of science and technology as no other President in this century.

When Adlai Stevenson raised the nuclear test ban issue in 1956, Senator Kennedy refused to commit himself even though he was viewed as a potential running mate for Stevenson. Nor did Kennedy take a stand on radioactive fallout hazards, which were in the forefront of public discussion in the period beginning with 1954. Sen. Estes Kefauver nosed out Kennedy as the

vice-presidential nominee and, when the test issue peaked in
the fall of 1956, Kennedy avoided involvement. Yet later as
President he was to seize the issue and to regard the Limited
Nuclear Test Ban Treaty of 1963 as one of his proudest
achievements.

In the area of defense politics Kennedy's political nose sensed
an issue that might get votes, and in 1958 he began to emphasize the significance of "the missile gap." He warned: "The de-
terent ratio during 1960-1964 will in all likelihood be weighted
against us." Presumably the 41-year-old Senator was taking
his cue from a close friend, columnist Joseph Alsop, who had
published the following projection of intercontinental ballistic
missiles:

	U.S.	U.S.S.R.
1960	30	100
1961	70	500
1962	130	1,000
1963	130	1,500
1964	130	2,000

Some of Kennedy's associates in the senate regarded these
figures as "authoritative"and used them to dramatize the missile
gap. Former Air Force Secretary Sen. Stuart Symington mounted
a barrage of criticism at the Eisenhower Administration for
doing nothing about the "gap."

"For many years, now, we have been living on the edge of
the crater," Kennedy intoned, and added: "In the years of the
gap, our exercises in brink-of-war diplomacy will be infinitely
less successful." The irony of the situation was that since 1956
President Eisenhower had authorized U-2 reconnaissance aircraft to overfly the territory of the Soviet Union, and no evidence had been found to verify deployment of a single Soviet
ICBM. But in 1958 intelligence estimates were still flabby and
permitted a wide range of interpretation of Soviet ballistic capability. The U.S. Air Force chose to credit the Soviet Union
with a maximum capability and "leaked" estimates to preferred

members of the press. Information about the U-2 operations were, however, kept in an ultra-secret category.

The Democratic Party swung behind critics of Eisenhower's defense policies and endorsed the missile gap and more spending on arms. In June, 1959, the Advisory Council of the Democratic National Committee published a report titled, "The Military Forces We Need and How to Get Them." Paul H. Nitze, later a defense official under Kennedy and Johnson, was a major author of the report, which called for "a crash effort to bridge the missile gap" and "an impressive additional expenditure of about $4 billion more a year on our strategic forces." The Democratic pamphlet proposed a total of $30 billion in defense increase over a four-year period—sweet music to the military-industrial complex, members of which distributed hundreds of thousands of copies.

Nuclear weapons definitely entered the vocabulary of J.F.K. in 1959 as the Senator drove hard to work up national support for his nomination in Los Angeles the next summer. Stevenson had not made any political hay with his test-ban proposals in 1956, but he had succeeded in driving the nuclear issue home to many Americans. The fear of fallout was not laid to rest by Administration efforts to calm the public. While President Eisenhower executed a massive U-turn in foreign policy and made overtures to the Soviets for a test ban, negotiations were stymied by Dr. Edward Teller and some of his associates. The nuclear scientist asserted that the Soviets might conduct illicit tests underground and that these would not be detected against a background of earthquake signals recorded by seismographs. Such clandestine tests, Teller argued, would give the Soviet Union a real advantage over the United States in the further development of nuclear weapons. Nonetheless, the test issue was kept alive, especially on a number of U.S. campuses. It was in the summer of 1959 that Kennedy first declared himself on nuclear tests.

Speaking at the University of Rochester on October 1, 1959, Kennedy warmed to his nuclear task by talking of "the crushing burden of the arms race," of nuclear war that would see "two Carthages destroyed," of nuclear pollution in the atmosphere and of the danger of other nations joining "the atomic club." But the cautious Kennedy did not commit himself on testing. A month later, on the University of California campus in Los Angeles, he spoke to the students on the specific problem of nuclear-test cessation. He urged a continued suspension of tests and a redoubling of efforts "to achieve a comprehensive and effective agreement to ban all nuclear tests under international control and inspection." This position set him squarely against that of another presidential candidate, Gov. Nelson Rockefeller. It may, however, have had its primary thrust directed toward another aspirant—Adlai Stevenson. Had Kennedy gone to the Los Angeles convention uncommitted on nuclear testing, he would have alienated an important liberal bloc of Democrats, many of whom looked upon the young Senator with disfavor. Kennedy had not endeared himself to the liberals during the McCarthy ruckus; they felt that he was of a conservative stripe.

The summer and fall of 1959 saw a new development in American politics. A year before, the Democratic National Committee had created an advisory committee of scientists who worked within the framework of the Democratic Advisory Council. This task force was headed by Dr. Ernest Pollard, a biophysicist with a strong sense of social conscience. Three Nobel prizewinners, Harold C. Urey, Polykarp Kusch, and Fritz Lipmann, were on the committee. Other prominent scientists gave their help incognito so that they would not embarrass their standing in government. It was the first time in U.S. political history that scientists formally associated themselves with a political party. The author, who participated fully in the work of the committee, observed at first hand the interaction of scientists and politicians as they mingled in conferences and at social events. Sometimes the meetings brought hard-line politicians into abrasive contact with leading scientists and some sparks were generated. I recall one scientist expressing dismay at the nuclear-test views of Senator Symington. The latter, a pupil of Dr. Edward Teller's school, took the view that a single illicit test by the Soviets could confer a supreme advantage on them. He emphasized this by dramatically running a finger across his throat. Privately the Senator from Missouri expressed his opinion that the scientists who disagreed with him were woolly-headed. Senator Henry Jackson had even stronger adjectives to describe them.

For their part some of the scientist advisers took the position that it was not sufficient for the Democrats to press for ever larger defense expenditures. They mourned the fact that the Eisenhower Administration had done so little to take the initiative in the matter of a test ban. They felt that this was the reason why the Geneva talks begun in August, 1958, collapsed. The United States had failed to do its atomic homework, and when disputes occurred at the conference table because of ambiguity about underground explosions and seismic disturbances the U.S. experts had no solid data at their disposal. The science advisers felt that something crucial was missing: huge appropriations were made for defense research, but only tiny driblets of money went into anything connected with what might be called research for peace.

In the fall of 1959 the science advisers to the Democratic Council came up with a proposal for a National Peace Agency. It included 17 suggestions, most of which centered on providing a technical base in test detection and inspection systems. Part of the philosophy of the scientists was that the Defense Department was lavishly funded and had immense physical facilities, including special laboratories, for generating data to support their requests for weapons systems; but the State Department had no such technical backup and was therefore often at a loss to champion the cause of peace. Indeed, the concept of peace research was something of a novelty.

Early in December, 1959, the leaders of the Democratic Party met in New York City for a review of policy. The late Trevor Gardner and the author represented the scientists at this conference. All the meetings took place in the Jansen Suite at the Waldorf-Astoria. When the Peace Agency proposal was introduced, former President Truman called it "a good statement" and it was approved as formal policy for the party. Senator Kennedy was not present but he had telephoned his approval of the proposal the night before. J.F.K. told Charles Tyroler II, a key man in the Democratic Advisory Council that he wished to be certain he was listed as signing the proposal. At lunch, Adlai Stevenson was enthusiastic about the Peace Agency, calling it "the best thing we've thought of in the past six years."

Ideas are one thing, party policy another, and legislation quite another. Led by Florida's Charles E. Bennett, Congressmen were quick to introduce bills to enact a Peace Agency. Getting the legislation into the Senate hopper was a move to be undertaken with care. Senator Humphrey was an obvious choice for the job; that was the trouble—there would be more impact if a less peace-minded man were to be "converted" to the cause. However, approaches in this direction met with failure. Therefore it was decided that an overture would be made to Senator Kennedy.

At the time the Senator was engrossed in the 1960 primaries, but he took time out to consider the legislation. He was none too happy about the title for the new agency, remarking, "The Russians have preempted the word *peace*." However, he agreed to back the bill. Then, just as he was about to do so, Senator Humphrey slipped an almost identical proposal into the Senate hopper. Kennedy was miffed and refused to introduce his own bill, claiming it would look like a "me too" move. Charles Tyroler II determined to effect a compromise and called a luncheon meeting in the Mayflower Hotel. I proposed splitting up the Peace Agency and separating out a part to be called The Arms Control Research Institute. Senator Kennedy agreed to this modification, and on March 8, 1960, he introduced his legislation on the Senate floor. He paved the way for it by giving a major speech on atomic arms the day before at the University of New Hampshire. "Push-button weapon systems based on 'instant response'—but capable of both mechanical and human error—could plunge the world into a nuclear holocaust through an act of inadvertence or irrationality. The galloping course of our weapons technology is rapidly taking the whole world to the brink." Kennedy underlined the meaning of these words with a statement that made news around the world. He said: "The world's nuclear stockpile today contains, it is estimated, the equivalent of 30 billion tons of TNT—about 10 tons of TNT for every human being on the globe."

Kennedy's New Hampshire speech tended to take the edge off his hard line on the missile gap. It sweetened him to groups interested in disarmament and it represented a strong overture to the scientific community. However, many scientists were still strongly attracted to their champion—Adlai Stevenson. I recall that at a meeting of the Democratic Advisory Committee on Science and Technology prior to the 1960 convention, we polled the membership by secret ballot on their choice of a nominee. With the exception of one ballot, all the scientists voted for Stevenson; the lone vote went to Lyndon Johnson.

Once Kennedy was named at Los Angeles, the scientists on the committee gave him their support and served as advisers during the 1960 campaign. Prior to that time they had prepared a series of policy papers for the Democratic Advisory Council and they had a final paper, "Deterrent Policies and Missile Systems," in galley ready for the printer. Then Kennedy designated his friend Senator Jackson chairman of the Democratic National Committee. The report never saw the light of day. Clearly this analysis, which looked forward to the day of the push button, was contrary to the philosophy of many arms enthusiasts. For example, the report questioned the value of fixed continental missile bases and of "an exaggerated overkill capability." One paragraph illustrates the tone of the scientists' report:

> In principle, then, mutual deterrence operates along the lines of a homicide machine. Two opposed parties control the mechanism of this lethal machine in such a way that when one party presses a button, the other responds by pressing another button; the result may be a common grave. In practice, deterrence is much more complex since the two parties are widely separated nations and the lethal machine consists of intricate

missile systems, alerted by complicated warning devices and
actuated by human decisions.

Fighting for the nomination and for the first place in American
politics, Kennedy kept hammering away on the "missile gap"
and the need for military strength. There could be little doubt
that if elected he would use crash programs to close the missile
gap and boost U.S. conventional forces as well. He had sig-
naled his stand earlier that year in a Senate speech, when he
called for stepped-up defense spending. Senator Kennedy
stated: "I am convinced that every American who can be fully
informed as to the facts today would agree to an additional
investment in our national security now rather than risk his
survival, and his children's survival, in the years ahead."

But the basic question remained, how well was the Senator
himself informed? Kennedy hit home at the missile gap time
after time in his 1960 speeches. He was not a member of the
Armed Services Committee, but presumably he was heavily
influenced by his close friends on that committee. He accepted
U.S. missile inferiority as gospel and never changed his stand
even though a sensational event occurred on May 1, 1960,
which should have spelled caution for him. On that day a U-2
plane, piloted by Francis Gary Powers came down on Soviet
territory. Within a short time there was good reason to believe
that the Central Intelligence Agency had for the first time succeeded in getting "hard" estimates of Soviet strategic capability
through photo-reconnaissance from high-flying aircraft. In July,
1960, Kennedy was given a 2½-hour CIA briefing on intelligence.

If Kennedy had any doubts about the missile gap, these
did not surface in the candidate's campaign oratory. For example, Kennedy called for "crash programs to provide ourselves
with the ultimate weapons (to) . . . close the missile gap" and
decried Eisenhower's term in office as "years the locusts have
eaten." President Eisenhower must have been hurt by the
charge that "it is quite obvious we obtained economic security at the expense of military security." Kennedy's opponent,
Richard Nixon, seemed incapable of responding to these barbed

attacks, possibly hoping that President Eisenhower would come to his aid. Had he done so, he might have generated sufficient authority to defuse the burning issue.

In view of this history it is interesting to examine President Kennedy's State of the Union message of January 30, 1961. He repeated what he had said on taking the oath of office: "Only when our arms are sufficient beyond doubt can we be certain beyond doubt that they will never be employed." Congressmen applauded this repetition which seemed like a blank check for open-ended defense funding. They also liked his promise of prompt action in stepping up the Polaris submarine program and in accelerating the entire missile program. However, there was no specific mention of a missile gap, and defense did not receive disproportionate space in the entire address.

The year 1961 was destined to be one marked by a seemingly endless series of B-52 and B-47 bomber crashes. On Inauguration Day a B-52 from El Paso exploded en route to Utah, but it attracted only local interest and did not make a dent in the political news. But on January 24 the President was shaken by news that a B-52 had crashed in flames 15 miles north of Goldsboro, N.C. The strategic bomber carried two nuclear weapons each packing the punch of 24 million tons of TNT—*i.e.*, 24 megatons. One weapon was jettisoned and parachuted to earth; the other went down with the plane and fell in a plowed field without exploding in a nuclear sense. One weapon was recovered and, to the astonishment of the experts, it was discovered that all but one of the "interlocks" or safety switches governing the electronic command to the bomb mechanism had been thrown. This news alarmed President Kennedy, who had been previously assured that the Strategic Air Command had taken all possible precautions to prevent an accidental detonation. He ordered an immediate review of the situation with emphasis directed toward making sure that the U.S. strategic missiles were "safed" to preclude any accident.

The North Carolina accident made it dramatically clear to the new President that he took office at a time when the weapon revolution needed to be fully understood at the highest levels of Government. One question he raised with associates was this: "How do we know whose accident it was?" In times of heightened international crisis an edgy chief of state might press the button first and ask questions afterward. President Kennedy thus had to face the realities of intercontinental missilery—the command and control of weapons for which decision-reaction times would be measured in minutes, not hours.

Bomber delivery of nuclear weapons has a built-in cushion of time in which an order can be given to get the B-52's off the ground and vectored toward their targets without committing the nation irrevocably. The two to three hours of travel time required before the jets lumbered to the point of no return provided considerable time in which to evaluate the crisis and make the final decision. President Kennedy was the first Chief Executive in history to be confronted with the stark challenge of "the button." Once given, the electronic order to launch hundreds of Minuteman ballistic missiles was beyond recall. Unlike bombers which could be allowed time to head for their targets before turning back, missiles once accelerated on course are like rocks thrown through space—they cannot be stopped. Even the alternative of sending out an electronic command to destroy the warhead is not an allowable option since this is a game that two can play. An enemy might hit upon this electronic signal and use it to blow up the warheads in counteraction. Thus, once the missiles were on their preassigned trajectories, World War III was started—and beyond control.

Only the President of the United States is authorized to press the button controlling the missile attack or reprisal. It has never been very clear who would give the command in the event that the Chief Executive was atomized by an enemy first strike. However, in the few times when President Johnson has been in a medical condition beyond the power of decision, the Vice President has been entrusted with a crisis satchel, a metal container which holds the key to unleashing the power of U.S. nuclear might. Ordinarily the container is only a few steps away from the President.

The physical existence of this device, like something conjured forth by the intermingled imagery of Poe and Milton, must have a profound psychological impact on the President. William Manchester relates that President Kennedy once remarked: "If you could think only of yourself, it would be easy to say you'd press the button, and easy to press it, too." No doubt the President was thinking in somewhat abstract terms of the clinical quality of a megadeath machine. It must be brain-numbing for any individual to realize that his finger may signal such nightmarish mortality.

Continuing a policy held over from the Eisenhower Administration, Kennedy went along with an informal nuclear-test moratorium while he tried to reach agreement on a treaty banning tests. His policy had been set forth in a letter that appeared in *The New York Times* on October 10, 1960. In it, he warned that he would, if elected President, not be the first to resume testing, that he would continue to negotiate, but he would set a time limit to measure progress; and in the event of no agreement he would consider the "prompt resumption of underground tests to develop peaceful uses of atomic energy, research in the field of seismic technology, and improvement of nuclear weapons."

Meanwhile in his first month in office, Kennedy had time to reassess the defense issue. His Defense Secretary, Robert S. McNamara, held a "backgrounder," or a session with the press operating under ground rules that did not allow any direct quotation or attribution. On February 7, 1961, the news broke that there was no missile gap, and it was quickly established that Mr. McNamara had said it. The furor was so great that it appeared the new Defense Secretary would never give another "backgrounder." It is important to stress the fact that Kennedy had campaigned on the basis of the missile gap. How then did Kennedy alter his stance once it became clear that there never had been a missile gap?

One way to answer this question is to look at the special message to the Congress on the defense budget that President Kennedy sent to Capitol Hill on March 28, 1961. "It has been publicly acknowledged for several years," the message read, "that this nation has not led the world in missile strength." It went on to specify a wide range of missile measures to strengthen the U.S. strategic deterrent, including:

1. 10 more Polaris submarines each armed with 16 missiles.
2. Development of a long-range (A-3) Polaris missile.
3. Doubling Minuteman production capacity.
4. Increasing fixed-base Minuteman deployment by some two thirds.
5. Development of a mobile Minuteman system.
6. Development of the Skybolt bomber-launched missile.

Kennedy's decision to boost the U.S. missile forces must have overjoyed the aerospace industry, but it may also have marked a turning point in the arms race. The U.S. decision was openly announced, and the Soviets could not have been in doubt about the build-up of our strategic missile strength. On September 18, 1967 (See Appendix XII on page 204 for the complete text of this speech.), Defense Secretary McNamara looked back on this decision and observed: "In 1961, when I became Secretary of Defense, the Soviet Union possessed a very small operational arsenal of intercontinental missiles." Explaining the U.S. decision to build a larger missile force, McNamara justified it as a "conservative" hedge against the possibility that the Soviets might produce more missiles in the future. But he stated: "Furthermore, that decision in itself—as justified as it was—in the end, could not possibly have left unaffected the Soviet Union's future nuclear plans." And he added, "Clearly, the Soviet build-up is in part a reaction to our own build-up since the beginning of this decade."

This astonishingly candid retrospection by a U.S. Defense Secretary before he left office raises the critical question of how the nuclear arms race might have gone during the '60's had President Kennedy pursued a more moderate arms policy. Hard-liners will point to Soviet intransigence and stoutly maintain that moderation would have made no difference in Soviet policy. But who can say whether U.S. initiative in building up massive missile forces did not compel the Soviet Union to follow suit?

President Kennedy did call for increases in military strength that amounted to $3.6 billion more than the previous Eisenhower budget. Actually the increase would have been more, but Mr. McNamara courageously hacked away at obsolete or ill-founded projects and effected big economies. For example, the Aircraft Nuclear Propulsion (ANP) program, on which the U.S. Air Force had spent in excess of $1 billion to build a nuclear-powered bomber, was summarily canceled. Scientists had long considered the ANP plane a technological monstrosity, but its budget was sustained by a combination of Air Force bullheadedness and congressional enthusiasm. Practically every year before the A-plane was killed, Senator Jackson told the press that he expected to see a Soviet nuclear-propelled plane in the air within a year.

A Soviet success and a U.S. failure were forerunners of Kennedy's venture into space during the spring of 1961. On April 12 Maj. Yuri Gargarin was launched into orbit aboard Vostok I to become the first human to travel round the world in ninety minutes. It was depressing news for the young President. On April 17 the ill-fated invasion of Cuba occurred. Although the machinery of the maneuver had been set in motion prior to Kennedy's inauguration, the new President could not avoid responsibility for the disaster—nor did he seek to. But his first spring in office was so dismal that he is reported to have said to Barry Goldwater: "What a lousy, fouled-up job this has turned out to be." The restless Kennedy mind was occupied with a message to the Congress on urgent national needs. In the course of work on this message, he conferred with a small group of advisers, predominantly military, who proposed that he take the initiative and announce a dramatic plan to send men to the moon. It was a weekend decision for Kennedy. Had he tarried in talking it over at length, Project Apollo might have died aborning. Most of his White House science advisers (including the members of his Science Advisory Committee) were known to have little sympathy for such a project.

President Kennedy addressed the Congress on May 25, 1961, and defined a new urgent national goal:

> *"First, I believe that this nation should commit itself to achieving the goal, before this decade is out, of landing a man on the moon and returning him safely to earth. No single space project in this period will be more exciting, or more impressive to mankind, or more important for the long-range exploration of space; and none will be so difficult or expensive to accomplish."*

Expensive it was to be. Estimates for the Apollo project place the total cost at roughly $30 billion. Kennedy was aware that this would be the price tag for the lunar venture because he had been given reliable cost estimates long before he made his decision. The Congress went along with Kennedy's Apollo proposal, partly because of sympathy for a President who had been badly battered in his first few months of office and partly because they looked upon space work as thinly disguised defense activity. Naturally, the aerospace industry was delighted with the new national space goal. It meant that the National Aeronautics and Space Administration would have a budget in excess of $5 billion per year. The meaning of the President's message was not lost on the arms-oriented Senators and Representatives.

Apart from the attraction of contracts that would flow from NASA and jobs to be created by them, Congress went along with the Apollo proposal because of the tried-and-true method of fund-getting—namely, the threat of Soviet competition. Apollo was to be the U.S. response to Sputnik and Vostok. We would beat the Russians to the moon! We would also boom the aerospace industry in California, Texas, Florida and other missile-associated states.

To the Cuban-troubled Kennedy, Apollo was more than a way of outdoing the Soviets in space. It was an excursion that would focus attention away from earth and provide a psychological uplift for the nation. Kennedy found little exhilaration in the earthly problems that beset him in his first presidential springtime. The young man in the White House was destined to come a cropper on another matter, which he had ranked as an urgent national need in his message of May 25.

"One major element of the national security program which this nation has never squarely faced up to is civil defense," he stated. "This problem arises not from present trends but from past inaction." He proceeded to spell out a new assignment of responsibility for civil defense, giving it to the Pentagon and recommending a national shelter program for the protection of the civilian population against the peril of radioactive fallout. He had in fact urged this measure even before he was elected to the presidency.

Khrushchev's belligerence during the summer of 1961 threw a scare into the American people. The White House hastily announced plans for a fallout program, and an atmosphere of near hysteria prevailed. People rushed to supermarkets to stock up on food, and get-rich-quick firms mushroomed in the shelter business. The Pentagon had no real time to formulate a shelter program, and the result was confusion. Anxiety increased early in July due to pressure of events in Berlin, and for the first time in dealing directly with Khrushchev, whom he had met in Vienna a month earlier, Kennedy had reason to weigh the U.S. response to Soviet threats. Finally, on the night of July 25 he gave a radio and TV report on the Berlin crisis. Calling for new defense expenditures, he emphasized:

> *"But even more importantly, we need the capability of placing in any critical area at the appropriate time a force, which, combined with those of our allies, is large enough to make clear our determination and our ability to defend our rights at all costs—and to meet all levels of aggressor pressure with whatever levels of force are required. We intend to have a wider choice than humiliation or all-out nuclear action."*

Public concern rose in August as the Berlin crisis deepened and the Wall was built dividing the city into two parts. On

September 1 the Soviet Union resumed atmospheric testing of nuclear weapons. The United States followed suit with an underground test series.

Against a background of heightened international tension Kennedy went to the United Nations on September 25 and made his famous "Damoclean" speech. He underscored the gravity of the moment with these words:

"Today, every inhabitant of this planet must contemplate the day when this planet may no longer be habitable. Every man, woman, and child lives under a nuclear sword of Damocles, hanging by the slenderest of threads, capable of being cut at any moment by accident or miscalculation or by madness. . . .

"The events and decisions of the next 10 months may well decide the fate of man for the next 10,000 years. There will be no avoiding those events. There will be no appeal from these decisions. And we in this hall shall be remembered either as part of the generation that turned this planet into a flaming funeral pyre or the generation that met its vow to save succeeding generations from the scourge of war."

Though the President called for stepped-up defense measures in the summer of 1961 and sounded a note of urgency in putting Strategic Air Command planes on continuous air alert, he did not suggest any cutbacks in the Apollo project. Nor did the Congress seek to reduce funds for this new space program.

Kennedy's bill on arms control was pushed through the Congress in the fall due to the urging of Senators Humphrey and Clark. In signing the bill that established the U.S. Arms Control and Disarmament Agency, Kennedy announced that its first director would be William Foster. The latter, a Republican who served under President Truman, was looked upon as a defensive selection designed to appease Congressmen who viewed the new agency as a less-than-wholesome addition to the federal family. This defensiveness became apparent in the appointment of military men and hard-liners to the agency's advisory committee and to its staff. The new agency was hardly off to a flying start as the cautious Kennedy was midway in his first year in office. The agency was soon to come under fire from congressional critics despite Kennedy's defensive moves, and it might have been wiser to have taken bolder action initially and to have retreated if necessary. The Kennedy caution was soon manifest in the selection of a successor to Allen Dulles as director of the Central Intelligence Agency. He picked Republican John McCone, a former Atomic Energy Commission chairman who, at his Senate confirmation hearing, faced charges of having tried to oust members of the faculty at the California Institute of Technology (where McCone was a trustee) because of their expressed views on nuclear testing. A militant anti-Communist, McCone ingratiated himself to powerful members of Congress who approved of his hard-line, no-nonsense attitude.

Khrushchev gave advance warning on October 17 that he planned to detonate a giant nuclear bomb equal in power to 50 million tons of TNT. Kennedy called upon the Soviet leader to forgo such a test, stating that "Such an explosion could only serve some unconfessed political purpose." Soviet weapons experts, confident of their technology, proceeded to test the superweapon on October 30. The huge atmospheric burst caused the President to issue a White House statement protesting that "It will produce more radioactive fallout than any previous explosion." Later analysis of the wind-borne atomic debris was to prove the White House incorrect.

The mighty Soviet bomb generated a power of 58 megatons—somewhat more than advertised, but actually only half its full power, which would have been greater than 100 megatons had not the Soviet experts taken precautions to minimize the radioactivity of the superbomb. They deliberately used a jacket of lead rather than uranium to envelop the inner core of the weapon. This was a very "sanitary" but unmilitary thing to do since it robbed the bomb of half its blast power. Uranium, as we shall see later, can double a superbomb's punch—but there is an unavoidable companion to this doubling of weapon power; in the process, immense amounts of radioactive fallout are generated. Uranium makes the bomb "dirty" and in a test operation poses operational problems as well as a global fallout hazard.

Although the White House made dire predictions about the dirtiness of the Soviet superbomb, it turned out that the mammoth explosion produced a third of the radioactive contamination of a 15-megaton bomb that the United States had tested on March 1, 1954. But there was no mistaking the fact that if the Soviets replaced lead with uranium they had in their possession a 100+ megaton weapon of fantastic kill-power.

Why had the Soviets elected to fabricate such a gigantic weapon? President Kennedy said: "The Soviet explosion was a political rather than a military act." Even the swashbuckling U.S. Air Force Chief of Staff, Gen. Curtis E. LeMay, downgraded the Soviet weapon, asserting: "I don't think that I am violating security to say that if we had wanted such a bomb we could have had it a long time ago." It is not difficult to think up reasons why the U.S. Air Force might not want the largest possible nuclear weapons. Their very size would inhibit the production of large numbers of strategic vehicles for delivering them, thus ultimately imposing limits on the strategic strike force. Weapons in the 100-megaton class tend to make incredible "numerical superiority" notions and thus they may be reckoned as hostile to the interests of air-power advocates.

Was the Soviet superweapon merely a political club? Could it be delivered? Herein I think we can get at the origin of the weapon. The Soviets started design of intercontinental ballistic missiles when there was no H-bomb. Therefore they worked on a huge ICBM capable of throwing a very heavy warhead over a long range. Then the H-bomb came along, giving them a lightweight warhead. Result: they had too big an ICBM, at least reckoned in terms of the warheads fashioned by U.S. experts for our missile tips. The Soviets salvaged part of their overaccomplishment by adapting the huge booster rocket to space feats and to orbital spectaculars which added luster to their technology, especially in the eyes of underdeveloped countries seeking an expeditious road to a modern economy. They also adapted their liquid-fueled rockets to carry high-yield nuclear weapons ranging in power to 60 megatons. Presumably their long-range bombers could carry even larger weapons, but by the early 1960's both great nuclear powers saw that bombers were on their way out.

I would think that while Khrushchev's immense nuclear blasts of 1961 had a political orientation, they also had real military significance as events in the true ballistic-missile era made evident. In a White House statement dated November 2, 1961, the President backed off a bit from his "political bomb" accusations and conceded that the Soviet tests could not be dismissed as "mere bluff and bluster" in "a campaign of fear." At the same time Kennedy asserted: "In terms of total military strength, the United States would not trade places with any nation on earth." This statement was in stark contrast to Kennedy's defense views of the year before when he had campaigned on "the missile gap." It is true that in his first year in office the new President asked for and got from Congress additional billions for defense, but appropriations are a long way in time from deployed military strength. We must conclude that President Kennedy was fully aware that it was the Soviet Union that had a "missile gap" and that the United States enjoyed a position of strategic superiority.

The President's shift in his assessment of U.S. defense vis-à-vis the U.S.S.R. did not go unnoticed. In a press conference on November 8, 1961, a reporter inquired: "I'd like to ask you, sir, what's happened since the campaign and now? Did you during the campaign possibly not have as much information as you derived later, or do you say, sir, that the improvement in our military position has resulted from the activities solely of your Administration?" In reply, the President fell back on the authority of General LeMay and Admiral Radford (two of the toughest hard-liners on defense policy) and ended up by saying that "statements that I made represented the best of my information based on public statements made by those in a position to know in the late years of the nineteen-fifties." His answer underlines the seriousness of a more general question: How can defense issues be debated in the hurly-burly of a political campaign? Is not the incumbent President in the best position to know the facts—not his power-hungry military leaders? Candidate Kennedy was not alone in thinking that there was a missile gap—the view was widely held on Capitol Hill, especially by members of the Armed Services Committees. But again, like military leaders, these Congressional leaders had a vested interest in promotion of "more defense," and a "missile gap" was a dramatic gambit to attract public attention.

The public furor over bomb shelters which President Kennedy had precipitated in the summer of 1961 subsided in the fall, and the President answered all questions about it by pointing to a civil-defense booklet that would be sent to every household by the end of the year. Within the Defense Department the booklet was first scripted by public-relations experts until it resembled a Gilbert and Sullivan production. When it finally emerged in print, it was a sad example of Government policy having outreached any well thought-out program. It appeared that the new President thought he could pull a lever and the machinery of a civil-defense apparatus would start up. As many Presidents before him had realized, this action at the top was not so easily transmitted downward through the echelons of bureaucracy. Late in the year, the President seemed reconciled to his ill venture on shelters when he remarked: "Let us concentrate more on keeping enemy bombers and missiles away from our shores and concentrate less on keeping neighbors away from our shelters."

To understand the President's enchantment with the civil-defense issue one has to recall that he was untried in the use of executive power. He assumed that a White House order could be promptly converted into action. But basically he was given some very loose-jointed advice on shelters. And underlying his decision was his personal confrontation with the Götterdämmerung apparatus—"the button." Any human compelled to live in constant proximity to such a lethal lever must inevitably be haunted by the thought: "What if deterrents fail?" In this context it was both natural and logical for Kennedy to look to the problem of home security.

But to the American people home defense against the superbomb appeared unnatural. They remembered the horror of Hiroshima, and they knew that the weapon which had fallen from the sky was now reckoned as a "low yield" bomb suitable only for certain battlefield applications. The man in the street could recall television pictures of huge craters gouged out of the ground, of mammoth mushroom clouds at Bikini and Eniwetok, and he reckoned his chances of survival were mighty slim. The Government had really done very little to persuade him otherwise, and the Kennedy civil-defense program, when it finally evolved, offered hope for survival against fallout only—provided you could get to and into a shelter. Apart from these factors the average American was so insulated against the possibility of any attack upon the continent—based on a century of citadel-like safety—that he preferred not to think about the reality of nuclear war.

Kennedy's first year was very jagged, marked by crises, disappointments, a sharp defense increase—indeed, very little to please liberals who supported him. However, his style and wit brought a new zest to the White House, and his youth afforded him some protection against criticism. One thing he did would have endeared him to many supporters had they known about it: Kennedy authorized a cutback in nuclear production. Apparently not wishing to invite the displeasure of defense enthusiasts, Kennedy kept the information secret until mid-1963.

According to Dr. Glenn T. Seaborg, whom Kennedy appointed chairman of the Atomic Energy Commission, a decision was made in 1961 to make an 18 percent cutback in the atomic production at three major AEC installations by June 30, 1964. The gradual reduction in output of the atomic plants was consistent with a public statement that the President made on September 26, 1961. In it he announced that 180 tons of enriched uranium would be made available for fueling peaceful nuclear reactors. This commitment was rather indefinite and obviously projected over a number of years in the future. Kennedy stated: "The capacity of the United States for producing enriched uranium is sufficient to meet all foreseeable needs for peaceful uses in addition to our defense needs." The fact that so much atomic material was earmarked for non-military uses could only mean that the stockpile reserved for military applications was much larger.

A single pound of highly enriched uranium (the Kennedy statement specified the peaceful allocation in these terms) is the equal of 8,000 tons of TNT. In practice, depending on the particular weapon design, the actual released energy is much smaller than this figure, which assumes that every single atom splits. Nonetheless, the explosive equivalent of the earmarked material could be estimated as sufficient to fabricate 15,000 bombs of Hiroshima size.

The question of sufficiency of the U.S. atomic stockpile had long been debated, but since the numerical value was kept highly secret, public discussion was foiled. Indeed, only a few congressional leaders had accurate information about the size of the atomic stockpile. Since 1946 the U.S. atomic stockpile has been watched over by the Joint Committee on Atomic Energy, a group of nine senators and nine representatives. Normally, one might think that the decision on stockpiling nuclear munitions would be a matter for the Joint Chiefs of Staff and the President. However, the ambitious Joint Committee switched from watchdog of the AEC to become its overlord and very quickly became policy-maker, forcing the hand of the AEC. Lack of leadership by the Atomic Energy Commission soon relegated this agency to a service function, fulfilling the military requirements as prescribed by proxy from Capitol Hill. It was the Joint Committee which championed a vast expansion of atomic production. A longtime member of the committee, Henry Jackson, took to the floor of the House in 1951 and pleaded for an "all-out" atomic effort, producing weapons "by the thousands and tens of thousands."

Congressman Jackson asked: "How can we conceivably not want to make every possible atomic weapon we can?" and he answered his own question: "I cannot, however, imagine any member of this House going before his constituents and saying that he is not in favor of making every single atomic weapon it is within our power to produce." The irony of the Washington

Democrat's colloquy with himself was that if any constituent asked one of some 400 Congressmen how many weapons had been produced and how many could be produced, no answers would have been forthcoming.

America's atomic production soared in the early 1950's until maximum plant capacity was reached in 1955. This did not satisfy some militarists. Again Jackson spoke out, this time as Senator, urging a new wave of atomic expansion. He did not succeed in his endeavor, but the huge plants at Oak Ridge, Tenn., Paducah, Ky., and Portsmouth, Ohio, kept turning out bomb material at full steam until 1961. Other production plants were located at Hanford, Wash., and on the Savannah River, S.C. The AEC investment in Senator Jackson's state of Washington alone totaled $1.2 billion. President Eisenhower was reluctant to turn off the atomic spigot that fed the pipeline to the U.S. nuclear arsenal. Thus it was not until Kennedy took office that a cutback was made.

Kennedy's action cut back but did not shut off atomic production; in 1967 it was half of full capacity and a year later it dropped to one third of maximum output. Few of the atomic pioneers who worked on the original A-bomb dreamed that the U.S. nuclear arsenal would ever swell to such fantastic proportions. I recall that when the late Dr. Oppenheimer headed up a task force to survey the long-term nuclear requirements of the United States, he made a stab in the dark and came up with an "unholy figure." At the time of his death in 1967 the U.S. stockpile had reached a total 20 times larger than the one Oppenheimer had pinpointed.

The irony of the Kennedy build-up of strategic striking power is that modern technology in the form of orbiting cameras aboard Samos satellites systematically uncovered the numbers of missiles in the Soviet strategic bases. Yet in the face of an "inverse missile gap"—with the advantage on the side of the United States—the Kennedy Administration continued its build-up of missiles forces. The appropriations for fiscal year 1962 involved a total force of 12 squadrons (600 ICBM's) of Minuteman missiles, subsequently raised to 800 in the next year and then to its present 1,000 level. The Polaris submarine fleet was raised from 29 undersea craft in fiscal year 1962 to 35 in the next year and then to 41 the year after that, bringing the total number of Polaris missiles to 656.

In his retrospection of September 18, 1967, Secretary McNamara stated: "But the blunt fact remains that if we had had more accurate information about planned Soviet strategic forces, we simply would not have needed to build as large a nuclear arsenal as we have today." But the fact is that the Defense Department did have more reliable intelligence on Soviet strategic strength than at any time in history. There was no missile gap; but it was not politically expedient to admit this fact. Instead, the myth was perpetuated and the arms race accelerated. Perhaps it was politically impossible for President Kennedy to stick with the Eisenhower budget on defense in view of his party's commitment to a "bomber gap" and a "missile gap." Perhaps the constituency of the weapons business was even then too powerful to be resisted. If so, then the "military-industrial complex" was fully joined with its political component.

Kennedy in his Inaugural Address stressed "arms beyond doubt"; quite evidently, his defense policies left little room for doubt.

III

THE STURDY CHILD
OF TERROR

"Then it may well be that we shall, by a process of sub-
lime irony, have reached a stage in this story where safety
will be the sturdy child of terror, and survival the twin
brother of annihilation."

—WINSTON CHURCHILL
House of Commons debate, 1955

President Kennedy in the year 1962 was to be confronted with
a situation in Cuba where the sturdiness of Churchill's "child
of terror" would be tested. It was to be the closest approach to
the atomic brink that the world had witnessed thus far in the
Cold War. If we are to understand the choices and the consequences involved in this Cuban confrontation, we must go back
and trace briefly the course of atomic events. In brief, we need
to look closely at how nuclear weapons have deterred the outbreak of general war.

The first decade of the postwar period was one of gathering
nuclear might in a world dominated by two great powers. Only
the United States and the Soviet Union could be rated as
potentially "great" in a nuclear sense. When Stalin's Joe I explosion occurred in August, 1949, the atomic competition was on
in dead earnest. The U.S. response to the breaking of its atomic

monopoly was to develop an H-bomb and to expand vastly its atomic production.

The Soviet stockpile of nuclear weapons was not militarily meaningful during the critical period of the Korean War. Although the United States seriously considered the tactical use of atomic weapons when the Pusan perimeter was shrinking, this defensive maneuver was not necessary. But the battlefield slugfest with the enemy brought home to military analysts the realization that nuclear weapons promised no cure-all for the conduct of ground warfare. If both sides possessed nuclear weapons in quantity then, an Army study concluded, thousands of these might have to be employed on the battlefield. How two nations might slug it out so fearfully on the ground and not resort to a strategic nuclear exchange was something that only an ivory-tower academician could contemplate.

Throughout the first atomic decade, the strategic problem on which we shall concentrate was much simplified by the sluggishness of "bomber-time." No leader of state was called upon to think in terms of pressing a button in a matter of minutes. The take-off to the point-of-no-return time for a bomber provided a buffer of a few hours in which the momentous decision could be debated, intelligence acquired and interpreted. From the standpoint of the United States there was little doubt that "atomic superiority" was still a comforting concept. But, as we have seen, the traditionalists in the Congress worried about the margin of superiority and propelled the Atomic Energy Commission into an expansion of plant capacity that would make the early postwar production look like a thin trickle of bomb stuff.

The United Kingdom attempted to enter the nuclear club on October 3, 1952, when it tested an A-bomb at Monte Bello Islands, Australia. But Britain, like France eight years later, could not really qualify for membership. The club was too exclusive to admit just any nation with the technical capability of making an A-bomb, or even an H-bomb. To be a full-fledged member one had to proffer other credentials. For example, a nation such as Britain could scarcely be considered a real nuclear power when its home base was so vulnerable to a handful of nuclear weapons. Any threat that it might wish to impose in a deterrent fashion would not have a high credit rating. We shall therefore confine discussion to the U.S. and the U.S.S.R. and, later on, to Red China.

In the early days of deterrence, U.S. policy was an extrapolation of Hiroshima-type thinking. This carried over even when the atomic monopoly was shattered. The U.S. Air Force gradually boosted the size of its Strategic Air Command with little public debate over "sufficiency" of the force level. Then the Eisenhower Administration began to take a "New Look" at atomic weapons under Adm. Arthur Radford's direction. On January 12, 1954, Secretary of State John Foster Dulles pronounced a policy of massive retaliation keyed to air superiority and overwhelming nuclear strength. The trouble with the strategic air-nuclear umbrella of Radford-Dulles design was that it was not leak-proof. The doctrine of responding massively and instantly was flawed because such an all-or-none response failed to answer international threats with anything but a nuclear thunderclap. Unless the Soviets were to stage a permanent retreat to passivity, one would have to expect a series of challenges that could not be answered with a big atomic stick. Another disadvantage of the Dulles doctrine was that it encouraged U.S. militarists to preach a counsel of preventive or preemptive war. President Eisenhower had to step in and resolve this issue by disclaiming any U.S. intention to strike first.

Shortly after Secretary Dulles enunciated his nuclear policy, an event occurred that radically altered the nature of war. It was the Bikini bomb test of March 1, 1954. This test, code-named *Bravo*, released the power of 15 million tons of TNT, of which some eight megatons had its source in the splitting of uranium atoms. In other words, it was a dirty bomb. Radioactive fallout from this explosion was deposited locally over an area of some 7,000 square miles. Due to winds which failed to live up to forecasters' predictions, this fallout came down on the Marshallese atolls of Rongelap, Alinginae, and Rongerik. Normally these islands would not have been downwind of the nuclear tests, since the testers tried to pick shot days when the winds aloft carried the radioactive debris over uninhabited parts of the Pacific Ocean.

A little tuna trawler, the *Lucky Dragon*, had innocently ventured near the test area and came within the pattern of the fallout. The Japanese boat was about 92 miles from Shot Island when gritty, whitish ash began falling on its decks and on the 23 crewmen. Fortunately, the *Lucky Dragon* lay somewhat north of the central tongue of fallout, which projected eastward from Bikini. Less happily, the men aboard the boat were unaware of the less-than-lethal fallout they received and they took no precautions to sluice it off the decks or to wash the strange dust from their bodies. Natives on the contaminated islands were evacuated 44 hours after radioactive debris settled to earth on Rongelap. None of the Marshallese died, although they sustained skin burns from fallout. One of the Japanese fisherman died after he returned to his home port, but radiation cannot be ascertained as the cause of death. However, beginning in 1963 follow-up studies diagnosed the presence of nonmalignant thyroid nodules, preponderantly in Marshallese children who were under 10 years old at the time of radiation exposure. Some two thirds of these children developed such growths on their thyroid glands. Most of the patients were brought to the United States, where subtotal thyroidectomies were performed at the New England Deaconess Hospital in Boston. Before the clinical manifestation of this thyroid abnormality, I had been struck by the possibility that it might be an indicator of fallout effects from continental tests in U.S.A. Accordingly, I published in *Science* magazine the proposal for thyroid surveys in the Troy-Albany area of New York, where a heavy fallout from a Nevada test had occurred. Clearly, areas closer to Nevada might be even better places to survey, but the secrecy imposed by the Atomic Energy Commission drew a curtain around fallout in places like Utah. Finally the Public Health Service looked into the problem and surveyed thyroid abnormalities in Utah children near the AEC test site. Seventeen children out of a sample of 2,100 exhibited palpable thyroid abnormalities, but as yet the Public Health Service has not reported on assignment of cause in these cases.

The real significance of the Bikini fallout is that nuclear weapons possess far greater lethality than that limited to such primary weapons effects as blast and heat. If we view the problem of weapons effects on a geometrical model, we can illustrate how they increase in radius or area of effectiveness. Since the blast and heat from a nuclear explosion travel out uniformly in all directions, we may define a sphere of effect. For example, the 13-kiloton Hiroshima bomb, assuming it to have a lethal radius of, say, 0.8 mile, would be a sphere—like a giant balloon—and the area stricken by this effect would be a plane intersecting this sphere. If now we wish to reckon the damage from a thousand-fold more powerful weapon—*i.e.*, 13 megatons—then we consider a sphere with a thousand-fold greater volume than the Hiroshima sphere. Geometry tells us that the radius of the bigger sphere would be 10 times greater than the 0.8 mile that applied to Hiroshima damage. This would be an area bounded by a circle 8 miles in radius; it would encompass about 200 square miles—quite enough to overlap the built-up area of most cities, but not overly large for metropolitan places like Los Angeles. Radioactive fallout behaves like a pancake, not like a balloon; the effect spreads out over a very large area. As a rule of thumb, one can say that for every 2 kilotons of bomb power, fallout may contaminate a full square mile to a serious or lethal level. On this basis a 13-megaton weapon could send a shower of such fallout over an area of 6,500 square miles—or over 30 times as much area as struck by serious blast damage.

Radioactive fallout also introduced a new dimension into the nature of war. The fallout material consists of many different species of atoms, some short-lived, others with a radioactivity persisting for days, weeks, months, and even years. An area dusted with almost invisible fallout poses an unseen, unsensed hazard to life above ground long after the radioactive mantle is laid down. Survivors lucky enough not to be badly irradiated on the first day would have to stay in a safe place until the surrounding territory "cooled" off enough to permit safe passage to less-contaminated areas. Added to this direct threat to human life would be the prolonged contamination of the food supply by a few long-lived atomic species such as strontium-90. Clearly, something quite new and different had been entered on the blood-encrusted pages of war's ancient history.

One would have thought that the vastly greater killing power of Bikini-born weapons would have produced some change in the bomber-force levels of the Strategic Air Command. Consider the facts: a single bomber could carry the equivalent of a load of 20 million tons of TNT, 10 times that dropped on Germany in all of World War II. This payload could "take out" an area of many thousand square miles. Surely this fact called for some reevaluation of the U.S. strategic strike force. But despite the enormous quantum jumps in weapon power, the U.S. Air Force, backed by powerful components of the weapons culture in Congress and in industry, continued its bomber build-up.

The first postwar decade ended with weapon development having reached a point where the mutual power of destruction was of continental dimension. A nation could destroy another but only at the risk of itself being subjected to lethal return fire. Hence Winston Churchill's "sturdy child of terror." But with all the imponderables of the deterrent apparatus, intelligence uncertainties, and human frailty—how sturdy was the child? And what would happen when the two great nuclear powers were joined by a third—namely, Red China? These questions, many years later, still remain unanswered. One thing seemed evident—the United States would be restrained from invoking its massive-retaliation policy in situations where the danger did not threaten its vital interests.

Secretary Dulles rather quickly backed away from his massive-retaliation policy but he was reluctant to abandon commitment to nuclear weapons. He shifted emphasis to tactical nuclear weapons to be used as a means of countering Soviet manpower in battlefield situations. In other words, big nuclear weapons would be invoked only for "last resort" purposes, and little ones would be used to stem the tide of conventional thrusts, especially if the Soviet Union attempted to invade the NATO countries. The need for such battlefield bombs was in fact the justification for keeping our A-plants running at full blast.

There were three big questions raised by reliance on tactical nuclear weapons:

1. How could one limit their use? This problem threatened to be most vexing if the aggressor also possessed similar weapons in quantity. With no historical precedent, with no established or even informal code of nuclear conduct, a nuclear conflict could become an incredible carnage—a small-scale mutual annihilation.
2. Would any potential in-between nation welcome U.S. nuclear firepower? Of course, this question flowed directly from the first; no nation would want to be caught in the crossfire of nuclear-armed armies. Nothing would be left standing after such liberation.
3. Could the small nuclear war be kept from escalating to a big one? In the day when Secretary Dulles looked upon the nuclear weapon as his ace in the hole to hold off a Soviet push through Europe, the problem of escalation focused on a limited nuclear encounter between the two great nuclear powers. The danger of this engagement's blowing up to strategic proportions—of the spark igniting the powderkeg—was increased because of the ballistic delivery of battlefield nuclear explosives. For example, a commander of ground forces might find his position hit by a nuclear warhead from a remotely-launched missile. His first thought would be to summon up firepower to prevent any further nuclear harassment. But this would automatically expand the area of conflict, especially since some missiles, like the Pershing, may be located 100 to 400 miles from the scene of battle. Moreover, since enemy missiles would not be refired from fixed installations, counterfire would have to use higher-yield warheads to saturate the probable launch sites. Both in land area and in weapon power the nuclear engagement would expand.

A report of the United Nations released October 10, 1967, dealt in part with the tactical use of nuclear weapons and described numerous war games or studies of tactical applications of these weapons in the European theatre. "Without going into the details of these studies," the report reads, "it can be firmly stated that, were nuclear weapons to be used in this way, they could lead to the devastation of the whole battle zone. Almost everything would be destroyed; forests would be razed to the ground and only the strongest buildings would escape total destruction."

Now that the nuclear club is no longer as limited as in Dulles's day, there is even greater danger of escalation. This potential was dramatized by the Israeli-Arab conflict of 1967. Had either side possessed a few nuclear weapons, even one, they might have been employed. Then the localized war could have escalated, depending on the political tensions of the major powers.

One great dividend of the New Look at defense in 1954 was that it stimulated debate about the use of nuclear weapons. More and more it became apparent that reliance upon weapons you could not use except in total war or at the risk of same was hardly sound defense policy. A war that neither belligerent could win was scarcely one along whose brink any nation would want to wander.

Perhaps it was the hysteria generated by Senator McCarthy, possibly it was the American mania for bigness, or just the traditional military requirement for more of everything—in any event, the United States clung to a blind policy of air-nuclear armament on an ascending scale. Stalin's death saw no letup in the Cold War. Khrushchev's control of the Kremlin might have been an appropriate time to reassess the U.S. policy toward the Soviet Union. But by this time the Cold War became a psychosis for many Americans.

Americans have always been "race" conscious, delighting in the thrill of competition, and in an international contest, in the sense of purpose which a national effort bestows upon the individual. A "bomber gap" therefore was made to order for contest-minded people. An "intelligence gap" made feasible "the bomber gap." Only in the absence of hard data on enemy capability and production could proponents of huge bomber fleets promote their cause. So successfully did they exploit the "bomber gap" during Eisenhower's presidency that they were able to push through Congress funds for a vast armada of strategic aircraft. Those who argued against such massiveness of the strategic strike forces were turned aside with the argument that bomber losses might be high due to air defense, and therefore superior numbers of aircraft were essential.

With this background on deterrent policy we rejoin the Kennedy Administration as it began its second year in office. Deterrence shifted to U.S. reliance on superiority in missiles and the "button" took on greater significance. Secretary McNamara was obviously aware of this fact when he testified before a congressional appropriations committee in the spring of 1962. Pointing out the differences between bomber and missile attack, the Defense Secretary stated that the United States could meet the threat by (a) developing quick-response retaliatory missiles capable of being launched in a few minutes or (b) developing "forces which can ride out a massive ICBM attack." McNamara stated a preference for the second option and expressed it in terms of Minuteman ICBM's deployed in underground silos and Polaris SLBM's stationed in lockers aboard nuclear submarines.

Mr. McNamara was to give a variety of Administration views on nuclear weapons in the Kennedy years. As a preface to them we may look behind the scenes in the White House, using the ear of an experienced reporter, Stewart Alsop. Based upon a long interview with the President early in 1962, Alsop wrote an article called "Kennedy's Grand Strategy," which was published in the March 31, 1962, issue of *The Saturday Evening Post*. In it Alsop maintained that:

> Kennedy inherited two basic doctrines on nuclear warfare. One, as we have seen, was that any war bigger than a brush-fire war would be a nuclear war from the outset. The other was that the United States would never strike first with the nuclear weapon. Under the Kennedy grand strategy, both doctrines have been quietly discarded.

Quoting the President, Alsop wrote:

> "Now we have got to realize that *both* sides have these an-
> nihilating weapons, and that changes the problem. Of course
> in some circumstances we must be prepared to use the nuclear
> weapon at the start, come what may—a clear attack on
> Western Europe, for example."

As background for understanding the President's thinking early
in 1962 we must realize that the tempo of Soviet testing late in
1961 had produced strong military pressure in this country to
resume atmospheric testing. In their massive test series, the
Soviet experts detonated more than 40 nuclear weapons, including 14 tests of over one megaton in power. The latter
brought the Soviet total of megaton-plus shots to 30 in contrast
to 20 such tests for the United States. It was understandable
that President Kennedy should be concerned about the weight
of Soviet nuclear power.

On March 2, 1962, President Kennedy made a radio-television
address on nuclear testing. He announced that the United States
would resume atmospheric tests. "Had the Soviet tests of last
fall reflected merely a new effort in intimidation and bluff, our
security would not have been affected," the President said. "But
in fact they also reflected a highly sophisticated technology, the
trial of novel designs and techniques, and some substantial
gains in weaponry." Hopes for a test ban were dashed. Furthermore, even if in the future, agreements could be reached, it was
clear that the advantage of arresting nuclear technology had
been lost. When the giants had feasted, then they might agree
to fast.

When the Alsop article on Kennedy's "grand strategy" appeared in late March, it raised anew the question of "first
strike" and "preemptive" war. When John Foster Dulles had
been queried about his retaliation policy, he had responded:
"One thing I want to make clear beyond the possibility of doubt
is that I don't believe you should tell the enemy in advance
just where, how, and when you plan to retaliate. The whole
essence of the program is that the action should be an action of

our own choosing and he is not to know in advance what it is, and that uncertainty on his part is a key to the success of the policy." Was Kennedy's new look at nuclear policy simply a restatement of this "keep 'em guessing" policy or did it imply more?

President Kennedy, worried by the challenge of the megaton, disliked strategic situations which left him no freedom of choice other than abject surrender or annihilation—or "choice between humiliation and a holocaust." Alsop quotes the President as saying: "In some circumstances we might have to take the initiative." Since initiative in retaliation is something of an anomaly, there appears some justification for concern over the meaning of Kennedy's views.

Mr. McNamara added fuel to the controversy on June 16, 1962, when he spoke at Ann Arbor, Mich., and advocated a "no cities" strategic bombing policy which was widely interpreted as support for a counterforce strategy. The latter means that strategic strikes are targeted on military, as opposed to civilian, installations—missile bases rather than cities. The worrisome aspect of this position was that a policy of counterforce *and* retaliation did not add up. Striking at enemy military strength after the initial exercise of that strength was tantamount to hitting at empty missile silos. Therefore, a counterforce strategy lent credence to fear that the United States had accepted a first-strike policy.

Is it not possible that Khrushchev became genuinely scared by the Kennedy-McNamara statements? After all, Khrushchev knew that there never had been a missile gap, that the Kennedy Administration knew this, but knowing it, had deliberately increased its strategic strike forces. Was the United States preparing to strike first? This must have been a much-debated issue in the Kremlin. Military planners have to assume the worst and this might mean but one thing—a U.S. first strike against the Soviet Union. To Russians conditioned by foreign thrusts at the Motherland, it was a kind of Pavlovian response.

Public controversy over the issue caused the Kennedy Administration to backpaddle vigorously. Counterforce philosophy was finally disavowed, but not without much confusion. To a certain extent the recurring theme of preemptive action or initiative represented a vocalization of Government official longing for the days of American invulnerability to attack and superiority in offense. It was not easy for many officials to accept the notion that the United States would have to coexist with nuclear nations. Perhaps to an even greater degree the stubbornness of a preemptive doctrine had its foundations in the classic pattern of military thinking. The cherished concept of victory and of war-winning was grievously assaulted by the prospect of mutual annihilation. Generals and politicians were loath to seem so unpatriotic as to concede that a "no win" policy might be the end result of a nuclear war. War became a contradiction in terms. If this was true for a system of two-party deterrence in which the nuclear might of the United States and of the Soviet Union were counterpoised, then it was even more true for a situation in which three or more nuclear powers were set in opposition. This was not a reality when John F. Kennedy dealt with the problem of deterrence in 1962. But, as we shall see, he was still worried about its prospect.

The domestic political scene was depressing to the President as the political campaign got into high gear for the off-year elections. Kennedy, always concerned about his "image," knew it was badly tarnished. He was still stung by the Cuban debacle of the previous year. Popularity polls, of which he was keenly conscious, showed that Kennedy's political stock had declined significantly. The young President stood in real need of a shot in the arm to boost his stock. The opportunity to recoup came in the form of new peril in Cuba.

Any preface to the Cuban missile crisis must take into account the strategic impact of the "missile gap" on Soviet thinking. With the vanishing of the gap in 1961, the Soviets were placed in a position of strategic inferiority; *i.e., they* were *publicly* known to be inferior to the United States in long-range missile strength. Khrushchev needed some means of redressing this inferiority, and this must have played a key role in the Kremlin's decision to send missiles to Cuba. If successful, this would constitute a politically impressive missile capability 90 miles off the Gulf coast.

Viewed from the interior of the Kremlin, the Cuban venture was probably not as great a gamble as it appeared to the United States. The Soviet rationale may have been fivefold:

1. Soviet deployment of missiles in Cuba might appear a tit-for-tat response to U.S. emplacement of Jupiter IRBM's in Turkey. If the Cuban venture had to be called off, it might form a lever for getting Jupiters moved out of Turkey.

2. Although of dubious military value, Cuban missile bases would give the appearance of restoring the balance of missile power lost as result of U.S. intelligence successes. Militarily, they would be analogous to the U.S. Jupiters in Turkey and Italy in that they would be temporary "gap-fillers" providing the semblance of strategic strength, shoring up the Soviet strike force until the home-based ICBM force could be deployed. Soviet planners, especially those fearing a U.S. first strike, could view the Cuban missiles as a shrewd gambit in the nuclear war game. If the U.S. was planning to strike first, it would have first to eliminate the Cuban base, 90 miles away, or strike at it simultaneously in an attack on the Soviet homeland—an exercise in timing that would give the Soviets advance warning of the blitz.

3. Khrushchev may have felt that President Kennedy would not take any strong action to interdict Soviet missile deployment in Cuba. At the Bay of Pigs, Kennedy had acted but had failed to follow through initial moves—this might have been the Kremlin's reading of the U.S. record. U.S. acceptance of the Berlin Wall must have encouraged Khrushchev's belief that he could get away with his Cuban excursion.

4. Soviet experts may have reckoned that the Cuban venture would not invoke any U.S. nuclear threat. Given the time scale and ocean mode of transportation involving a hundred ships, there would be opportunity for a variety of U.S. challenges at a non-nuclear level. Soviet authorities knew that their ships would pass through the Skagerrak on their way to the Atlantic and that U.S. naval intelligence maintains constant surveillance of such shipping. A massive logistics effort, replete even to shipping prefabricated concrete arches for missile buildings, could not escape detection.

5. The men in the Kremlin probably fixed the time scale of the

operation based on the ending of the missile gap. U.S. versions of the Kremlin initiative put the time as late spring 1962 but this seems too late for the kind of effort mounted in the Cuban venture. In any event Soviet understanding of the off-year national elections was hardly likely to be acute. Had they reckoned fully with the politics of this particular election they might have timed their venture differently.

According to various eyewitness accounts, the United States first became aware of emplacement of Soviet missiles in Cuba on the afternoon of October 15, 1962. U-2 photos showed unmistakable evidence of missile sites in western Cuba. The Cuban crisis ended on the morning of the 28th. President Kennedy commemorated the 13-day period of crisis by bestowing a silver calendar, the days appropriately marked, upon each of his colleagues in crisis. The world settled back as the "first" nuclear confrontation was resolved without resort to nuclear arms. Kennedy's "triumph" paid off at the polls and in elevation of prestige.

Those close to the President during these days of crises report that he viewed the episode as a true nuclear confrontation. Dean Rusk, his Secretary of State, spoke of "a flaming crisis" and is reported to have stated that a misstep might have meant "incineration" of the entire Northern Hemisphere. The question to answer is not whether there was in fact a real military crisis threatening the lives of millions of Americans, but what motivated the principals as they balanced on the tightrope of decision. Khrushchev may have justified his provocative act on the basis that the United States had deployed missiles in Turkey and Italy. But the fact that Khrushchev appeared to be overbidding in the Cuban move undercuts the idea that he was merely seeking an equity exchange—Cuban bases for Turkish bases. Later, when the United States threatened an invasion of Cuba if the missiles were not promptly removed, a mutual pullout of missile bases was publicly proposed. The unacceptability of this arrangement serves to illuminate the Cuban crisis in a strange light.

We now know that President Kennedy had in fact issued an

order in August, 1962, for the removal of the U.S. Jupiter missiles from Turkey, but by mid-October no steps had been taken to implement this command. Walter Lippmann and U Thant had offered compromises on missile exchanges; imagine how they might have reacted had they known that that which Kennedy refused to consider publicly he had already authorized privately! If North America's fate might be nuclear incineration, how much did this count in crisis?

In his radio and television report to the American people on the Soviet arms buildup in Cuba on October 22, the President stressed the strategic importance of the Cuban missiles. Yet was this new development any more dangerous than the situation several years earlier when the United States was reported to be on the short end of a missile gap? In the early days of the Cuban crisis McNamara was not alarmed about the Cuban deployment. He is reported to have said: "A missile is a missile. It makes no great difference whether you are killed by a missile fired from the Soviet Union or from Cuba." Mr. McNamara may well have pointed out that the military threat of land-based missiles in Cuba was less serious than Soviet "Polaris-type" submarines in the Caribbean. Kennedy's statement of October 22 stressed that "Our own strategic missiles have never been transferred to the territory of any other nation under a cloak of secrecy and deception." But are not U.S. Polaris patrols really exercises in practiced stealth where secrecy and concealment are prized? However similar their military firepower, Soviet missiles on Cuban soil and in submerged submarines off Cuba had radically different political firepower. After spending a few days with the crisis managers, Mr. McNamara apparently saw the difference.

From a purely military viewpoint, soft-based IRBM's (intermediate range ballistic missiles) like our Jupiters in Turkey were highly vulnerable and obsolete installations. General LeMay stated: "The Jupiter is a very vulnerable missile. It is not hardened at all. It sticks up like a sore thumb. It could be knocked out with a rifle." The Soviet installation of IRBM's in Cuba, 90 miles offshore, was tantamount to challenging a lion by inserting one's head in its mouth. It did not change the ability of the U.S. Strategic Air Command to inflict unacceptable losses on the Soviet homeland—and it was this capability that was absolutely fundamental to the nuclear deterrent policy.

But from a political viewpoint, meaning domestically, Kennedy was soft-based to Republican counterfire. This is a point that most authors and commentators have overlooked or minimized in discussion of the Cuban crisis. Kennedy's political liabilities in the Cuban crisis were formidable.

First, he had tilted with the Republican presidential candidate, Richard Nixon, capitalizing on a charge that the Eisenhower-Nixon Administration had tolerated Communist encroachment in Cuba.

Second, in the face of Republican charges that the Soviets were deploying offensive missiles in Cuba—claims underlined by Sen. Kenneth B. Keating's specifics as to missile bases—the President had countered with reassurances that such bases were purely defensive and that if the situation should prove otherwise, "This country will do whatever must be done to protect its own security and that of its allies."

Third, the Bay of Pigs rankled in the presidential bosom and demanded psychological countermeasures.

Finally, the President needed some uplift in the sagging campaign which threatened to produce a Republican majority in the House of Representatives.

For these reasons, the President's hand was more or less tipped as he faced the challenge of Soviet intervention in Cuba. The timing of the crisis was critical. Anything short of success in dealing with the Cuban crisis could be deadly at the polls—success had to come before the election. Given this combination of circumstances, it is not surprising that politically-minded men in the White House would seek to manage a crisis in such a way as to produce maximum political value for the President. Crisis managers will manage to find crises.

The Kennedy mythology is now about a light-year deep, so that such a suggestion may seem bizarre. But when a compromise was offered in a mutual withdrawal of IRBM's, Russia's from Cuba and ours from Turkey, was this so unthinkable that it was promptly dismissed? If, in fact, millions of American lives were at stake and the North American continent might be incinerated, was not such a trade-off a small price to pay in the deadly game of deterrence? Reckoned in the short term and in the framework of domestic politics, the trade-off was unacceptable. But we must remember that in terms of our national security posture, little would have been sacrificed because the Jupiters in Turkey were already obsolete and Kennedy had in fact ordered them removed. Politically, the President could not afford the Republican attack which would follow such a "deal" with Khrushchev.

Khrushchev backed down and withdrew his IRBM's from Cuba. It was Kennedy's triumph and it came just in time to save his Democratic majority in the House. But somehow the sturdy child of terror has never been the same since. Dean Rusk characterized the confrontation as "eyeball to eyeball," but in reality the eyes of the two protagonists were thousands of miles apart. Communications were often difficult and tardy, and in a moment of crisis the State Department relied on liaison between a trusted news reporter, John Scali, to deal with a member of the Soviet Embassy in Washington.

During the days of the Cuban crisis Soviet weapons experts were conducting an extensive series of tests at three sites— Novaya Zemlya, Semi Palatinsk and a rocket area in central Siberia. Some 50 nuclear tests were made in a span of nine weeks—a drumfire arranged to perfect and prove out weapons prototypes and designs of 50 tests that had been executed the year before. Out of these came lightweight warheads of high megatonnage, but both the warheads and their ICBM carriers were in short supply as Khrushchev confronted the immensely powerful overkill of U.S. bombers and missiles. Though he might deal a crippling but far-from-mortal blow to the U.S. homeland, the Soviet leader knew beyond doubt that his own nation would thereafter cease to exist as part of the 20th century. Moreover, his position in Cuba was untenable in the face of overwhelming conventional firepower that could be summoned from the U.S. mainland. He wisely chose to back down from a confrontation.

Charles J. V. Murphy, military analyst for *Fortune* magazine, has observed: "Probably never before in history has a head of state entered a war situation so well informed of the adversary's strengths and weaknesses as was Kennedy in October, 1962, or, for that matter, with so absolute a knowledge of the overwhelming advantages that lay with him across the board." Given such consoling intelligence, the Cuban situation qualified as a low-risk opportunity for White House crisis managers to stage a scenario of large proportions, yielding a great political payoff.

But what if the scenario should be replayed with today's Soviet nuclear might as part of the script? How would Kennedy have played the scene when there would be no doubt of the mortal blow that the United States would suffer? Would politics prevail? Would the contest between two rival political parties in the United States loom larger than the nuclear issue? This is something that President Kennedy was not called upon to face, and we cannot know the answer.

General Omar Bradley summed up the Cuban crisis in a single sentence: "In Cuba, they (the Communists) tested us to see if we were prepared to go to nuclear war and found we were." This is surely an overly simplistic retroview of the confrontation. Khrushchev was in no position to make a nuclear challenge stick: he knew it and he knew we knew it. The missile gap was in our favor and the crisis site was in our own backyard where we had overwhelming air-sea power of conventional type to intimidate any aggression directed toward our shores. It was really a one-sided nuclear confrontation.

Looking back on the Cuban crisis, McNamara responded to a Senate inquiry on the use of nuclear force by stating: "The greatest danger was not that Khrushchev would deliberately launch nuclear war, but that the situation might have gotten out of control if conflict had started." But many Americans concluded that the Soviet Union had stepped back from the brink of nuclear war, and the Kennedy Administration found this an agreeable conclusion.

What will be the ultimate price of the Kennedy victory in Cuba? Did it not precondition America to crisis—and to the assumption that no one will dare to risk war with the United States? Many Americans, reluctant to think at all about nuclear war, look upon Cuba as proof that "nuclear war is too horrible—it will never happen," or "they backed down once, they won't fight." In the Cuban cockpit, Khrushchev had few choices after his initial miscalculation on the missile venture. But what of the true crisis in which provocation is not so close to our shores and the enemy's ICBM's pose an undisputed kill power?

Sen. Richard B. Russell, chairman of the Armed Services Committee pondered the question in the course of appropriations hearings on the fiscal year 1968 budget. "I hope I am not an obscurantist or an anti-intellectual," observed the Senator, "but it seems to me that our war gaming on ICBM exchange is based on so many assumptions and counterassumptions and is so conjectural that we are likely to outsmart ourselves in trying to work it out and come to some decision." Senator Russell's observation was made in the context of discussion of ballistic-missile defense systems. These compound the uncertainties of deterrence and make more hazardous the problem of crisis management when a handful of men make war or peace decisions. Crises in the future may be much more fearful and complex than the one that occurred off our shores in October, 1962. Not only has the vast apparatus of nuclear war-making graduated to a sophistication once relegated to the world of H. G. Wells, but the instruments of atomic devastation have come into new and untested hands.

President Kennedy was deeply concerned over the prospect that nuclear knowledge might diffuse to many countries. He was hopeful that a nuclear test ban treaty might slow up the atomic arms race, and a year after the Cuban crisis he celebrated the signing of a Limited Nuclear Test Ban Treaty. Under this agreement nations pledged themselves not to test nuclear weapons in the atmosphere, in space, or in the ocean. Since noncontaminating underground shots were permitted, the arms race was not arrested; both the United States and the Soviet Union continued their nuclear programs, but the atmospheric fallout was virtually eliminated. Fear of fallout subsided, and this, coupled with the interpretation following the Cuban crisis that the Soviets would always knuckle under when the chips were down, induced a false sense of security for many Americans. Nothing deterred the Red Chinese from developing and testing their own A-bomb in the atmosphere. Nor did anything stand in the way of the Red Chinese H-bomb—a development that we shall describe in the next chapter.

President Kennedy took note of China's potential as a nuclear competitor during a press conference on August 1, 1963. Noting China's huge population and difficult geography and social conditions, he said:

". . . so that we find a great, powerful force in China, organized and directed by the government along Stalinist lines, surrounded by weaker countries. So this we regard as a menacing situation.

"In addition, as I said, that government is not only Stalinist in its internal actions, but also has called for war, international war, in order to advance the final success of the Communist cause. We regard that as a menacing factor. And then you introduce into that mix, nuclear weapons. As you say, it may take some years, maybe a decade, before they become a full-fledged nuclear power, but we are going to be around in the 1970's, and we would like to take some steps now which would lessen that prospect that a future President might have to deal with.

"I would regard that combination, if it is still in existence in the 1970's, of weak countries around it, 700 million people, a Stalinist internal regime, and nuclear powers, and a government determined on war as a means of bringing about its ultimate success, as potentially a more dangerous situation than any we faced since the end of the Second War, because the Russians pursued in most cases their ambitions with some caution."

What did the President have in mind when he referred to

"steps" which might be taken? It is true that, at the time, Kennedy was much concerned with the problem of nuclear proliferation—or "diffusion" as he preferred to call it—but there were certainly no signs that Red China would sign the test ban pact or any other international agreement on nuclear weapons. Stewart Alsop has given us an intimate glimpse into what may have been on the President's mind. Writing in *The Saturday Evening Post* (Jan. 1, 1966) Alsop recounts a conversation that the President had with "one of the Government's leading experts on the Far East" a few days before his assassination.

According to Alsop, the official told President Kennedy that it would not be possible to reach an accommodation with Red China. The President then asked: "Do you think this country should permit Communist China to become a full-fledged nuclear power?" The adviser gave a negative answer and suggested: "It should be technically possible, at this stage in their nuclear development, to destroy the Chinese nuclear plants in such a way that it will seem an atomic accident. This could be done as a surgical operation, without nuclear weapons, using high explosives. We could have plans for you, with various optional means of taking out the plants, in the near future."

There is no evidence that the President went any further in this matter or that he intended to do so. One would have thought that the White House would have been fumigated to remove Bay of Pigs advisers from the woodwork. But that such plans should even be proposed to a President of the United States is a remarkable episode in the history of a democracy. The notion that our country would seize the initiative in "taking out" Red China's atomic plants illustrates American impatience in dealing with world events. But there is also something contained in Kennedy's press remarks that indicates a point of change in the Cold War. Organized opposition to the threat of Russian Communism had been the main sustainer of the weapons culture in the Cold War. Would it be possible to substitute China for Russia as a new Communist menace? The thoughts and questions were premature as long as Red China was a nonnuclear power, but as Kennedy anticipated, Communist China would someday possess nuclear weapons. The first A-test, signaling a new era for the Middle Kingdom, came slightly less than a year after Kennedy's death. Later another event occurred that attracted little attention: *Jupiter missiles were removed from Turkish soil*. The Turkish government is reported to have sought U.S. assurance that Polaris submarines carrying equivalent firepower would patrol the eastern Mediterranean waters. Such was history's footnote to "a flaming crisis."

IV

RED CHINA

No. 3

"Let China sleep.
When she awakes the world will be sorry."
—NAPOLEON

When President Kennedy found that Khrushchev was willing to commit the Soviet Union to a nuclear test ban, he realized that he might have to do some arm-twisting to get the U.S. Senate to ratify a test ban treaty. That is why in the summer of 1963 Kennedy took his case to the American people so that they would in turn persuade the Senate to approve the nuclear pact. It was in the course of this domestic persuasion that Khrushchev engaged in bitter attacks on Mao Tse-tung and let the world in on some facts about Red China. There could be no doubt that Khrushchev knew a Red Chinese A-bomb was in the offing and that he deeply regretted having helped to accelerate the development. He feared having Red China as a nuclear-armed neighbor, for he knew that the advent of a third nuclear giant made for fearful company.

The U.S. Senate did ratify the treaty which banned the testing of nuclear weapons in three environments—space, the ocean, and the atmosphere—but there was extended debate on the treaty as arms advocates worried about illicit tests the Soviet

Union might conduct. By this time the total explosive power of all weapons tested by the two nuclear giants equaled almost half a billion tons of TNT. When Adlai Stevenson had first proposed a halt to testing, the total weapon yield was very much less and the Soviets had not conquered the technology of multi-megaton weapons. The United States then had a decided edge in the nuclear technology, an advantage much slimmed when an agreement on testing was finally reached.

Red China and France were notably missing from the ranks of the more than 100 nations that signed the Test Ban Treaty in 1963. Neither the United States nor the Soviet Union could persuade the two countries to sign up; both had in their own way contributed to Red China's ability to make an A-bomb. The United States provided the scientific education for 95 of Red China's 228 top-rated scientists in its Academy of Sciences, the tally being taken for the year 1962. This education was actually extended to a much larger group of Chinese who studied in the United States before the exodus began back to Mainland China. For some the training was simply that of the standard type given in U.S. colleges and universities; for others, like Ch'ien Hsueh-shen, it included advanced research at the Massachusetts Institute of Technology and the California Institute of Technology. Dr. Ch'ien headed up CalTech's Jet Propulsion Laboratory research in 1950 prior to being deported. Knowledgeable experts believe that some 1,500 top Chinese scientists, trained in the U.S.A. and in Europe, have returned to China since 1949.

The Soviet Union played host to hundreds of Chinese scientists and gave them advanced training in atomic science at its big Dubna Joint Institute for Nuclear Research north of Moscow. Nothing could have been more valuable to Red China as it struggled to organize its society after the October, 1949, takeover by the Communist regime. At that time Red China's scientific situation was exceedingly primitive. Dr. Ch'ien San-ch'iang, one of China's foremost nuclear experts and policy-makers, later reported: "At the time of the liberation, there were only a few nuclear scientists in China and two laboratories."

Few knowledgeable scientists, viewing the Red Chinese nation as it was in 1949, would have predicted that it would test its first A-bomb in 1964 and detonate an H-bomb in June of 1967. Yet we now know that Chairman Mao launched his country's 12-year Plan for Scientific Progress in 1955. In June, 1958, the Red Chinese leader asserted: "It is entirely possible for some atom and hydrogen bombs to be made in ten years' time."

One reason why it is still so hard for most Americans—even some expert scientists—to understand that Red China succeeded in its big Atomic Jump Forward is that we had in the course of the postwar years greatly exaggerated the difficulty of making nuclear weapons. It was made to appear that only the most advanced technological nations like the U.S., the U.S.S.R., Britain, and France could possibly make A-bombs. Furthermore, we had in mind that Red China would laboriously follow in our footsteps, duplicating all the effort we have expended on the atom in the postwar period.

We failed to realize that Red China, despite her perilous economic status in 1955, started out on its atomic project with certain advantages that we did not have when we began work on the A-bomb. First, Red Chinese experts knew that a bomb *could* be made. As Gen. Leslie R. Groves, wartime military commander of the U.S. atomic bomb project, summed it up shortly after Hiroshima:

> The big secret was really something we could not keep quiet, and that was the fact that the thing went off. That told more to the world than any other thing that could be told to them. It was something that we did not know until we had spent almost $2,000,000,000 and had worked about three years.

Second, the Red Chinese did not have to repeat our mistakes or follow our wartime blind alleys to their dead ends. U.S. experts spent much time and money on techniques and processes that no one would want to spend money on today. For example, we built a $350 million plant at Oak Ridge, Tenn., that we would not build the same way today. We know better methods of making A-bomb material—and so do the Red Chinese.

Third, a vast amount of nuclear information was freely available by 1955 and great improvements in atomic production had been made. New atomic plants would be more productive than those we designed before Hiroshima.

Fourth, Red China had resources of uranium minerals which it had already exploited, although it shipped these to refineries behind the Iron Curtain and later had to develop its own processing plants.

Fifth, and most important, Chinese experts knew before they began work on the A-bomb that a revolutionary nuclear development, the hydrogen bomb, would be a cheap shortcut to impressive nuclear firepower. It will be necessary to explore the technology of the H-bomb in some detail before the immense advantage of this weapon to Red China becomes apparent. Without the H-bomb "shortcut" Red China could hardly aspire to being more than a noisy cricket in the Nuclear Clubhouse.

To these five points we should add another—one which Edwin O. Reischauer, former U.S. Ambassador to Japan, stresses: "It should always be remembered that great capacity for hard work on the part of the Chinese people, their eagerness for learning, and their tremendous organizational abilities make Mainland China a land with great economic potential."

Red China set out to build nuclear weapons knowing full well that it could not equal equal the vast complex of atomic-production plants that the United States built after the war—much less even equal the wartime construction. But it apparently saw no military requirement for building up a huge arsenal of A-bombs. Red China opted to develop the A-bomb, to manufacture a modest number of these and to convert them into H-bombs of vastly greater power. To understand this sequence of events we need to look at how the United States built up its own stockpile of nuclear weapons.

There are basically two roads to travel in making material useful in A-bombs. One is to use uranium, convert it into a gas and then process this gas to remove from it the valuable atoms which qualify as A-bomb fuel. The other is to purify uranium in metallic form, arrange tons of this metal inside the core of an "atomic oven" and "cook" it until small amounts of a new atomic species, heavier than uranium, are produced. This new material—an artificially created element called plutonium—also qualifies as a bomb material. Because the Chinese chose the first process, we shall concentrate on it here, reserving discussion of plutonium for the next chapter.

During the war, U.S. experts traveled both roads to the production of bomb material because they did not know which would pay off first. In fact, at the site in Tennessee, where facilities were constructed for processing uranium gas, they tried a number of different methods—again, not knowing which would turn out most successfully. We shall describe the process that worked best—and which the Chinese also chose to use. The first U.S plant of this kind was built at Oak Ridge, Tenn., at a cost of $500 million. Located on the banks of the Clinch River, the wartime plant was a colossus—the world's largest factory. It was code-named K-25 and resembled a giant U, a half mile long and having some 44 acres of roof area. Inside the four-story structure miles and miles of corrosion-proof pipes snaked about in a maze of thousands of electric pumps and half a million valves. This inner plant might be likened to a huge distillery lying on its side. To those in the area who never got to look inside or even to thousands who worked three shifts round the clock to keep the monstrous distillery humming continuously, it was a mighty strange plant. One of the strangest things about it was the fact that apparently the same stuff—a greenish gas—went into and came out of the plant. Many were convinced that the whole operation was a New Deal boondoggle to make jobs.

Even today the Atomic Energy Commission keeps certain details of the Oak Ridge process highly secret, but the principles involved in the operation are well known. The uranium

gas that is pumped into the Oak Ridge plant is uranium hexa-
fluoride, or "hex" for short. During the war our uranium came
from the rich veins of pitchblende in the Belgian Congo; now
the bulk of our uranium is mined in the United States in the
form of a relatively low-grade ore. This is converted into
"yellow cake," an oxide of uranium, which in turn is purified
and chemically converted into hex—the feed material for the
Oak Ridge plant. The hex feed contains two kinds of uranium
atoms, chemically identical but physically different in weight.
The lighter species, called uranium 235, or U-235, constitutes
only 0.7 percent of the total number of uranium atoms; the
rest, or 99.3 percent, are a heavier species called U-238. The
whole purpose of making the atoms travel through hundreds
of miles of pipes in the Oak Ridge plant is to separate one
species from another and finally to produce a hex gas that is
highly enriched in U-235. The desired concentration of U-235
in the final product was in excess of 90 percent. Summing up:
the task at Oak Ridge was to boost the "hex" from an initial
0.7 percent U-235 content to over 90 percent purity.

Any gardener knows that if you throw dirt up against a
sieve, fine soil passes through while the pebbles and rubbish
are separated out. Physicists used ultrafine sieves within the
pipes, or diffusers, of the K-25 plant to effect a separation of the
two kinds of uranium atoms. Because of the infinitesimal size
of the gaseous atoms, the dimensions of the holes in the sieve
had to be exceedingly minute and they had to be uniformly
microscopic; otherwise the gas would gush through the sieve.
A sieve section the area of a dime would have to contain many
millions of holes, but to be effective many acres of this sieve
material, or barrier, had to be used. Since the two forms of
uranium differed so slightly in weight (about one percent difference) a single pass of gas through a barrier would produce
at best only a very slight increase in concentration of U-235 on
the far side of the barrier. We can visualize the separation process occurring at the barrier surface as follows: the U-235 atoms,
being slightly lighter than U-238 atoms, possess a bit more
speed and knock about faster; this means they bounce up

against or jostle the barrier more frequently and consequently have a better chance to pass through the tiny holes. Plant designers arranged to have the hex gas pumped through thousands of stages in sequence, thus gradually producing gas richer and richer in U-235 content. The entire system had to be leakproof so that the diffusing gas would not be lost; this was an engineering challenge at the time, but only because there had been no technical requirement for such leakproofness prior to the war.

The K-25 plant produced only a trickle of bomb material during the war and, in fact, even this was not highly enriched, so that it had to be reprocessed by other plants. But this was because many bugs had to be worked out of the process and improvements made in control of the entire production plant. Still the early postwar years saw no booming production at Oak Ridge. But as process improvements and design changes were made, the resulting production from the revamped K-25 plant became impressive. However, a stockpile of weapons numbered in the low hundreds did not impress the Joint Chiefs of Staff or the Joint Committee on Atomic Energy. Late in 1947 the Congress authorized a step-up in atomic production, and by the spring of 1948 a $700 million atomic construction program was under way. This first wave of atomic expansion was followed by a second when President Harry S Truman announced on December 1, 1950, that additional diffusion plants would be built at Oak Ridge and a vast new plant would be located near Paducah, Ky.

Sen. Brien McMahon, who had linked his political career to atomic energy, spearheaded a drive for a third round of plant expansion when he delivered an impassioned speech on September 21, 1951. He called for "a sweeping variety of atomic weapons—one model that takes the place of a thousand bazookas, another that makes unnecessary a hundred depth charges, yet another that would substitute for TNT stacked as high as Pike's Peak." Alarmed by the Korean war and the specter of a human sea of massed armies, the chairman of the Joint Committee on Atomic Energy proposed "an atomic army and an atomic navy and an atomic air force—in place of the conventional defenses," promising that this would "mean fewer men under arms."

President Truman did not go along with the full $5 billion per year atomic increase championed by the Atomic Committee, but in 1952 he approved a third atomic expansion. A new uranium separation plant of the Oak Ridge gaseous diffusion type was authorized for construction near Portsmouth, Ohio. When the Portsmouth plant was complete, the AEC's uranium separation plants added up to a capital investment of $2.5 billion. It would be wholly wrong to conclude that, since this amount was five times the cost of the original K-25 plant, atomic production was increased five-fold. If we look at the total electric power consumed in running the plants—a better but by no means complete index—then the complex of plants at Oak Ridge, Paducah, and Portsmouth had a capacity sixteen times that of the early postwar K-25 capability. Running full blast, as the three huge production complexes did in the mid-'50's, the electric-power consumption was 6 million kilowatts. At one time this amounted to 12 percent of the electrical demand in the U.S.A.

How was this prodigious consumption of electricity related to production of bomb material? The Atomic Energy Commission clamped a tight security lid on this information, and it was not until June 14, 1967, that the AEC released the pertinent data and then in a rather oblique manner. AEC press release K-125 contained the following information:

GASEOUS DIFFUSION PLANT COMPLEX
PRODUCTION CAPABILITY

Electric Power Usage	Annual Production of Separative Work
Megawatts	Millions of Kilogram Units
2,000	6.9
3,000	9.9
6,000	17.0

The public could hardly benefit from such a technical revelation, but to a physicist it meant that at full power the AEC production plants could turn out 85 tons per year of bomb material. If we include additional bomb material, plutonium, from other AEC production sites, then this amounts to a total annual production of almost 10,000 low-power A-bombs per year.

One way to arrive at the maximum size of the U.S. nuclear stockpile is to use data on the procurement of uranium. Over the past 20 years the AEC has paid $6.1 billion for 289,285 tons of uranium oxide, which yielded a quarter million tons of purified uranium. This amount of feed material would allow production of 1,000 tons of bomb material, enough for a stockpile in excess of 100,000 A-bombs. The actual weapons stockpile is not this large because (a) some material is diverted to fuel uses aboard nuclear submarines and in civilian atomic power plants, (b) some medium-power weapons require considerably more material than a low-power A-bomb, and (c) bomb material is kept in reserve, uncommitted to a specific weapon. Nonetheless, the U.S. atomic arsenal contains a truly incredible quantity of firepower. On April 21, 1964, Sen. John O. Pastore, chairman of the Joint Committee on Atomic Energy, disclosed: "Today we count our nuclear weapons in the tens of thousands."

The average citizen may justifiably exclaim at the size of this stockpile. And he may ask why its size had been surrounded by so much secrecy. After all, if we seek to deter another nation by implied force of nuclear arms, it would seem reasonable to advertise one's nuclear strength. There might have been reason to conceal weakness but not such nuclear muscle as the U.S. accumulated. Two reasons probably accounted for the U.S. policy of strict secrecy on the atom. First, ever since Hiroshima our atomic program has been treated as a thing apart from the regular business of our nation. Even in the Defense Department, high officials had to receive special clearance to receive nuclear information. Second, a policy of secrecy goes hand-in-glove with the weapons culture's grasp on our society. In the absence of secrecy a democracy can function normally by exposing issues to the test of controversy. Anyone who takes the trouble to read congressional hearings on defense appropriations will find blank spaces in the printed record where deletions have been made in the interests of national security. For example, in the latest defense hearings the unit price of a F-111A aircraft is deleted. Would this information help a potential enemy? In the case of the atomic stockpile, I suspect that if the facts had been disclosed at an early date there would have been a public outcry over the swollen size of the nuclear arsenal. Secrecy thus serves to insulate issues from the give-and-take of public discussion, and in such an atmosphere weapons may multiply almost without limit.

Given the national costs involved in building up the U.S. nuclear arsenal and the estimates on the size of the A-stockpile, it would seem that any attempt by the Red Chinese to challenge the United States in the nuclear field would be doomed to failure. Red China's economy and the growing demands of a huge population would argue against diverting men, money, and material to atomic weapons. If, at best, China could only muster a plant capacity less than that of the K-25 plant, would it make any sense even to try for a place in the atomic competition? Three factors, one political and two technical, probably played a dominant role in Mao's decision to go nuclear.

First, leaders of the Chinese Communist Party undoubtedly attached high value to the political impact that a nuclear explosion inside the Bamboo Curtain would have on other Asian countries. The implied power would be more important than any real nuclear capability.

Second, technical experts in Red China knew that improvements in the production of A-bomb material in gaseous-diffusion plants made it possible for a plant half the size of the K-25 wartime installation to produce a ton of product per year. Furthermore, the cost of such a plant might be less than $200 million.

Third, weapons specialists knew that while the number of A-bombs producible from a $200 million plant might be small compared to U.S. production, the nuclear material could be fabricated as triggers to detonate an H-bomb and thus give Red China a potent weapon in world propaganda.

In essence, it is the author's contention—published incidentally long before Red China tested its first H-bomb—that Chinese experts resolved to leapfrog their nuclear development, bypassing the arduous and extremely expensive duplication of our Oak Ridge-Paducah-Portsmouth production facilities. Instead, they would make a production facility adequate for making big atomic bombs which would be used to trigger H-bombs. They would, in effect, settle for some hundreds of these superbombs rather than try to build up a stockpile numbered in the tens of thousands of A-bombs.

To understand why this alternative was so attractive to the Red Chinese, we need to examine the technology of the H-bomb and to look at some nuclear economics. In the case of the United States, the H-bomb project was given official authorization by President Truman on January 31, 1950. However, such a superweapon had been thought about by U.S. scientists even before the A-bomb project was launched. In the 1930's physicists speculated about the nature of the fabulous outpouring of energy from the stars, especially from the closest one, our sun. They concluded that deep within the core of a star, atoms of hydrogen moving about at high speed because of the stellar temperature bumped into each other occasionally in a head-on collision in such a way that they fused together, forming an atom of helium. This, they theorized, was a very slow "burn" and involved no danger of a disastrous explosion. On the other hand, their calculations showed that if one could bring about a "fast-burn," then man might have within his power a fantastic explosive. But they realized it would be hopeless to try to make an H-bomb before one had first made A-bombs big enough to heat up hydrogen to a point where it would undergo fusion.

By 1948 bigger A-bombs were in hand and still more powerful ones were in prospect. When Russia tested its first A-bomb in August, 1949, it served to trigger a U.S. effort to outdistance the Soviets, not only in nuclear production but also in weapon power. To the experts who brainstormed the hydrogen problem in 1949-1950, the H-bomb seemed far from attainable—and, if it could be made, almost prohibitively expensive. For one thing, unlike the fusion inside stellar cores, the H-bomb would require a special kind of hydrogen for a fast-burn.

Just as uranium atoms are found in a light and heavy species, so too, hydrogen, the lightest of all elements, is made up of two kinds of atoms. Ordinary hydrogen, symbolized as H-1, is the most abundant form, so plentiful, in fact, that for a long time scientists did not think there was any other kind. Then in 1932 Prof. Harold C. Urey discovered heavy hydrogen, or H-2, also known as deuterium. This heavy hydrogen was to play a role in the H-bomb, but still another form of the light element, one not found in nature, was of critical importance. Tritium, or H-3, is the "unnatural" species of hydrogen that produces a fast-burn in the H-bomb. And it was the difficulty of producing tritium that caused the weapons experts so much trouble back in 1950. Physicists knew that they could manufacture tritium in the same plants that produce plutonium; all one needed to do was to use another light element—lithium—and "cook" it in the atomic oven. Then a nuclear reaction would spawn tritium, but on a weight-for-weight basis, production would be 80 times less than for plutonium; therefore the tritium would be a very expensive production item.

The cost-production problem associated with tritium was just one of the technical nettles which worried the H-experts. Even with a good supply of the rare tritium they did not know if the A-bomb trigger would ignite a fusion reaction in tritium. They knew from laboratory experiments that the fusion of deuterium and tritium atoms could produce energy. The nuclear reaction was easily written down as

$$H-2 + H-3 = He-4 + n$$

where He-4 stands for helium and n is the nuclear symbol for a particle called a neutron. The nuclear energy released in this fusion process is imparted to the neutron and the helium atom; these fly apart with tremendous speed. The neutron carries off four fifths of the total energy, which equals 17.6 Mev (this is the abbreviation for "million electron volt," a special energy unit used in nuclear physics) so that we speak of 14-Mev neutrons coming from the fusion reaction. Such neutrons are extremely fast and penetrate through solid matter with the greatest of ease, so much so that the bomb-makers had to worry about how to trap these particles inside the bomb; otherwise they would speed off into space and rob the explosion of concentrated energy.

Suffice it to say that during the first year after Truman's go-ahead on the project, the H-bomb was a very "iffy" proposition. Then weapons expert Dr. Edward Teller came to the conclusion that "a thermonuclear bomb might be constructed in a comparatively easy manner." The word thermonuclear is physicist-language for "heat-induced," and when it is used as above it means "H-bomb."

On November 1, 1952, the United States conducted its first test of a full-scale thermonuclear device. The site for the test was Elugelab Island, a low-lying sandy projection of the Eniwetok Atoll in the Marshall Islands. At this remote spot in the far Pacific a 25-foot cube, starkly black against the dazzling sand, had been built to house a device that was festooned with instruments. The contraption, code-named MIKE, exploded at the prescribed time with incredible power—the equal of 12 million tons of TNT stacked up in a single pile. A new word—the megaton—came into man's vocabulary, meaning the equivalent of one million tons of TNT. The 12-megaton MIKE explosion equaled the TNT that could be packed solid in a line of boxcars stretching from San Francisco to Chicago.

The MIKE device was too bulky to be used as a military explosive, but the weapons experts quickly used the data from the test to design a more compact weapon, which could be carried in a heavy bomber. On March 1, 1954, such a weapon was tested at Bikini Atoll; its explosive power was 15 megatons. It was this bomb, code-named BRAVO, which produced the radioactive fallout described earlier. The new superbomb was not only spectacularly explosive but it was also incredibly cheap. To understand this, we need to explore the nature of the superbomb's energy sources. It is really more appropriate to call it a superbomb than an H-bomb because, as the fallout demonstrated, most of the weapon power derived from fission of a heavy element rather than from fusion of a light element. However, the name H-bomb is generally used and we shall use the term interchangeably.

The new weapon's vast power came from a whitish, slightly blue, powder made up of fine crystals of the simplest chemical compound known to man and a from a brownish-black metal, the heaviest atom in nature. The powdery light salt is known as lithium deuteride; it is formed by heating the light metal lithium in a closed vessel into which is introduced heavy hydrogen gas. Lithium is an element more abundant than tin but less so than copper and it is available commercially in 500-pound drums at $9.50 per pound. The heavy metal is simply ordinary uranium. It can be the kind that is used as feed material by the AEC, costing no more than lithium, or it can be uranium metal recovered as waste from the "tailings" or discards of the Oak Ridge diffusion plants, in which case its cost is merely that of recovery.

This double package, the light powdery salt and the heavy metal, is involved in a complicated set of nuclear reactions that need not concern us here. We should mention, however, that the lithium, like hydrogen and uranium, is composed of a light and heavy atomic species which have different nuclear properties. However, these atoms are easy to separate and only a small amount of the separated lithium is required; once the nuclear reaction starts, it reaches a point where ordinary or unseparated lithium works very well in the bomb.

Because of its importance to the Chinese nuclear program, we shall describe the H-bomb mechanism very briefly, omitting technical details and concentrating on the economics of the weapon. Inside the bomb, lithium serves as a source of instantly-made tritium; it is generated when the A-bomb trigger explodes and releases a great burst of neutrons. The neutrons strike the separated form of lithium, split it asunder and

and release tritium. The latter then reacts with deuterium in a fusion reaction. If every atom in a pound of lithium deuteride split and every tritium atom fused to a deuterium partner, then this single pound of salt would release energy equal to 29,000 tons of TNT—*i.e.*, 29 kilotons, or more than twice the power of the Hiroshima explosion. In practice such perfection cannot be achieved, but it is reasonable to think of a pound of the whitish crystals releasing five kilotons of energy.

We have seen that the fusion reaction releases neutrons that are exceedingly speedy. These fast neutrons are of double utility in the superbomb. First, they split ordinary lithium to form more tritium, thus reducing the requirement for having the more expensive separated lithium in the bomb. Second, the speedy neutrons split or fission U-238 atoms, thus making a previously thought worthless material into a bomb fuel. Because of these nuclear mechanisms, the H-bomb turned out to be a surprisingly cheap weapon. Measured in dollars per pound of explosiveness it is a dirt-cheap weapon.

Consider first the cost of an A-bomb, one powerful enough to serve as an atomic trigger for an H-bomb. Such a bomb probably costs about $350,000 if mass-produced and releases energy equivalent to 100 kilotons or 0.1 megaton. That means a ton of TNT equivalent is available at $3.50. If we now add several tons of lithium salt and uranium, boosting total weapon cost to, say, $600,000 we can get explosive power equal to 10 megatons. That figures out to be 6 cents per ton of TNT!

Given such supercheap explosiveness, any cost-minded person would be foolish to build up a vast stockpile of expensive A-bombs or to build the plants for turning out the required bomb stuff. The obvious course would be to make production plants sufficient to make enough material for a quantity of big A-bombs and use these as triggers for superbombs. There is now solid evidence that Red China took this beeline course to the H-bomb.

Even so, China's conquest of the atom could not have been an easy one. Its national economy was stretched taut trying to keep up with elementary demands of an emerging agricultural and quite technologically backward society. As we have seen, Red China sought aid from its Communist neighbor, and on October 15, 1958, the two countries concluded an "Agreement on New Technology for National Defense." This Sino-Soviet agreement included, according to Peking, "a sample of an atomic bomb and technical data concerning its manufacture." However, technical cooperation between the two Communist powers dissolved a year and a half later. No Soviet A-bomb was ever transferred to Red China, but this does not mean that the Soviets did not give their Asiatic comrades a helping hand. We know that Russia engineered complete factories for the Chinese and exported to them valuable plant material and equipment. This included hydrogenerators, steel pipe, motors, controls, and numerous items useful in constructing an Oak Ridge-type diffusion plant. But there is no evidence, other than some rumors, that the Soviets gave technical aid specifically to help the Chinese in the construction of a diffusion facility.

A U-2 aircraft flying high over Red China photographed territory in Kansu province where an appendage of the Great Wall hooks down to the Yellow River. The object of the reconnaissance was to survey activities around Lanchow, an industrial city of 1,200,000 people. Photo-analysts inspecting the U-2 blowups could hardly believe their eyes—there on a plain overlooked by high mountains of the Wu-ch'uan-shan range was a huge rectangular plant under construction, the like of which was to be found nowhere in the Orient. Diffusion plants are not uniquely identifiable from aerial photos, but the size of the installation suggested that the Chinese were building an Oak Ridge plant. To be sure, it was not the size of the wartime K-25 plant—more like the K-27 addition to it—but it was an impressive piece of construction.

Subsequent intelligence made it clear that the huge Lanchow plant was designed to produce enriched uranium for A-bombs This information was hard for some skeptics to swallow; they felt that the Chinese were not up to the task. Where would they get the uranium? The miles and miles of corrosion-proof pipe? The endless array of valves, pumps, and controls? And, of course, the necessary kilowatts of electricity?

Red China, as we have noted, had been shipping uranium ore to Communist countries. We know that it continued to do so, but demanded part of the purified uranium in return. Furthermore, it launched a "keuikuanra," or race-for-uranium, which resulted in ore finds in the Kiangsi and Kwangtung provinces along with producing mines in Sinkiang. Red China managed to produce enough "yellow cake" to feed its Yellow River plant. Hydrogenerators, one of which came from the Soviet Union, located upstream on the Yellow River, provided 150,000 kilowatts of electrical power—not as much as required by the K-25 plant but adequate for the Lanchow plant's initial needs. The steel plants Russia had given to Red China must have been most useful in supplying the special pipe in which the greenish hex gas diffused. Much of the instrumentation and control equipment must have been adapted to "Chinese copy" techniques in small industries.

But where did the Chinese get their "barrier"? Without this critically important "sheet of holes" to effect separation of the uranium atoms, the Lanchow plant would be a bust. Details of this fragile barrier are still kept highly classified by the Atomic Energy Commission. The AEC developed special automated processes for manufacturing acres of the precious barrier. It is still a mystery as to how the Lanchow experts solved their problem. Perhaps it was through sheer Coolie patience and hand work, but somehow or other they produced the required acres of micro-pored barriers.

Enriched uranium from the Lanchow plant was drained from the final diffusion section and chemically converted from the fluoride form to pure metal. Flat cakes of this bomb material were handed over to metallurgists, who in turn transformed them into split hemispheres which form the "nuke," or nuclear core of an A-bomb. The critical material traveled westward to the test center on the Takla Makan desert. In the late summer of 1964 reconnaissance U-2's spotted a test tower being erected at Lob Nor, a dry lake, and U.S. authorities knew that Red China would soon make its first A-test.

On October 16, 1964, Red China became the first Asiatic power to test an atomic weapon. Invisible fragments of the bomb cloud traveled eastward, and high above the Pacific Ocean some radioactive debris was scooped up in special filters aboard U.S. aircraft. The filters were rushed to a U.S. analysis center that had much experience in long-range nuclear detection. Analysis showed that the first Red Chinese A-bomb had been roughly 20 kilotons in power—and that it contained enriched uranium.

Many U.S. experts were genuinely shocked when they heard the news—not so much that Red China could develop a bomb but that it had succeeded in producing enriched uranium. All four nuclear powers before China had used plutonium in their first A-test. Red China had done it the smart way—a route which we thought only an industrialized society would elect to take.

China's nuclear progress since its first shot is summed up in the following chronology:

TEST NO.	DATE	WEAPON POWER	REMARKS
1	Oct. 16, 1964	20 kilotons	Tower shot
2	May 15, 1965	20-40 "	" "
3	May 9, 1966	200 "	10,000 ft. altitude
4	Oct. 26, 1966	20-40 "	Ballistic burst
5	Dec. 29, 1966	300 "	Contained lithium
6	June 17, 1967	3 megatons	Atmospheric shot

Except for Test No. 4, which was an operational test of a ballistic missile, there is a steady increase in weapon power. In two years and eight months after the first A-test, Red Chinese experts succeeded in detonating a lithium-uranium bomb at least two hundred times more powerful than the weapon that blasted Hiroshima.

Production at the Lanchow plant has been improved and augmented to a two-bomb-per-week schedule, meaning low-power A-bombs. The Chinese nuclear stockpile at the end of 1967 would have exceeded 100 of such weapons, but it is very probable that priority has been assigned to the development and production of H-bombs. It would not be very surprising to find an early Lob Nor test in the multimegaton range, designed to have political impact on the outside world. Given China's present nuclear capability, and not allowing for any new production plants, Peking should have at its disposal in 1970 a stockpile of 100 H-bombs.

Nonetheless, a stationary stockpile is by itself not a military threat. To be effective as weapons, the nuclear explosives must be deliverable to their targets. The fact that Chinese Test No. 4 was an operational trial of a ballistic missile, albeit of intermediate range, indicates that their experts are double-tracking their weapons development, putting the missile and the warhead on parallel paths. U.S. experts, especially those in the Military Establishment, have generally taken the position that the Chinese will require many years to build up an ICBM force capable of challenging that of the U.S.A. If one looks at the costs for U.S. Strategic Retaliatory Forces, they are discouraging for a nation like Red China. For example, U.S. funds expended over the past seven years total $60 billion for our modern strategic delivery systems. When all the costs are counted, it turns out that a single missile such as Minuteman runs at least 10 times the price of its nuclear warhead. In fact, this is a rock-bottom multiplier for missile-to-warhead costs; for some systems described in Chapter 6 it is much higher.

Whenever U.S. experts in the official defense community appraise the initial capability of another competitor, they seem to be bedazzled by the cost and complexity of our own weapons systems. Furthermore, they assume that another nation will be just as perfectionist and sophisticated in weapons development as we are and will therefore have to pay the same price. For example, our ICBM's have been developed to a point where their accuracy is one-half mile or less—to be more precise, we mean that 50 percent of the thrown warheads land within a circle one mile in diameter. The guidance systems for such accuracy are highly complex gadgets that have required years of development. But would Red China's missile experts set their sights on the same accuracy? If they have in mind targeting a city like Los Angeles, Chicago, or Philadelphia, then a half-mile accuracy is not necessary—one can use a cruder and cheaper guidance system that can be developed in much less time.

U.S. estimates of enemy capability are often colored by what I call "weapon ego." Having been the first to develop the A-bomb, the United States found it comforting to assume that other nations would take many years to develop the same weapon. The longer it took, say Russia, to make the bomb, the greater would be the difficulty of the task and the higher would be America's status as a weapon-maker. For example, shortly after Hiroshima, Gen. Leslie R. Groves predicted to a congressional committee that "one nation could catch up and produce a bomb, if they did it in complete secrecy, probably within fifteen to twenty years—more likely the latter." Then, double-thinking his prediction, the general added: "It may be that instead of this being twenty years it should be forty to fifty." China was not even on the list of nations that General Groves thought might be capable of making the bomb.

Once a nation demonstrates it knows how to make a new weapon, we continue to rate them as scientific pygmies and then, almost as though afflicted by a national schizophrenia, we flip-flop and view them as technological giants. This was the techno-history of our atomic-missile experience with the Soviet Union and it will probably repeat itself in the case of Red China. It hardly requires comment that the pygmy-to-giant transformation represents self-interest in various groups within the weapons culture that stand to profit from contracts that result when "gaps" develop and must be filled. An example of this is our initial disbelief that the Red Chinese could test a nuclear-ballistic missile, the subsequent long time-scales assigned to their operational status, and then a clamor for Nike-X to defend us against Chinese ICBM's.

If the United States deploys a "thin" Nike-X defense, of the type discussed in Chapter 7, to counter the threat of Chinese missiles, then a number of consequences may follow. For example, it certainly raises the prestige of Red China if the world's top-rated technological power finds it necessary to erect ballistic defenses against a Chinese attack. It may even force China's neighbors to accelerate their own defense preparations. Japan, for example, is considering development and deployment of its own ballistic defenses. These would in turn require nuclear warheads and make another nation "go nuclear."

Chinese experts might respond to the deployment of Nike-X by feinting with ICBM development and opting to take other strategic approaches to the United States. One rather obvious and sinister approach is through the soft underbelly of the U.S.—the Gulf of Mexico. Chinese submarines could transfer nuclear explosives to shrimp boats which would then chug into Gulf ports in Texas or Florida. These Trojan shrimp boats could unload their nuclear cargo directly to refrigerated trucks. These, adorned with an outer stack of shrimp containers, could be dispatched to Detroit, Washington, St. Louis, and a dozen other U.S. cities. The weapons could be pre-set to explode on a fixed time schedule depending on the staging of the attack and the nature of the blackmail involved. Naturally, there are grave risks and difficulties in this underbelly route, but our shores cannot be sealed off against such nuclear invasion.

Another mode of nuclear attack that would render ballistic missile defense futile is that of offshore nuclear explosions. Submarines or even surface ships, such as grain cargo carriers, could approach to within several hundred miles off the Pacific coast. Each vessel could easily carry many H-bombs or a few "hyper-bombs"—*i.e.*, gigantic lithium-uranium bombs 10 times more powerful than Khrushchev's 100-megaton bomb. No such bomb has been tested yet (how could it be safely exploded?), but there is no theoretical upper limit to this weapon's explosiveness and, with a 100-megaton bomb in hand, larger weapons can be engineered. The blast-heat from these surface or sub-surface bursts would not extend damage to continental U.S.A., but the prevailing westerly winds would sweep fallout over much of the United States, enveloping the western and central states in a mantle, largely invisible, of radioactivity. If this sounds like something out of H. G. Wells' *War of the Worlds*, the reader is warned that it is definitely not fiction.

Moreover, the Oriental mind may devise strategic plans that do not even focus on mainland U.S.A. but rather concentrate on fomenting nuclear trouble of a different kind. Consider, for example, Red China's role as a country willing to sell, loan, or give nuclear explosives to countries like Cuba. Conceivably this could be done under the guise of peacetime applications of thermonuclear energy; after all, the United States has advertised its Project Plowshare and talks of using nuclear explosives to dig a canal across the Panama isthmus. How would the United States react to the presence of nuclear explosives in Cuba? Or, in the event of another Arab-Israeli war, how would we view Chinese nuclear aid to the Arabs?

The fact is that these questions loom much larger now that China is a nuclear power. The whole framework of deterrence is altered by the fact that a third great land power possesses nuclear weapons. Neither Britain nor France qualifies as a great nuclear power because of their limited geography. Because they count Red China as Nuclear Power No. 5, many people fail to perceive that it greatly complicates the deterrent equation. Even with France and Britain possessing nuclear weapons, the U.S. and the U.S.S.R. really considered deterrence a two-way matter. But with China in the picture it becomes a three-way proposition. Robert Oppenheimer's graphic illustration of the U.S. and the U.S.S.R. as "two scorpions in a bottle" focused on a pair of contestants. Adding a third sting-tailed member to this nuclear company is not an act that makes for much harmony.

The present Chinese nuclear scorpion is not like the other two, and its behavior may not conform to theirs. Both the United States and the Soviet Union have much to lose if nuclear war breaks out, and it is the forecertainty of this loss that deters nuclear aggression. But deterrence depends on a nation's having the utmost respect for that which it might lose—and on knowing beyond doubt that it could be lost. Deterrence works best where the opposing powers have comparable Gross National Products per capita. The U.S. and the U.S.S.R. are industrialized, but China is only semi-industrialized and has a G.N.P. per capita one thirtieth that of the United States. For example, electrical energy use is a measure of industrialization, and in the case of Mainland China its electrical consumption on a per capita basis is a hundredth that of the U.S.A. Urbanization is another measure of how far a nation has climbed the industrial ladder; here Red China is clearly agricultural, having four fifths of its population devoted to food production and only a seventh of its people living in cities of any considerable size.

Red China's value system must be linked to its culture, to its people, and to its good earth. And its psychology must be that of invincibility based on centuries of contempt for conquest. China has a monomania which holds that it is the one civilization on the planet and that all other people are barbarians—technologically adept but barbarians nonetheless. If we are to judge how deterrence may work applied to Red China we need to ask two questions:

First, do Chinese leaders understand the power of modern weapons?

Second, how much do they value their people?

Answering the first question is not easy because it involves looking into the mentality of Chinese leadership. The aged leaders, survivors of The Long March, are not apt to absorb the tough technology of nuclear weapons. Particularly, they are unlikely to comprehend the strange dimension of radioactive fallout, which is an instrument-sensed hazard, evaluated in dial readings marked in radiation units. It may require some time for appreciation of this subtle hazard—especially that of crop contamination and land-use denial—to percolate through to the higher echelons of command. Blast and heat are readily sensed, and the color movies of China's nuclear tests have undoubtedly conveyed the significance of these primary weapon effects. Comprehension of the fallout threat is something that may take much longer. Yet it is precisely this effect that is most potent in attacking an agricultural country like China.

Secretary McNamara has spelled out nuclear deterrence as applied to Red China in his testimony on fiscal year 1968 appropriations for the Defense Department:

> *"China is far from being an industrialized nation. However, what industry it has is heavily concentrated in a comparatively few cities. We estimate, for example, that a relatively small number of warheads detonated over 50 Chinese urban centers would destroy half of the urban population (more than 50 million people) and more than one half of the industrial capacity. Moreover, such an attack would also destroy most of the key governmental, technical, and managerial personnel, and a large proportion of the skilled workers."*

In the same testimony Mr. McNamara defines nuclear deterrence as applied to the Soviet Union and speaks of 80 to 120 million fatalities and destruction of up to two thirds of Soviet industry. I would think that such a deterrent would indeed deter. The men in the Kremlin would have to be insane to "accept" such punishment in response to obvious aggression. But 50 million Chinese represent just 6 percent of the total population of Red China. Would the anticipation of such loss deter the Red leaders?

During the course of congressional hearings on mainland China's economy, Sen. Jacob Javits wondered about this very question. He said: "Somehow or other our people think the balance of terror will work with the Russians, but we wonder about people who talk about expending 300 million casualties and still being able to survive." Senator Javits was referring to Mao Tse-tung's assertion of 1957: "We aren't afraid of atomic bombs. What if they killed even 300 million? We would still have plenty more—China would be the last country to die." A decade later, Mao has not rephrased his words, but China remains inscrutable so far as deterrent experts are concerned. No one on this side of the Bamboo Curtain knows what price Peking might be willing to pay.

The further that Red China climbs on the rungs of the industrial ladder, the more it will have to value and the more our sophisticated deterrent doctrine should work. In addition, the more that Chinese leaders learn about the lethal effects of nuclear weapons, the more they should appreciate the certainty of fallout mortality. Here the United Nations has quite tardily studied the problem of nuclear warfare and released a report of the Secretary General on October 10, 1967. The U.N. report concluded:

> There is one inescapable and basic fact. It is that the nuclear armories which are in being already contain large megaton weapons every one of which has a destructive power greater than that of all the conventional explosive that has ever been used in warfare since the day gunpowder was discovered. Were such weapons ever to be used in numbers, hundreds of millions of people might be killed, and civilization as we know it, as well as organized life, would inevitably come to an end in the countries involved in the conflict. Many of those who survived the immediate destruction, as well as others in countries outside the area of conflict, would be exposed to widely spreading radioactive contamination, and would suffer from long-term effects of irradiation and transmit, to their offspring, a genetic burden which would become manifest in the disabilities of later generations.

This single paragraph encapsulates the knowledge that must sink into the conscience of the world.

No discussion nuclear deterrence can dismiss the grave internal problems of Red China, which may generate great pressures demanding some form of venting. The combination of a swelling population and restricted agriculture is not a happy one for China or for the world. China's arable land, limited as it is by terrain and climate, will be called upon in 1980 to feed one billion people. One acre will have to provide food for four people. Mao's "walk on two legs" policy of simultaneous development of industry and agriculture, so set back by reverses in the Great Leap Forward, becomes a precarious national posture as China attempts to compete in an arms race.

In the United States the emergence of Red China as Nuclear Power No. 3 had a curious history. At first there was much reluctance to believe that this semi-industrialized nation could develop its own A-bomb. Then there was doubt that it could follow up this breakthrough with any significant nuclear production, and at the same time official circles in Washington discredited Red China's ability to make weapons systems capable of delivering the new weapons. Gradually these views changed and underwent drastic revision when the Chinese H-bomb proved that Communist China was not an amateur in modern technology. But I suspect these technological developments were less significant than political considerations involving Vietnam, the Cold War, and the machinations of the "military-industrial-political complex" on the home front.

No war in Vietnam could persist for as long as it has without throwing into prominence the role of Red China. The momentum of the Cold War was sustained for the first two decades of the postwar era by the specter of the Soviet Union. With its post-Khrushchev moderation, the U.S.S.R. has loomed as a less compelling adversary in the Cold War, and consequently Red China becomes inflated as successor to the Soviet Union. Most recently, we have witnessed a rather weird gyration of U.S. defense policy in which a "thin" ballistic-missile defense has been announced to counter the threat of Red China's future nuclear missiles. But, as we shall show, the U.S. ballistic undertaking is primarily a response to pressure from military-industrial-political forces, and Red Chinese nuclear strength is used as a convenient rationalization for the defense program.

V

THE HONEY-VENOM

"Nuclear technology is advancing so rapidly that the cost of building a minimum nuclear capability is decreasing dramatically every year in terms of capital expenditure, of human skills, and of time."

—DEFENSE SECRETARY ROBERT S. MC NAMARA
October 22, 1964

Red China's success in developing nuclear weapons was all the more impressive because it was the first semi-industrialized country to become a member of the nuclear club. President Kennedy did not live to see China become a nuclear power but, as we have noted, he worried about the prospect. His concern was that nuclear weapons would spread—or diffuse, to use his favorite word—to smaller countries. Regarding this possibility he said in 1963:

"I ask you to stop and think what it would mean to have nuclear weapons in so many hands, in the hands of countries large and small, stable and unstable, responsible and irresponsible, scattered throughout the world. There would be no rest for anyone then, no stability, no real security, and no chance of effective disarmament."

Sen. Robert Kennedy has carried on in the tradition of his President-brother and has warned of the dangers of nuclear diffusion. For example, in a Senate speech in 1965, he drew attention to the peril where nuclear weapons might be used in disputes over Cyprus, the Gaza Strip, or the Rann of Kutch. "There could be no security," he stated, "when a decision to use these weapons might be made by an unstable demagog, or by the head of one of the two-month governments that plague so many countries, or by an irresponsible military commander, or even by an individual pilot." Senator Kennedy cautioned that "it is far more difficult and expensive to construct an adequate system of control and custody than to develop the weapons themselves."

Behind the fears expressed by the two Kennedys lurks a hazard which is of a technological nature and to which we have only alluded up to now. It is the alternative method of making bomb material through the use of machines known as nuclear reactors. To understand why the product of these machines, plutonium, is a honey-venom—a boon and a peril—we need to go back to the wartime days and revisit the atomic scientists as they struggled with the task of making an A-bomb.

Scientists knew that the gaseous-diffusion process for separating uranium atoms, sorting out the U-235 species from the more abundant U-238 variety, would be an expensive and time-consuming gamble. In the race against time to develop an A-bomb before Hitler succeeded, the Oak Ridge method of manufacturing bomb material might not pay off. Therefore they looked into all possibilities that gave a glimmer of hope in providing an alternative route to bomb material. One rather "far out" possibility seemed worth investigating; it was a method of transforming the heavy, unwanted U-238 atom into an entirely new atom which would have nuclear characteristics like the valued U-235.

To accomplish this conversion of U-238 into a bomb material, physicists hit upon the following scheme: If one bombarded ordinary uranium, which we know is 99.3 percent U-238, with neutrons, then laboratory experiments using cyclotron-generated neutrons showed that a new atom, U-239, was born. This newly formed "unnatural" atom then proceeded to disintegrate radioactively, creating a brand-new element called neptunium.

Uranium is the 92nd element, the last, on the Periodic Chart of Elements. Neptunium, element No. 93, was therefore something quite new in nature's scheme of things. As it turned out, this artificially formed atom of neptunium was also radioactive, disintegrating rather soon to form still another new species called plutonium. The latter is element 94. The specific atom produced by this intricate sequence of nuclear events is plutonium-239 or Pu-239. It would, the scientists predicted, have properties like U-235, which was to be so laboriously separated out from U-238 in the Oak Ridge plants.

It was all very well to produce invisible trace quantities of this bomb material in cyclotron experiments, but how could it be produced in quantity sufficient to make A-bombs? Using cyclotrons was out of the question; it would cost too much to make enough of these atom smashers to supply the necessary neutrons for converting uranium into plutonium. Physicists saw a possible source of neutrons in the splitting of the uranium atom. Laboratory experiments showed that when uranium atoms fissioned, the disruptive process was accompanied by the release of neutrons. No one knew just how many were emitted in a single fission, but if more than two neutrons were released it might just be possible to build a machine in which there would be a self-sustaining chain of fissions. Each generation of uranium atom-splittings would produce enough neutrons to fission another generation, and so in a chain reaction. And in the process, if it could be achieved, there might be enough neutrons available to bombard the "useless" U-238 and convert it to useful plutonium. This "wild idea" appealed to the imagination of physicists like Enrico Fermi, a brilliant Italian scientist who was scientifically ambidextrous—he could on one hand carry out marvelous experiments in the laboratory and, on the other, devise brilliant theories on the structure of the atom's core or nucleus. Equally intrigued by the possible chain reaction was Leo Szilard, a Hungarian-born physicist with a flair for stabbing in the dark and coming up with ideas for new ventures. Another fellow Hungarian, Eugene P. Wigner, shared enthusiasm for neutron experiments but concentrated on theoretical calculations. The trio formed the intellectual spearhead of U.S. research on the nuclear chain reaction in 1940-41.

When the physicists tackled the job of seeing if a chain reaction could be achieved, they knew from cyclotron experiments that it would be hopeless to attempt anything so straightforward as piling up a great mass of uranium. No matter how large a pile, even one as large as the Great Pyramid, and no matter how pure they might get uranium, there was no hope for an automatic chain reaction. Physicists knew why this was so hopeless; the U-235 atoms would split when hit by neutrons produced in fission, but the U-238 atoms would not. Since there exist 139 of the U-238 atoms for every U-235 atom, the chain reaction was squelched. It was as though the fluffy dry tinder (U-235) was dampened by the presence of wet logs (U-238) so that nothing would start to blaze (chain react). Somehow or other the tinder had to be insulated from the wet logs.

The dilemma facing the scientists in trying to insulate one atom from the other was that they were intimately intermingled in natural uranium. Separating them from each other was the monumental task for the diffusion plants. Therefore some "trick" had to be invented. Physicists hit upon the idea of interspersing chunks of uranium inside a great cube of graphite. The principle underlying their scheme was that the graphite, which is the light element carbon, would serve to bounce neutrons around and slow them down, keeping them wandering around inside the pile and not colliding too frequently with the uranium atoms. Laboratory data showed that slowed-down neutrons would be less likely to get lost in U-238 and more likely to split U-235 atoms. It was a clever plan, and in the summer of 1942 work was started in a squash court under the West Stands of the University of Chicago athletic field to assemble a large cube of graphite in which uranium would be positioned at points carefully calculated on the basis of small-scale experiments with uranium-graphite blocks. The work was carried out in the greatest secrecy so that nobody outside the atomic project would know what was afoot. Incidentally, the greasy graphite impregnated the soles of scientists' shoes, and bootblacks in the neighborhood (only infrequently, because few scientists paid to have their shoes shined) knew that something queer was going on at the university.

The story of the world's first successful chain reaction has been told many times and needs only to be pointed up by recalling the date: December 2, 1942. The world marks this date as the point in time when science crossed the threshold of the Atomic Age. Not many people are aware that the success of this chain reaction had been assumed. For example, Eugene Wigner had been working all that year on calculations of a plutonium-production pile of very high power. The first pile, or chain reactor, which flickered briefly on December 2, 1942, produced one-one hundredth of the power needed for an ordinary household electric light. The West Stands pile contained 385 tons of graphite and 40 tons of uranium; its power was raised to 200 watts before it was dismantled.

On January 9, 1943, Dr. Wigner issued his report CE-407 "Preliminary Process Design of Liquid-cooled Power Plant Producing 500,000 Kilowatts." CE stood for Chicago Engineering and the report number 407 was given very limited distribution even within the guarded area of the atomic project. Wigner, a slightly-built, soft-voiced physicist had dreamed up a design for the world's most powerful power plant. Like the West Stands pile, the new machine would be constructed of blocks of graphite. But because it would run at such a high power level, some provision had to be made to remove heat from the device. This heat is given off when the atom splits and its fragments fly apart and collide with other uranium atoms nearby. Unless this uranium were cooled, it would continue to heat up until it melted and, of course, then the chain reactor would be ruined. In addition, since the split atoms of uranium are highly radioactive, any melt-down of the uranium would be extremely hazardous. With these hazards in mind, Wigner designed uranium fuel elements in the form of short cylinders clad in air-tight cans of aluminum. These were centered in aluminum tubes which ran horizontally through the massive array of graphite. Cold water, pumped through these channels, served to remove heat from the uranium fuel elements. This was the basic design of three huge reactors that were built in the state of Washington near the town of Hanford.

The Du Pont Company, which built the uranium-graphite reactors on the banks of the Columbia River, was reluctant to accept Wigner's design, but after some delays agreed to it, reducing the power level to half the design value. The vast heat generated inside the reactors was unwanted during the war and it was simply discarded by allowing the coolant water to return to the Columbia River. The product desired was plutonium which gradually, atom by atom, built up in the uranium inside the reactor core. After "cooking" in this atomic oven for some months, the uranium cylinders were pushed out of the pile, dumped into hoppers and allowed to "cool" underwater. Then when much of the intense radioactivity had spent itself, the aluminum was chemically removed from the uranium and the latter was sent through a long "canyon," where remotely controlled instruments tended the isolation of the trace amounts of plutonium from the dissolved uranium. Thick barriers of concrete many feet deep protected workers from the penetrating radiation. Finally, the plutonium was shipped in carefully controlled amounts to the weapons laboratory at Los Alamos, N. Mex. No shipment could be permitted to contain in a single package more than a few pounds of plutonium. Too much—an overcritical amount—would automatically chain-react, although not explosively. To work in an A-bomb the plutonium metal had to be highly purified and machined into hemispheres. These, when mated together to form a hollow sphere, would be designed to be just below the critical point. By fitting this baseball-sized sphere inside an ingeniously-contrived cocoon of high-explosive charges, weapons experts managed to produce a nuclear explosion.

The TNT cocoon is exquisitely fashioned out of separate prismatic wedges of high explosive which fit together to form a perfect sphere. Each TNT wedge, or "lens," is equipped with a detonator, and these are all interconnected so that an electrical impulse blows them up at precisely the same instant. Then the inwardly bound explosive wave is neatly focused by the action of the lenses and squeezes the hollow plutonium core or "nuke" into a solid mass. The "nuke" achieves criticality, a chain reaction rips to completion, and in less than one millionth of a second the solid metal core becomes converted into an ultrahot gas—like the fiery center of a star. A single pound of plutonium is the equal of 8,000 tons of TNT if every atom splits, which does not happen in practice, and it takes on the order of 10 pounds or so to form a critical mass.

The selfsame pound of bomb material can be persuaded to give up its vast energy slowly, in an orderly manner, over a long period of time by using it as nuclear fuel in a chain reactor. A single pound of nuclear fuel can produce the same heat as 2,300,000 pounds of coal, and in this statistic we can appreciate the honey nature of plutonium, whose venom quality in a nuclear weapon is quite apparent.

When the reactor experts designed the huge Hanford plants, they knew full well the peacetime potential of a nuclear reactor. But the wartime mission was to produce bomb material, so they bypassed the problem of using reactor heat for power purposes. That could come later—after the war was won. But by the same token, physicists knew that civilian power reactors, whose heat produced electrical power, could never be made without a Jekyll-and-Hyde character. Neutrons, so important to the reactor's operation, could always be put to use making plutonium. This dual nature of reactors worried Leo Szilard even before the end of the war. I recall many after-hours sessions with him and a few associates in the Metallurgical Laboratory, the name given the atomic project at the University of Chicago, when the future of atomic energy was discussed. Once the A-bomb was public knowledge, Szilard was free to commit his thoughts to papers that did not bear a SECRET stamp. I have in my files one of Szilard's earliest memoranda, dated August 14, 1945, one paragraph of which reflects his concern about the postwar hazard of civilian power development:

The Suppression of Atomic Power Development—

If Russia, the United States, and other countries were willing to forgo the use of atomic power for peacetime purposes, one could have a system of control that would be fairly simple since it would be almost sufficient to control the movements of raw materials. Ores of uranium would have to be mined under control and transported to some "neutral" territory. Whether or not it would be permitted to have in a neutral territory installations of certain limited types of atomic power plants is a question of minor importance. It appears likely that if the major powers were willing to forgo the use of atomic power, a system of controls could be set up without encountering too great difficulties.

Here we see that Szilard had implicitly assumed that the control problem would be virtually impossible if nuclear power were to proliferate around the world. Part of Szilard's concern over the hazards of atomic power plants turned out to be premature. He, along with the majority of scientists, assumed that with the ending of war, scientists and engineers would team up under government sponsorship and bring reactors to a state of technical maturity.

The early postwar period of atomic development was marked by great optimism about the splendors of cheap and abundant nuclear power. The success of the Hanford plutonium production reactors made it seem likely that the generation of electrical energy by new designs would come about rather quickly. For a number of reasons nuclear power underwent a prolonged period of gestation. Scientists either had underestimated the technical difficulties of taming reactor power for civilian applications or they had overestimated the proficiency of engineers. Furthermore, the Atomic Energy Commission dillydallied in its postwar development of peaceful uses of the atom, giving greater priority to military applications. In its birthing process, the AEC came under intense congressional fire, with the result that the new agency became timid about taking bold new steps on its own.

Optimism about civilian atomic power gradually subsided,

and then, on December 8, 1953, President Eisenhower gave his famous "Atoms for Peace" address before the United Nations. "The United States knows that peaceful power from atomic energy is no dream of the future," said the President. "That capability, already proved, is here—now—today." This announcement caught scientists by surprise, as indeed it did all but a few AEC officials who had gotten a brief glimpse at Eisenhower's text. In its seven-year history the Atomic Energy Commission had not pushed nuclear-reactor development vigorously enough so that economic power was just around the corner. Certainly the technical facts did not justify any belief that it had turned that corner. We know, of course, that it was not a reality for another decade.

President Eisenhower told the United Nations: "Who can doubt, if the entire body of the world's scientists and engineers had adequate amounts of fissionable material with which to test and develop their ideas, that this capability would be rapidly transformed into universal, efficient, and economic usage?" This nuclear proliferation was the very thing which frightened scientists because of the honey-venom nature of reactor fuel. Had anything happened since 1945 to make such a global nuclear sharing safe? Eisenhower proposed that the nations of the world pool their uranium fuel resources, making "joint contributions from their stockpiles of normal uranium and fissionable materials to an International Atomic Energy Agency." The latter would be set up by the United Nations to be "responsible for the impounding, storage, and protection of the contributed fissionable and other materials." As for safeguards, President Eisenhower stated: "The ingenuity of our scientists will provide special safe conditions under which such a bank of fissionable material can be made essentially immune to surprise seizure."

A short-lived flurry of speculation and hope centered on a technical process for rendering fissionable material safe, but this did not hold up. The U.S. Atomic Energy Commission was embarrassed by the sudden swoop of the Eisenhower approach; it was not ready to implement the grandiose plan of atom pooling—practical reactors were still being developed and realistic safeguards eluded ingenuity. The rocky road to peacetime nuclear power seemed to be full of detours and offered no short cuts. Bringing other nations into the nuclear activity might be a useful exercise in international cooperation, but the United States could not expect the Johnny-come-lately countries to produce a sudden surge that would advance reactor technology.

President Eisenhower's atoms-for-peace proposal caught the AEC off guard, but it recovered sufficiently by 1955 to hold an international conference in Geneva. This meeting featured a U.S. disclosure of much previously secret reactor technology. This deluge of atomic data somewhat overwhelmed the delegates, especially those from under-developed nations. The bright promise of President Eisenhower's U.N. speech of December 8, 1953, was grayed by the realization that smaller nations faced very high technical barriers before they could enter the promised land of abundant nuclear power.

The United States generously offered to make available nuclear fuel, specifically enriched U-235, to "friendly countries" in their pursuit of A-power. In 1956, for example, the U.S. Atomic Energy Commission authorized the allocation of 22 tons of nuclear fuel, measured in terms of U-235 content, for transfer to eligible foreign countries. But while fuel might be available, the state of the reactor art was not advanced enough to allow nations to build practical power producers. Few nations could afford the luxury of installing power plants which had no economic advantage over coal- or gas-fired electric plants.

The turning point came in the mid-1960's when the General Electric Company looked over its cost data and came to the conclusion that the technology would permit nuclear power plants to be more economic than coal-fired-steam electric plants. The U.S. Atomic Energy Commission was caught somewhat by surprise by General Electric price schedules for nuclear electric stations. Three times in less than two years it had to revise its estimates of how many nuclear electric kilowatts would be generated by 1980 in the United States. At present the projection calls for 150,000,000 kilowatts of electric power of atomic origin in the U.S.A. As of January 1, 1968, the United States has 18 nuclear power stations generating 3,680,000 kilowatts. Forty-eight more electric reactors were ordered or announced; their total means 37,000,000 more kilowatts for the U.S. power grid.

All the U.S. plants will be under strict regulation and control so that no plutonium product from the power stations will find its way into unauthorized channels. In 1980, for example, the annual U.S. production of plutonium by the electric power industry will exceed 100 tons. Since even a few pounds of this nuclear material would be coveted contraband, the degree of inspection and control of domestic plutonium will have to be quite precise. The situation overseas for Free World countries will probably involve an equal quantity by 1980. However, the difficulty of extending controls outside U.S. borders, if American fuels are involved, is subject to great political handicaps.

No foreign country wishes its nuclear fuel tied to the apron strings of another power, if such an arrangement can be avoided. One way to be fuel-independent is to build nuclear reactors run on natural uranium, which is available on the world market. However, U.S. reactor designs have embodied reliance on nuclear fuel that is partially enriched. The use of fuel with a two or more percent U-235 content, a concentration produced by Oak Ridge-type separation plants, has technical advantages that U.S. reactor designers value. Reactors using enriched fuel are being built by General Electric and Westinghouse in India, Japan, and other countries. Two U.S.-built reactors at Tarapur, India, are scheduled to produce a total of 380,000 kilowatts of electricity by 1969.

Transfers of nuclear fuel to foreign nations take place under a system of international agreements, backed up by various safeguards. Initially, the United States entered into bilateral agreements known as "Agreements for Cooperation for Civil Uses of Atomic Energy." Three dozen such agreements, involving seven tons of U-235 fuel, were made by the United States through the year 1966. To provide assured flow of fuel, commitments were made for over 200 tons of nuclear material. Recent U.S. policy has been directed toward programs handled by the U.N. through its International Atomic Energy Agency, which has headquarters in Vienna.

Safeguarding the custody of nuclear fuel is a complex matter because the material must be kept under surveillance in many forms and in a variety of sites. Nuclear fuel elements are not simply introduced into reactors and then "burned" up until all the valuable U-235 is consumed. Long before this point can be reached a number of technical barriers intervene; one is physical decomposition of the rod or fuel-element structure, another is the build-up of "poisons" or split atoms, which rob neutrons from the chain reaction. This means that fuel rods must be discharged from the reactors and then chemically processed to remove the unburned nuclear fuel. To be sure that no U-235 or plutonium is being "siphoned off" in fuel reprocessing, it is necessary to have on-the-spot inspectors.

Nuclear inspectors play very much the same role as bank examiners who go over "the books," except that their job is more sophisticated. They have to be sure when they check on a vat or a storage tank or an inventory of fuel rods that the U-235 and plutonium content is assayed correctly. This is far more difficult than merely adding up columns of figures and striking a balance. And it promises to be even more difficult in the future. As Dr. Glenn T. Seaborg, chairman of the Atomic Energy Commission, has observed: "The material-control procedures that have worked effectively in the past may not be entirely adequate when special nuclear material is available in larger amounts and more widely distributed, because present management uncertainties are too large to guarantee that significant quantities of fissionable material could not be diverted without detection." No doubt Dr. Seaborg had in mind the fact that current projections call for a hundred-fold increase in the Free World nuclear generating capacity by 1985. A diversion of nuclear fuel amounting to a fraction of one percent, insignificant in 1966, would be much more serious in the future.

The U.S. Atomic Energy Commission has carried out 700 nuclear-reactor inspections in 29 countries during a span of eight years. At the present time the International Atomic Energy Agency is supervising the application of safeguards in some 50 different sites in 23 countries. Research and development is being encouraged in discovering and perfecting new schemes and techniques for foiling even the most diabolic means of thwarting inspection procedures. For example, the AEC has developed a "safing" procedure using special copper tapes that are placed on reactor apertures to seal off the insertion of fuel rods. Any tampering with the reactor breaks these seals, and special X-ray techniques have been developed to reveal if the copper tapes have been removed and replaced.

Technical ingenuity cannot counter circumstances in which outlaws seize possession of a nuclear installation or in which a nation abrogates international agreements. In other words, there is no technical panacea for political instability. This problem will be exacerbated as nuclear reactors spread to smaller and less responsible powers and as the sheer number of reactor installations multiplies. Presumably a special advisory panel to the AEC had this in mind when it reported in 1967:

> Safeguards programs should also be designed in recognition of the problem of terrorist or criminal groups clandestinely acquiring nuclear weapons or material useful therein. Although such illegal groups are more likely to steal finished components or weapons than divert materials from peaceful programs, criminal organizations may be attracted to divert such materials if a black market develops, as it is likely to. It should be recognized that political and social restraints would not influence terrorist, insurrectionist, or criminal groups. Therefore, criminal sanctions, *e.g.*, fines and prison terms, are essential elements of an effective safeguards program.

We shall pass over the nightmare of a band of renegades swooping down a la Pancho Villa on some nuclear outpost. It is sufficient to raise the issue of a nuclear black market developing in the trade of nuclear material.

The world is going to be in very serious trouble when a

nuclear black market occurs, because then even quite minor powers may find it possible to get their hands on bomb material. They would be able to do this without paying the entry fee of building up the expensive facilities and acquiring the technological know-how to obtain pure nuclear material. Today we may take comfort in the fact that mere possession of nuclear material does not give a country a weapon capability. But with the passage of time, weapon designs will also enter the black market and also even weaponeers skilled in the making of nuclear explosives. If nuclear bomb material becomes an item of illicit commerce, we must expect that nuclear mercenaries will peddle their ghastly trade.

Quite apart from clandestine nuclear activities involving purloined, smuggled, or deviously acquired nuclear fuel, more and more countries will face great temptation as their domestic economy switches over to dependence on nuclear power. Many nations are poor in fossil-fuel resources, so that they will come to depend on uranium power as a source of cheap electricity. Furthermore, this flameless, fumeless energy source will assume greater popularity as atmospheric pollution increases and imposes penalties on human life and even on agricultural production. In addition, many nations are short of fresh water, and here the nuclear reactor holds great promise as a combination power plant and desalting machine. For example, the United Arab Republic has plans for a 150,000-kilowatt nuclear electric plant at Borg-el-Arab for desalting water. Israel has also planned a dual-purpose reactor installation that will provide kilowatts and desalination of salt water.

Pakistan is turning to uranium power and already has a 70,000-kilowatt reactor at Rooppur, and a 132,000-kilowatt plant in Karachi is scheduled for early completion. So it goes; nations all around the world seek the boon of atomic power to aid them in their industrialization. Countries like Japan, further up the scale of technological advancement, want uranium power as a means of sustaining their economy and reducing their dependence on foreign energy resources. Lacking adequate coal and petroleum, Japan projects an ambitious nuclear program.

It plans to build at least one 350,000-kilowatt nuclear power plant each year for the next seven years. Japan's target is an initial 2,500,000 kilowatts of electrical power, and this will be increased precipitously so that by 1985 Japan projects a need for 100,000 tons of natural uranium to fuel its A-power industry. Japan has only a few thousand tons of uranium in its domestic ores and it must look elsewhere for fuel to stoke its nuclear furnaces. One of its companies, Mitsubishi, has contracted with Canadian uranium companies to assure the flow of the modern fuel to Japan.

Nations such as Japan will undoubtedly try to become self-sufficient in uranium power, and there is a technological wrinkle that will greatly ease their fuel worries in the future. This is the development of a nuclear reactor which actually produces or breeds more nuclear fuel than it burns up. Such breeder-reactors are not yet practical as power producers, but the principle has been demonstrated and some experts are hopeful that within 20 years power breeders will be developed. It is the long-range scarcity of uranium that adds urgency to the development of the breeder. Free World resources of natural uranium available for less than $10 per pound of "yellow cake" are estimated at 1,365,000 tons. These resources double if one pays $15 or more for a pound of yellow cake concentrate, but then fuel prices go up and so does the cost of the electricity produced. But if power breeders work out it may be possible to double a reactor's fuel supply in seven years. The great value of breeding is that it allows much fuller use of uranium energy. Without breeding, one is confined to using the U-235 portion of uranium's energy—and that is just one part in 140 of the total—and whatever conversion of U-238 to plutonium can be accomplished in existing reactors. But at best one is restricted to a few percent of uranium's energy. When breeding is achieved, it becomes possible to tap the energy of the U-238 atoms so that the price you can afford to pay for natural uranium is no longer a limiting factor in nuclear-power economics.

Breeding dramatizes the Jekyll-Hyde nature of a nuclear power installation, showing as it does that a peacetime reactor is also a potential bomb producer. But whether or not breeding is achieved does not alter the fact that any nuclear-electric plant can produce plutonium. As the nuclear industry booms in various countries, a vast amount of plutonium-honey will accumulate in many nuclear hives. Many nations will have within reach the essential material for making A-bombs. Some nations, like Sweden and Israel, are in this situation. They have the honey in the hive, but for political reasons they prefer not to make a nuclear test. They have the plutonium technology at hand, as well as the plutonium, and they have enough weapon know-how. They are, in effect, silent members of the nuclear club. Sweden obviously would tarnish its peaceful image if it tested, and Israel would arouse the Arab world. Except for the noisy test that proclaims a nation to be a member of the nuclear club, Sweden and Israel are practically in the door.

Five nations have conducted hundreds of nuclear tests. Nuclear weaponry is in its third decade, and while still to reach maturity, it is no longer in its infancy. Given the back-door entrance to the nuclear club which reactor-produced plutonium provides, we must expect that membership in the once exclusive organization will grow. The Limited Nuclear Test Ban Treaty of 1963 was, in President Kennedy's words, "the first step in a journey of a thousand miles." It did not prevent Red China from testing. And as Sen. Robert Kennedy has remarked: "But we have not yet taken the second step. The world has not moved, beyond the limited nuclear test ban itself, to halt the proliferation of nuclear weapons."

The United States announced on August 17, 1965, terms of a Non-proliferation Treaty, which would attempt to keep nuclear weapons from spreading to nonnuclear nations. Under this treaty the nuclear powers would agree not to:

1. transfer, either directly or indirectly, nuclear weapons into the control of a nonnuclear power.
2. assist such a "have-not" nation in the manufacture of nuclear weapons.
3. act so as to increase the number of nuclear powers in the world. This injunction carries with it the understanding that nuclear

weapons are not to pass out of national control to any regime or organization.

Article II of the treaty specifies corresponding obligations for the "have-not" nations. There is a basic asymmetry in the agreement in that nonnuclear powers are enjoined to forgo a nuclear capability which has become a mighty power symbol. And to insure that the nonnuclear powers do not misuse civilian uranium power, they are subject to inspection of reactor and fuel-processing facilities. Presumably no nation enjoys having inspectors roaming over their territory. Certain countries equate inspection with espionage, maintaining that inspectors transgress and seek military-industrial secrets. On-site inspection was the big stumbling block to a test agreement that would ban underground detonations. The Soviet Union refused to budge on this matter and the United States was unwilling to ratify a treaty that could not be policed except by remote detection of illicit tests. Thus under the Test Ban Treaty of 1963 underground tests are allowed so long as they do not produce objectionable atmospheric contamination beyond the territorial borders of the tester. The inspection problem has also been a sticking point in reaching agreement on a nonproliferation treaty, but there have been some indications from the U.S. Government that it might agree to depend on unilateral verification systems, specifically those made possible by orbital reconnaissance.

Another issue that complicates the nuclear problem is the peacetime uses of nuclear explosives. The AEC has budgeted $20 million for its Project Plowshare research in 1968. Plowshare work includes the underground detonation of nuclear explosives for:

1. nuclear excavation. Such applications would embrace the use of nuclear charges to dig a sea-level canal across the Central American isthmus, to remove earth for domestic rail cuts through rocky terrain, to make new coastal harbors, and to engineer access to reservoirs for water storage.
2. nuclear-physics research. The intense neutron bursts available

in subsurface explosions may be used in nuclear physics and in producing new atomic species lying beyond uranium in the periodic system of elements.

3. natural resources, primarily fuels. An experiment code-named Gas-buggy was designed to stimulate production of natural gas from underground reservoirs. It is hoped that the heat generated by underground nuclear explosions can be used to release useful fuel from oil shale and tar sands.

If Plowshare explosives prove to be economically useful in large-scale engineering projects, they may find application in underdeveloped countries. Such introduction of nuclear explosives into nonnuclear territory would require strict international controls to prevent the devices or information about their technical nature from falling into the wrong hands. Again, the honey-venom duality of the explosive atom is evident.

An ironical twist of events in 1967 highlighted the U.S. attitude toward a non-proliferation treaty, or NPT, as it is abbreviated. This was the U.S. decision to build a Chinese-oriented ABM system. Defending the decision, Paul C. Warnke, Assistant Secretary of Defense for International Security Affairs, asserted on October 6, 1967: "We came to the conclusion that our Chinese-oriented ABM deployment should make it easier, and not harder, for countries in Asia to sign the NPT. The increased credibility of the United States deterrent, which we would expect to result from our deployment, should make even clearer the lack of any need for independent national nuclear forces in Asia." Instead of reassuring our allies, it appeared that U.S. action on Nike-X did just the opposite. It tended to magnify the significance of Red China as a nuclear power and to raise the issue of ballistic-missile defenses for our allies, both in the Far East and in Europe, as well.

Defense Secretary McNamara, sizing up the proliferation problem in 1966, stated: "I will say that within the next ten years, seven to ten nations would fall into the category that I call threshold nations, meaning by that nations which have within their power, by applying their own technology and their own economic resources, the capability to develop nuclear weapons." Since Mr. McNamara is known to have been consistent in his appraisal of this problem and held similar views when he was President Kennedy's Defense Secretary, we can understand why Mr. Kennedy remarked at a press conference on June 24, 1963:

> *"When Pandora opened her box and the troubles flew out, all that was left in was hope. Now in this case, if we have a nuclear diffusion throughout the world, we may even lose hope."*

VI

THE DETERRENT
SWORD

"The chessboard is the world, the pieces are the phenomena of the universe, the rules of the game are what we call the laws of Nature. The player on the other side is hidden from us. We know that his play is always fair, just, and patient. But we also know, to our cost, that he never overlooks a mistake or makes the smallest allowance for ignorance."

—THOMAS H. HUXLEY
A Liberal Education

Playing the deterrent game, especially in a world of three great nuclear powers and an assortment of minor ones, is an elaborate chess game in which *your* pieces may be moved by an uninvited associate. The play, unlike Huxley's apt phrasing for a non-nuclear world, may be grossly unfair, catastrophically unjust, and most precipitous.

Those who deter and are deterred play an intercontinental tournament, one which goes on every minute of the day and night, in which intelligence as to the other's strength and weakness is apt to be faulty. Many books have been written about deterrent doctrine, and the literature abounds with analyses made by operations analysts, war-gamers, and defense intellectuals. However, when the chips are down and hard decisions have to be made, the men at the center of the stage are the political leaders. These hardheaded men are apt to find wargaming a heady intellectual exercise. We should recall that Kennedy's Cuban crisis, as chronicled by at least three men close to the scene, fails to illuminate a single war-gamer on the stage or in the wings.

This is not to say that computer analysis of U.S. *vis-à-vis* enemy capability is not fundamental to the structuring of our strategic forces. Each year when the Secretary of Defense makes his presentation to the House and Senate committees, he brings with him a thick report which embodies statistical tables of damage we can inflict versus damage we may incur. The congressional committees really do not know what to make of these analyses, and they may be forgiven if they fail to comprehend the megadeaths so neatly printed out by the high-speed, solid-state computers.

Take, for example, the following table which Mr. McNamara used in his testimony before the House Appropriations Committee in defense of the Fiscal Year 1968 budget:

Number of fatalities[1] in an all-out strategic exchange[2] (assumes no Soviet reaction to U.S. antiballistic-missile deployment)

[In millions]

	Soviets strike first; United States retaliates		United States strikes first; Soviets retaliate[3]	
	U.S. FATALITIES	SOVIET FATALITIES	U.S. FATALITIES	SOVIET FATALITIES
U.S. programs:				
Approved	120	120+	100	70
Posture A	40	120+	30	70
Posture B	30	120+	20	70

[1] Fatality figures shown above represent deaths from blast and fallout; they do not include deaths resulting from fire-storms, disease, and general disruption of everyday life.

[2] The data in this table are highly sensitive to small changes in the pattern of attack and small changes in force levels.

[3] Assumes United States minimizes U.S. fatalities by maximizing effectiveness of strike on Soviet offensive systems.

Later we shall examine a companion piece to this table to illustrate the cost and effectiveness of a ballistic missile defense,
but for the moment we shall simply explain that the Congress
is being shown the results of Pentagon computer print-outs for
three programs:

APPROVED: Meaning that already authorized by the Congress.
POSTURE A: A $12.2 billion "total damage-limiting package."
POSTURE B: A $21.7 billion "defense package."

In effect, the Defense Secretary is telling Congressmen the
basic facts of nuclear life and death. They are quite brain-
numbing and present the legislator with unprecedented choices.
If a Soviet first strike can kill more than half the population,
the United States has been "killed." To talk of recuperation
after such a mortal hemorrhage is to indulge in fantasy. But
what about "Postures A and B," which would spare the lives
of 80 to 90 million Americans? For the $12.2 billion expenditure
this would mean spending $150 per life saved; this is certainly
not an excessive price. But before jumping to the conclusion
that security can be purchased so cheaply we must reckon with
enemy responses to U.S. defense innovations. This we do in
the following chapter. Here we shall look at the power to deter
based on the cutting edge of the nuclear sword, not at the protection which a defense shield may afford.

Basic deterrent policy is keyed to a mutuality of terror—of
a common anticipation of and regard for the penalties invoked
in the event a nuclear war is triggered. Mr. McNamara speaks
of this in terms of "assured destruction," which he defines as a
capability:

> To deter deliberate nuclear attack upon the United States
> and its allies by maintaining, continuously, a highly reliable
> ability to inflict an unacceptable degree of damage upon any
> single aggressor, or combination of aggressors, at any time
> during the course of a strategic nuclear exchange, even after
> absorbing a surprise first strike.

Recognizing that it would be folly to risk underestimation of
U.S. strategic capability by enemy intelligence, Mr. McNamara

admits that there has been a deliberate policy of advertisement of our retaliatory power. This publicizing of our nuclear strike force stands in stark contrast to classical secrecy on military force levels. Even so there is a considerable margin of uncertainty that remains—and the advent of ballistic missile defense widens this margin—by which an aggressor may miscalculate.

Consider, for example, the Soviet Union in a hypothetical contemplation of a first strike at the United States. What factors must be sized up by the planners in the Kremlin?

First, there is the key matter of target doctrine. Do Soviet strategists direct the strategic blow at U.S. civilian or military targets? If they are rational, they must plan an attack which aims to deny the United States the power of returning fire at an unacceptable level. This means targeting U.S. missile bases, bomber bases, and Polaris submarines as well as certain command and control facilities.

Second, assuming a strike at U.S. bastions of strategic strength, the next question is: "What is the force level needed to take out of action *sufficient* U.S. retaliatory capability?" By sufficient, we mean great enough to keep damage to the Soviet Union down to an "acceptable" level. We postpone discussion of the extent to which a Soviet ballistic missile defense might blunt U.S. return fire.

Soviet experts know that any first strike at the United States has to be staged with ballistic missiles. Resort to manned bombers would sacrifice the whole element of strategic surprise and would allow the United States to pummel the Soviet Union with immediate broadsides fired from Minuteman ICBM bases. Thus in our discussion of a strategic U.S.-S.U. exchange, the issue hinges on missile exchange. Only these vehicles of destruction strike quickly enough to make their mark in the time scale of nuclear blitz warfare. Bombers lumbering to their targets might well arrive after the war was over—not that any decision would have been reached by then, but that the lethal blows would have been dealt.

The U.S. strategic force that Soviet experts have to target

include 1,000 Minuteman missiles, which are located in our western states, and the Polaris-Poseidon missiles that happen to be on station. Normally this would include 30-plus submarines, each equipped with a locker of 16 missiles.

U.S. planners have deployed the Minuteman force so as to minimize ICBM vulnerability to attack. One approach is purely numerical—enough ICBM's are deployed so as to outbid an enemy, forcing him to buy an exorbitant number of attacking missiles to kill the Minutemen. A second technique seeks to reduce vulnerability by locating each missile far enough from its neighbor so that a single attacking weapon cannot strike at more than one ICBM. Finally, each ICBM is stored, ready-to-fire, in what is called "a hardened configuration," meaning that it is housed below ground in a concrete silo. The latter is designed to protect against a blast overpressure of more than 100 pounds per square inch. Certain technical features of the Minuteman may be noted: the guidance systems permit last-minute retargeting, and the solid-fuel propulsion system permits rapid fire.

The problem faced by Kremlin planners in targeting the Minuteman complex is essentially one of assigning enough missiles with sufficient warhead power so that there is a high probability of imposing more than 100 pounds per square inch of blast pressure on the buried ICBM's. Back in the early 1960's when missile and warhead technology was less sophisticated than it is today, not counting tomorrow, Soviet planners would have had to assign many attacking missiles to each Minuteman silo. The number of Soviet missiles needed to be launched would depend upon the warhead power and the missile accuracy. For example, a 10-megaton warhead and an accuracy such that 50 percent of the warheads impact within three miles of the silo would mean that 14 missiles would have to be expended for a 90 percent probability of making one kill. No military man in his right mind would think of contesting in a strategic nuclear exchange where he had to expend fourteen missiles to knock out a single ICBM. Prudent assessment of improvements in missile guidance dictates caution about invulnerability through hardened bases; inevitably missilery would reach higher accuracy until at last only a few—perhaps just one—launched missiles would be required to knock out a Minuteman base. Put another way—the hardened base would soften with the passage of time as ICBM's became increasingly accurate. Such was the gist of testimony that I presented to a congressional committee in the spring of 1960—opposing the viewpoint of Gen. Curtis E. LeMay, who held that the ICBM's were safe against enemy attack.

In the late 1960's and certainly in the early 1970's we may expect further refinements in the attacking power of offensive ICBM's which may jeopardize the security of silo-housed ICBM's such as Minuteman missiles. For example, the Soviets are known to have heavy throw-weight capability and they may capitalize on this by fitting multiple warheads to single ICBM's. These clustered warheads might simply follow divergent ballistic paths and bracket a target. The advantage would be that the defender would have a complex job of interception, and the attacker would have a higher probability of having at least one of the warheads hit within a kill radius of the target. The attacker does lose something in total megatonnage deliverable when he splits up his payload into multiple packages, but this is offset by the fact that a miss with one big warhead is a total loss, whereas if two out of three separate warheads miss, a kill may be made with the single hit. To illustrate the problem, we may assume that a single big warhead has a power of 20 megatons and produces 100 pounds per square inch of overpressure out to a distance of one and three-quarter miles. Using the same nose cone for three individual warheads might involve halving the total megatonnage—i.e., each warhead would be three and a third megatons in power. The smaller warhead would still be able to impose the 100 p.s.i. kill power out to a distance just a little under one mile. Despite the halved megatonnage of the triplet warheads, they would spread their kill-punch over 50 percent more area than the single warhead with twice as much power.

Because missiles cost so much more than their warheads,

The Weapons Culture

probably 20 to 40 times more, weapons experts have been attracted to the idea of incorporating a number of maneuverable individual warheads within a single nose cone. The acronym MIRV, standing for Multiple, Independently targetable, Reentry Vehicles, has been given for the U.S. missiles being developed for strategic bombardment. Each warhead can be directed toward separate targets, even cities. Such an offensive technique would sorely tax the defender's ability to intercept the incoming warheads. The lesson to be learned from the forgoing is that any deterrent system which has fixed geographic coordinates is vulnerable to attack. Furthermore, numbers alone cannot guarantee that an aggressor will be deterred from attacking, and once an attack is underway it may panic a spasm of retaliatory fire. Minuteman missiles are of the prompt launch "out of the hole" type; in time of acute crisis, they may be dispatched out of fear for their survival. A spasm-prone ICBM system like Minuteman is not the ideal instrument of deterrence. Undersea-launched missiles like Polaris-Poseidon have the advantage of mobility and concealment. Barring some quite unforeseen technological development that would make undersea platforms vulnerable, the Polaris-Poseidon system should continue to confront Soviet military leaders with an unresolvable dilemma. Even if Soviet ICBM's knock out the great majority of Minuteman sites, the Soviet Union will remain exposed to the withering return fire from undersea nuclear platforms. We can probably trust the U.S. Air Force, jealous of its strategic mission, to keep U.S. citizens informed as to technological developments that might render sea-borne deterrents vulnerable.

In meeting the challenge of the missile age, the U.S. Air Force has been humiliated into burying its strike force underground and to the care-taking of shiny ICBM's which need an occasional polish and an electronic tune-up but no massive operational tests. While Minuteman costs should not in any sense be played down, they are smaller than the overall costs for manned strategic bombers. In a very real sense technology has been the worst enemy of the U.S. Air Force. Missiles move so swiftly that propelling them even faster is of no real value. Their flight times are measured in minutes, whereas bombers mark their trips in hours. Bombers can carry heavier payloads than ICBM's like Minuteman or Polaris, but they are easily destroyed if caught on the ground. In flight the high vulnerability of a bomber to missile-fire is a matter of comparative speed; the winged plane even at supersonic speed is no match for the ground-launched interceptor-missile.

Anyone who looks back in time and surveys the build-up of the U.S. strategic strike forces of the bomber era may justifiably ask why such vast power was allowed to proliferate once the cheap megaton was born and fallout became a new dimension of war. The fact is that attack levels were allowed to escalate to the tens of thousands of megatons. One explanation, that bombers would experience high attrition over enemy territory, and therefore large numbers would have to be used to insure penetration of Soviet defenses, was surely evasive. The fact is that prior to the breakthrough of the lithium-uranium bomb, the U.S. Air Force measured weight of bomb loads in kilotons. With the breakthrough to the cheap megaton, there was a compelling need to reexamine the whole question of damage achievable with strategic bombardment. But the Air Force had programmed its bomber production and had cemented its ties with Congress and with industry. Here secrecy about nuclear weapons was an absolute prerequisite for the Air Force; without it, the public might learn the new facts about superexplosives and superlethality and question the prodigious numbers of B-52's that were scheduled. By the time that the bonds of secrecy were sufficiently loosened to permit the public to glimpse the real situation, it was too late. By then huge numbers of bombers had been produced and were a *fait accompli.*

Weapon lethality underwent a historic change at Hiroshima. Previously a five-ton weight of bombs delivered just that weight of explosives to a target. But in the summer of 1945 a single B-29 bomber acquired the capability of hauling a 20,000-ton weight of TNT in its bomb bay. Ton for ton, nuclear explosives were 4,000 times as powerful as TNT. During the next decade

A-bombs became more powerful and yielded greater explosiveness per ton of bomb weight, but this gradual improvement in weapon potency was dwarfed by the H-bomb breakthrough. As a result the B-52 bomber could accommodate the two 20-megaton bombs; a single jet bomber therefore packed 2,000 times the punch of the B-29.

The lithium-uranium superbomb's power is not fully gauged by comparing it on an explosive scale with a TNT bomb. A 20-megaton bomb bursting on the earth's surface can shower an area of almost 10,000 square miles with a lethal mantle of radioactive fallout. The radioactive sting of the superweapon can be felt over an area 50 times larger than that hit by blast and heat. Fire-power beyond the imagination of all but a demented militarist was placed in the hands of Air Force generals. It was only the technical challenge of the ballistic missile that put an end to B-52 production, 25 of which could transport nuclear explosives equal to a billion tons of TNT.

Nothing sustained the bomber build-up so much as the fear of Soviet air supremacy, which became translated into a much-heralded "bomber gap." This appeal to the American competitive spirit focused public attention on outproducing the Soviets and thus obscured the fundamental issue of "how much" strategic nuclear power was adequate for deterrence. With aircraft plants booming in Washington, Kansas, Texas, and Georgia, industrialists, legislators, and worker-constituents formed pressure groups interested in promoting increased aircraft production. Traditionally the Congress is used to accepting the weight of military authority without probing too deeply into the basis of this authority. When nuclear firepower so transformed the nature of war, making the general as much a stranger to the megaton as the congressman, there should have been a searching inquiry into the sufficiency of strategic force. Years later, with reference to Vietnam but with equal pertinence to strategic power, McGeorge Bundy observed: "Nothing is less reliable, in hard choices of this sort, than the unsupported opinion of men who are arguing the value of their chosen instrument —in this case military force. We must not be surprised, and still

less persuaded, when generals and admirals recommend additional military action—what do we expect them to recommend?

If the Congress was accustomed to put blind faith in military
authority, it did not change its ways once the atom revolution-
ized the ways of war. Perhaps the Congress felt that it did its
duty when it created a special Joint Committee on Atomic
Energy or perhaps it assumed that the union of science with
the military lent a rationality to strategic-force determinations.
If so, the legislators erred, especially if they felt that scientists
were allowed to invade the policy rooms of the Joint Chiefs
of Staff. The Defense Establishment compartmentalized science
to its service and used it at its own discretion. When scientists
on their own initiative challenged strategic doctrine, it was at
their own peril. As we have seen, this was Dr. Oppenheimer's
unforgivable "crime" and for it he was punished accordingly.
Had he not been publicly humiliated and set down from his
prestigious position, his voice in public affairs might have questioned too severely "how much was enough" in air-atomic
power.

The military-civilian pressure groups pressed the bomber-gap
issue after Stalin's death in 1953, and the U.S. strategic bomber
command grew and grew. A total of 1800 B-47 and 850 B-52
bombers (not to mention 383 B-36 aircraft purchased at a cost
of $2.5 billion) filled the bomber gap. Finally, when the hard
facts emerged, it turned out that the Soviets had deployed a
long-range force of only 120 Bison jet heavy bombers and 70
Bear turboprop bombers. The bomber gap that never really
existed was passed by without a post-mortem. The same leaders
who championed the bomber gap hit hard on a missile gap
which impended in the second term of the Eisenhower Administration.

As usual the gap-prophets sounded the direst notes of alarm
about lagging in a missile race. In 1956, for example, Trevor
Gardner, an assistant Air Force secretary under Eisenhower,
warned: "The intercontinental ballistics missile is probably the
greatest single advance in weapons that will be attained by any
country in the next ten years. The nation that gets it first may

be in a position to determine the kind of world we live in for the next generation." The mystique that first possession of a weapon confers a supreme advantage on a nation is the equivalent of victory in a race. It overlooks completely the fact that modern defense systems represent colossal engineering undertakings that require years for development and additional years for production, deployment, and operational readiness. We have already seen that the missile gap was just as fictitious as the bomber gap, but there continues to be an appeal to superiority in numbers of missiles, based on revised estimates of Soviet missile strength and throw-power.

Going back to our earlier discussion of deterrent doctrine, we must stress that adequacy in the U.S. second-strike missile force is or should be the determining factor in reckoning U.S. force levels—not how many missiles the Soviets may have. Testifying before a House of Representatives appropriations hearing in 1964, Defense Secretary McNamara stated: "The basic objective of the management system we are introducing and trying to operate is to establish a rational foundation as opposed to an emotional foundation for the decisions as to what size force and what type of force this country will maintain." Mr. McNamara made it painfully clear to bomber enthusiasts that he thought of strategic deterrents in terms of missile fire-power. As the first generation Atlas ICBM's and stop-gap intermediate range missiles like Jupiter phased out, this firepower was concentrated in the deployed Minuteman and Polaris missiles. Although the Defense Department never announced it as official policy, the specific level of adequate return fire from these missiles was set at 400 megatons. The smallness of this figure, compared to the tens of thousands of megatons once carried by strategic bombers, is now being decried by those who seek to exploit a megaton gap.

If Soviet experts accept the 400-megaton figure as accurate, then their problem is that of so staging a first strike that it knocks out U.S. strategic-missile firepower to a point where the return fire is reduced to an "acceptable" level. Suppose, for the sake of argument, that the Soviet strategists decide that they can "accept" return fire of 100 ballistic missiles on target. On this reckoning they must be capable of knocking out about 90 percent of the U.S. strategic retaliatory capability. This means targeting over 1,000 sites not only accurately but also time-phasing them to arrive nearly simultaneously on target. To strike an all-at-once blow at the bastions of U.S. retaliatory power, Soviet missiles would have to be staged to arc over the polar region at different times, giving the U.S. early warning system a graduated awareness of the attack. Such an unmistakable alert would in fact be certain to trigger a massive prompt response. Whether the Soviets had 500 or 5,000 attacking missiles, this would not prevent solid return fire far in excess of the Pentagon's rock-bottom level of 400 megatons.

The fundamental point in this back-and-forth discussion of U.S. vs. U.S.S.R. missile capability is that it is not really a race for numerical superiority that can tip the scales in either's favor. Mr. McNamara has pinpointed this issue very acutely with the observation: "Now, in strategic nuclear weaponry, the arms race involves a particular irony. Unlike any other era in military history, today a substantial numerical superiority of weaponry does not effectively translate into political control or diplomatic leverage." The concept of having enough of anything is rather foreign to the military mind and it is equally alien to civilian minds of the congressional-industrial complex. An example of military-civilian hostility to what we may call nuclear sufficiency is the American Security Council-Mendel Rivers report mentioned in Chapter 1. This report is really an outcropping of the military-industrial-scientific-congressional complex. It epitomizes the inability of the preatomic mind to adjust itself to the new dimensions of the present era just as it illustrates the coalition of forces against which Eisenhower's Farewell Address warned. The argument put forth in the report may be summed up as follows:

1. In the past the United States possessed a five-to-ten-fold superiority over the U.S.S.R. in strategic firepower, measured in megatons.

2. In the summer of 1967 the U.S. and the U.S.S.R. were nip-and-tuck in the megaton race.
3. In the early 1970's the Soviet Union will possess a four-to-one, or possibly greater, megaton advantage over the United States.

The prospect of the United States being on the short end of a megaton gap is calculated to compel the American people to back a stepped-up arms program to restore the balance of power in our favor.

President Kennedy addressed himself to this question in the course of a radio-television interview (December 17, 1962) in which a question was asked about his reaction to a newspaper ad of the Douglas company urging a $2.5 billion program for a nuclear delivery system. Detailing the missile systems in existence, the President responded:

"There is just a limit to how much we need, as well as how much we can afford to have a successful deterrent.

"I would say when we start to talk about the megatonnage we could bring into a nuclear war, we are talking about annihilation. How many times do you have to hit a target with nuclear weapons?

"That is why when we are talking about spending this $2.5 billion, we don't think that we are going to get $2.5 billion worth of national security."

If the generals, admirals, and academicians fail to perceive the absurdity of the megaton gap that they promote, it is possibly because they are accustomed to pre-atomic arithmetic. They count megatons as they would add up numbers of tanks, or guns, or torpedoes; national security is added up like punching keys on a cash register. However, the coin of national security has changed: Billion-dollar defense outlays may not buy more security—they may even purchase delusion. U.S. defense increases may provoke corresponding Soviet outlays for arms, the use of which would spell gross devastation. In an analysis of the U.S. arms race with the Soviets, Secretary McNamara incised the issue as follows: "Whatever be their intentions, whatever be our intentions, actions—or even realistically potential actions—on either side relating to the build-up of nuclear forces, be they either offensive or defensive weapons, necessarily trigger reactions on the other side. It is precisely this action-reaction phenomenon that fuels an arms race."

But Mr. McNamara's thinking is not shared by former members of the Joint Chiefs of Staff who authored the American Security Council's July, 1967, report. Judging from their emphasis on a "megaton gap," they reject the finiteness of a deterrent force and wish to build up a nuclear strike force without limit. The only measure of limitation they appear willing to accept is that U.S. forces always be superior to those of any hostile power.

A basic difference between Defense Secretary McNamara and his Joint Chiefs is that he concentrates on deterring the outbreak of a nuclear war while his military leaders plan to fight and win the war. The latter position is one that the military planners have to assume since, otherwise, deterrence might be interpreted as pure posturing. We must appear to the enemy as an implacable adversary willing to go the limit. Yet if deterrents fail, the course of conflict is apt to be an uncontrolled convulsion of attack and counterfire, the latter coming more as a reflex action than as a deliberate response to some level of provocation.

Wars in the past have known the agony and the luxury of time. The agony, the protracted and seemingly endless succession of months and even years of battle, is an obvious and dreaded character of armed conflict. The luxury has been due to the sluggishness of battle which allows time for damage assessment. But now ballistic missiles blur the dimension of time. Consider, however, the implications of the "time constants"—to use a physicist's phrase in electronic circuitry. A ballistic missile takes, say, 25 minutes from takeoff to touchdown. This brief span of time is in fact a minimum, for if one attempts to make a ballistic vehicle go much faster it arcs into orbit and is much delayed in being summoned back to earth, having to be retro-thrusted in the proper plane. The latter procedure severely limits the number of times per day that

an orbiting vehicle can be recalled to earth so as to impact
on or near a specific target. While the total launch-to-target
time is 25 minutes for many military situations, it is not
the awareness-to-action time. Due to over-the-horizon radar
and midpoint detection systems, an attacked nation may possess
intelligence of a strategic strike before the hostile ICBM's have
reached their zenith hundreds of miles above the arctic icecap.
As the minutes tick off and radars gather intelligence about the
trajectory of the incoming missiles, high-speed computers project their course and predict their impact points.

How do the decision-makers of the attacked nation respond
to such minute-by-minute information? War-gamers have spent
endless hours going through various attack "scenarios" in which
they play the game. One high defense official who participated
in many of these exercises told me: "It's all very boring—it
happens so slow that you have time to go to the men's room,
return and check on the hostile missiles, and so forth." Perhaps
the artificial exercise is tedious, but I know that the real thing
would be far from routine.

Let us assume that the U.S. decision-maker No. 1, whoever
that ill-starred President may be, is whisked away from the
vulnerable White House and is safely sheltered in the military
redoubt built deep underground at the Pennsylvania state line.
Let us also assume that U.S. intelligence machinery functions
as expected, and the trajectory and target-impact data are fed
to the command post and promptly displayed on an electronic
war map projected in front of the President. There he sits
watching the miraculous perfection of electronic systems duti-
fully absorbing, digesting, interpreting, and finally displaying
the "parameters of the attack situation." As commander-in-chief
of the Armed Forces the President occupies the cockpit of
decision—it is his to command.

The reader may conjure up any attack situation he wishes.
It may be 100 hostile objects 1,000 miles "out" or 500 such objects 5 minutes from impact . . . whatever he wishes . . . inevitably the hostile objects get converted into target data on
the illuminated display screen. . . . Minuteman sites under at-

tack light up. . . . City targets are displayed. . . . The map of the United States becomes a surrealistic chimera. . . . Anticipation becomes reality as the display changes color indicating IMPACT. . . swiftly the installed bomb blast-heat sensors define the "yield" . . . computers, remembering stored vital statistics, read out probable mortality . . . even fallout figures appear as computers project wind vectors and calculate lethality. . . . And then the "national returns" start coming in, printing out mortality-casualty data. . . . Industry is not forgotten—percent capacity destroyed appears on the screen. . . .

By this time the much-publicized "hot line" is burned out and the "button" becomes all. The President himself has few options for decision—assuming that the command and control systems are operative and missile-base commanders have not, out of fear having their birds destroyed in their concrete nests, given the order to launch—because the whole dimension of time has been compressed. If the attack is light, his option of heavy strikes against the remaining hostile launch sites, may insure that the enemy, sensing the counterfire, will launch more ICBM's in order to prevent loss of strategic striking power. If the attack is heavy, then lashing back at empty missile silos is an act of futility—the targets then become cities. The President has no elbow room for negotiation; he simply carries out the retaliation as promised on page one of the Book of Deterrence.

The scenario just scripted was one that may seem unreal to many an American, but it was all too real to President Kennedy. Less than a year before his death in Dallas, the President expressed his personal view of just such a situation. Referring to "five or six minutes to make a judgment" of a Soviet attack, he said:

"Once he fires his missiles, it is all over anyway, because we are going to have sufficient resources to fire back at him to destroy the Soviet Union. When that day comes, and there is a massive exchange, then that is the end, because you are talking about Western Europe, the Soviet Union, the United States, of 150 million fatalities in the first eighteen hours."

No U.S. President, imprisoned in a subterranean cubicle of reinforced concrete, is apt to wax philosophical, but he might contrast his own blastproof shelter with the naked vulnerability of his nation and its population being mercilessly pummeled by the simultaneous impact of weapons of a thousand-fold more deadly than those that struck Hiroshima. Historically, one of the first conclusions reached by atomic scientists was that the United States had developed in the nuclear weapon something of a Frankenstein monster. Because of its high urbanization and closely woven pattern of its industrial society, the United States appeared to the postwar-emergent scientists as highly vulnerable to its own weapons-offspring. A number of them recommended a program of industrial and urban dispersion that would reduce U.S. vulnerability to nuclear attack. There is no need to recite the history of civil defense in the United States; suffice it to say that weapon lethality spiraled upward much faster than any countervailing progress on home defense. Furthermore, any substantial gains on the home front could be offset by increases in the enemy's strike force. The megaton and its concomitant fallout conspired to make much of the U.S. population vulnerable to even small-scale nuclear attack directed at metropolitan areas.

As few as six high-yield nuclear weapons deliberately exploded so as to cast their fallout shadows over the megalopolis which stretches from Washington, D.C., to Boston could embrace a population of 38 million in a lethal grip. How would a U.S. President respond to this statistic being flashed on the electronic display in his underground sanctuary? The whole thrust of my argument here is that once nuclear war breaks out it will carry the decision-makers before it like tiny chips in a maelstrom. No one will have time to conduct such a war —least of all an enemy who may not be so affluent in having an instantaneous damage-evaluation-prediction system. To play the war game properly, both sides should have similar systems —perhaps it now becomes necessary for the United States to make a bizarre pact with potential enemies and equip them with the nuclear antennae, sensors, computers, and display systems so that there is symmetry in the game. But even this electronic sophistication would not solve the ultimate problem—namely, that of finding some independent referee or umpire to decide the "winner." Presumably only those noncombatants not caught in the crossfire of a nuclear exchange would come in this category.

Some commentators on nuclear war hold that its ravages would be so extensive as to pollute the entire planet with toxic radioactive effluents. Bad as the effects of nuclear weapons are, they are mitigated by time and distance. It is true that the stratospherically dispersed remnants of the bomb cloud do travel to the four corners of the world. No person living on earth and no baby born is without measureable amounts of bomb products in his or her skeleton. But there is a vast gulf between radioactivity which is only detectible and that which is serious or lethal. A nuclear war that emphasized dirty weapons would see the fallout concentrated within the continent or subcontinent under attack. Tongues of fallout would be carried tropospherically and deposited at greater distances within the latitudinal zones where the detonations concentrated. However, the fallout from even a very heavy attack on, say, the United States would not be of military significance to the residents of the Soviet Union. In general, one would expect that it would reach maximum values at least one hundred times lower than the lethal level. And since this intercontinental fallout tends to stratify in latitudinal zones, a war between the U.S. and U.S.S.R. would confine the most serious radioactivity to the North Temperate Zone. While there is some leakage of fallout between the northern and southern hemispheres, this would be far less than that trapped above the equator.

Predictions about the global impact of radioactive fallout can be given with some degree of confidence. After all, the United States has for well over a decade studied exhaustively the patterns of fallout around the world and has analyzed the specific behavior of debris from a variety of detonations. The latter has been facilitated by "tagging" a nuclear weapon with telltale atomic species, such as tungsten, which can then be systematically traced as it diffuses around the globe and percolates down to the southern latitudes. It is found, for example, that stratospherically-transported debris from nuclear tests above the equator produces a 10-fold lower intensity of a long-lived species like strontium-90 in South America. A total of almost a billion tons of TNT equivalent has been set loose in nuclear explosions to date, so there is actually quite a good deal of evidence on which to make estimates.

However, the localization of intense fallout within a nation's borders would have the effect of laying siege to a whole continent. To be sure, the vagaries of the wind would not produce a uniform mantle of fallout over a region and there would be, because of targeting doctrine, large areas less severely dusted with radioactivity, but many metropolitan areas would find themselves pinned down by the aboveground hazard of fallout. The length of this pin-down time would vary from one community to the next, but it would range from a few days to a few weeks before the fadeaway of radioactivity would permit limited above-surface excursions. Nonetheless, the persistence of penetrating radiation from the invisible debris must be considered as a community attempts to return to normality. Each day's exposure, though not serious in itself, would add to the subsequent day and to the next. Body cells act like imperfect adding machines, remembering previous insult, though not fully, and totalizing each day's dose of radiation. Without adequate instruments to monitor the radiation received, a person would be playing tag with eventual death by living aboveground. He might flee to a safer "cooler" place if he knew that such a sanctuary existed and that he could make the trip without excessive exposure—and that when he got there he might find shelter and food.

The extent to which the United States might receive assistance from foreign countries is highly debatable. Fear of radioactivity might discourage many a good Samaritan. Canada might escape the direct ravages of a nuclear attack on the United States and, with its happy proximity of fuel supplies to its wheatlands, could provide critically needed food. But how many survivors might make their way across the border and be accommodated on Canadian soil is an unanswerable problem.

Many computer-based studies have been made of the consequences of a nuclear attack on U.S.A. But a computer only does what it is instructed to do; it cannot supply answers when important data inputs are omitted. No one really knows how to predict the full consequences of nuclear war within the boundaries of an attacked nation. Computer studies cannot spell out what happens to a society when it is ripped apart at the seams, especially in terms of predicting how recuperation may take place. One of the world's most brilliant scientists, Dr. Eugene P. Wigner, of Princeton, sought to find as many answers as he could. He feared that America might be subjected to a devastating attack and that, if it were possible for him to do so, he ought to apply his wits to the problem of civil defense. He headed up an intensive study of the problem for the National Academy of Sciences and in 1965 he produced the first results of this study, code-named Project Harbor. But when his report saw the light of day, it was subjected to critical assessment by scientists who disagreed with basic conclusions of the task force. The debate carried over into 1967 without resolution of the basic differences between the pros and the cons.

Fundamental to the Harbor study is a conviction that a nation subjected to a first strike must seek protection for its population in the form of underground shelters. The Wigner task force of some 60 eminent scientists came up with a proposal for tunnel systems that would cost $38 billion for all U.S. cities over a quarter million in population—a cost estimate attacked by critics as being much too low. The Johnson Administration has given no indication that it is willing to recommend such a national shelter system. Instead, the Department of Defense nurses along a politically nonprovocative program of marking and stocking existing qualified building spaces within urban areas. Such a shelter program is designed to provide protection primarily against fallout. There appears to be little public support for any more ambitious shelter program, and the Defense Department has given no indication that it proposes anything beyond a fallout-only system of shelters.

The biggest drawback to a shelter program is the weakness that you have to be in a shelter if you are to be protected. A nation that is vulnerable to a first strike has no guarantee that it can get its people to shelter in advance of nuclear impact even if shelters are available. Even an aggressor, though possessing the advantage of ordering a population to shelter, might tip his hand in the process. So far the Soviets have not undertaken a national shelter program; should they do so, it would raise the issue for the United States of finding a proper response to such an act. The strategic analysts in the Defense Department would have to evaluate the extent to which a Soviet shelter program would reduce mortality in the event of attack and how much additional retaliatory fire, if any, would be required to assure destruction at the preshelter level. Suppose, for example, the Soviet shelters protected their urban population up to blast pressures of 15 pounds per square inch. Such shelters would protect their inhabitants out to a distance of slightly over two miles from ground zero (the point on the earth's surface directly under the explosion) for a one-megaton bomb exploded at optimum altitude. This corresponds to a knockout area of some 14 square miles in which mortality would be high. An unsheltered population would sustain high mortality over an area of 58 square miles. The larger Soviet cities would therefore have to be targeted with more warheads or with higher megatonnage. Smaller Soviet cities already overhit with a one-megaton bomb would not have to be retargeted. Since a Soviet hardening of its population would require massive engineering and considerable time, response to it could be gradual and is already anticipated in the entry into the U.S. strategic arsenal of multiple warheads and weapons of improved yield.

The U.S. civil response to a massive Soviet shelter program cannot be predicted with any certainty. It is, however, quite doubtful if the American people would underwrite a vast system of blast shelters; what is "good" for the Soviet Union is not necessarily good for the United States. In this case, if the Soviet initiative on shelters provokes an increase in U.S. strategic strike-power, it can hardly be regarded as "good" for the Soviet Union. Building a permanent system of underground shelters would bring the American people in daily contact with the grim foreboding of nuclear war—a subject they would rather not think about or would prefer to relegate to the military.

The elements of our militarized economy which seek to promote further increases in strategic power to fill a megaton gap may find that unlike the bomber and missile gaps, a megaton gap is hard to sell. If the average American is asked to support a program designed to achieve megaton superiority, he may end up getting some inkling of what a megaton really is; if so, the megaton gap-makers may fall into a credibility gap. When the layman grasps what the prefix mega- means—*i.e.*, a million tons of TNT, a million deaths—he may think his world has gone mad. He may come to the unwelcome conclusion that he is in fact living in a weapons culture. While he is unlikely to become pacifist, he may think things through and realize that some abatement, not escalation, of the arms race is in order.

For two long decades the United States sharpened and resharpened its deterrent sword and, while there was no outbreak of nuclear war, the Damoclean instrument did not put an end to conventional war. Nor did it in any sense impede four other nations in their quest for nuclear power. With the entry of Red China into the ranks of nuclear powers, it became clear that deterrence was a game that many could play and the rules were somehow concealed from the players. During these many years of armament, the United States became increasingly a captive of the weapons culture and found itself unable to resist new techno-military ventures. When, finally, technology gave hope of finding a shield to match the sword, the United States and the Soviet Union plunged into a new domain of weaponry—ballistic missile defense.

VII

THE NUCLEAR SHIELD

"The so-called heavy ABM shield—at the present state of technology—would in effect be no adequate shield at all against a Soviet attack, but rather a strong inducement for the Soviets to vastly increase their own offensive forces."

—ROBERT S. MC NAMARA
September 18, 1967

The U.S. decision to deploy Nike-X, the U.S. Army's ballistic defense against intercontinental missiles, was foreshadowed in November of 1966 when Defense Secretary McNamara revealed that the Soviet Union had begun a limited deployment of ballistic defenses on its home soil. The intelligence pinpointing this defense of Moscow and a few other points in the Soviet Union came from photographic data obtained by U.S. Air Force satellites. Despite the highly secret nature of these photographs, Secretary McNamara had reason to believe that the information was being leaked to newsmen; he therefore took the initiative and announced the new development himself.

Throughout 1967 pressure built up to respond to this Soviet move by deploying Nike-X. Mr. McNamara stubbornly and courageously fought to counteract the powerful forces of industry, the demands of the military and "scientist-hawks" in the Pentagon and the firepower directed at him from Capitol Hill. But there was one pressure that was irresistible—namely, that involved in White House considerations of election-year politics. Following the disclosure of Soviet ABM deployment, prominent Republicans—presidential "hopefuls" among them—strongly advocated immediate action on U.S. ballistic-missile defense. With this issue now given a political slant, the White House became vulnerable to a 1968 campaign attack that the incumbent Administration had failed to provide adequately for the nation's security. Such Republican "missile attack" involved political warheads whose punch was measured in megavotes, not megatons. Mr. McNamara's department was confined to megaton warheads, but President Johnson had to handle the political warheads.

Thus when Mr. McNamara announced on September 18, 1967, the U.S. decision to deploy a thin ABM defense, called the Sentinel system, it came as no real surprise. What was something of a shocker was the disclosure that the defense system would be built to protect against possible miscalculation on the part of Red China. Careful reading of Mr. McNamara's speech on the thin ABM shield (see Appendix XII) makes it clear that the Defense Secretary has little faith in Nike-X; indeed he argues this case so convincingly that one is led to the conclusion that a Chinese-oriented ABM system is a ruse or at best a rationalization for a decision that was primarily political.

Two additional developments, coming shortly after the Nike-X decision, throw new and rather strange light on the U.S. defense venture. McNamara's colleague, Paul C. Warnke, who is in charge of international security affairs, attempted to explain the U.S. ABM decision in a speech delivered October 6, 1967. His explanation centered on Secretary McNamara's concern for a "situation in which there is the danger of a preemptive attack." Mr. Warnke went on to explain:

> "In a crisis which they had brought on, if the Chinese came to believe that the United States might attack, they might be tempted to launch a preemptive strike, hoping to bring down at least a part of the American house in the face of total destruction, or even only the destruction of their nuclear forces, which at the moment of crisis they feared we were about to wreak on them."

This amounts to a frank admission that the policy of nuclear deterrence, which we have lived by during the past years, would not apply to Red China! Mr. Warnke went on to further explain: "This danger will pass when China develops, as the Soviets have done, a secure second-strike capability." It would appear that the strain of rationalizing the ABM decision agonized Mr. McNamara's associates. Given the 5 to 7 years required to deploy our Nike-X system, Red China could also deploy a secure missile-attack system, so on this basis the decision makes little sense.

The other sequel to the ABM decision was little noticed by the public; it came in the form of a "Letter to the Editor" published by *The New York Times* on October 22, 1967. Written by Dr. Richard L. Garwin, Columbia University professor of physics and director of the IBM Watson Laboratory, the letter commented on the implications of the MIRV (Multiple, Independently targetable Reentry Vehicle) development:

> The very possibility of MIRV's and the long delay involved in building either more offensive forces or a defense of our ICBM force have compelled (if not persuaded) Secretary McNamara to initiate the deployment of a defense of Minutemen, to be effective against Soviet missiles by perhaps 1973.

Now Dr. Garwin is a member of the Defense Science Board, the highest scientific advisory body in the Pentagon, and he therefore has access to the most secret defense data. If Nike-X is to defend Minuteman missiles, it is certainly not against the threat of Chinese attack.

We shall discuss the so-called "Chinese-oriented" system briefly and focus on the "thick" or full-scale Nike-defense. The grave danger exists that the "thin" Nike-X system represents a first installment of the $40 to $50 billion defensive system. As Secretary McNamara commented in this regard: "There is a kind of mad momentum intrinsic to the development of all new nuclear weaponry. If a weapon system works—and works well— there is strong pressure from many directions to produce and deploy the weapon out of all proportion to the prudent level required." True to form, once the "thin" Nike-X decision was announced, Congressmen pleaded for a commitment to a "thick" system.

Make no mistake about it, the complexities—both military, technical, psychological, and political—involved in the thick nuclear shield are enormous. Portraying the problem in terms of a deterrent sword and a defensive shield is in itself a very great oversimplification. For example, we may enumerate the following points to illustrate how intricate the problem is:

1. It is by no means certain whether the Soviets plan to deploy a heavy ABM system. So far the intelligence data indicate a relatively light defensive array. But if the U.S. opts for a heavy system, this may prompt the Soviets to do likewise; we may therefore be encouraging a new arms race.

2. Any defensive system is founded on assumptions about the nature of the offense it is intended to counter. An enemy may choose to depend on alternative modes of attack that outwit the ABM system. Defense is more or less static while offense has many options. The French learned the truth of this inflexibility when Hitler stabbed at the heart of France by skirting the Maginot Line and attacking with numerically inferior forces.

3. The performance requirements for an effective ABM system are extreme and may be incapable of adequate operational testing. Two highly qualified defense experts, Dr. Jerome B. Wiesner, former science adviser to President Kennedy, and Dr. Herbert F. York, former research-and-development chief in the Pentagon, contend that "a 90-percent success in interception constitutes failure in the inverted terms of thermonuclear warfare." Thermonuclear weapons are so devastating in their effects that a defensive shield would have to be virtually leakproof or impenetrable.

4. Given the fact that a Nike-X shield would be penetrable, one must provide for "leakage." This means that even the most expensive Nike-X system would require a back-up of a shelter system to protect the civilian population against weapons that penetrate the defense. As we have noted, several years ago shelters were rejected by the American people; given the present civil strife in metropolitan areas, it seems improbable that nuclear-weapon shelters will enjoy popular support. Ghetto-dwellers need a different kind of shelter.

5. Deployment of a thick Nike-X system can be countered by the

Soviet option of building more ICBM's to override the defense. This point was made most impressively by Secretary McNamara in his fiscal year 1968 testimony before Congress. The essence of his analysis appears in the following columns:

Number of fatalities in an all-out strategic exchange (assumes Soviet reaction to U.S. anti-ballistic-missile deployment)

[In millions]

| | Soviets strike first; United States retaliates | | United States strikes first; Soviets retaliate | |
	U.S. FATALITIES	SOVIET FATALITIES	U.S. FATALITIES	SOVIET FATALITIES
U.S. programs:				
Approved (no response)	120	120+	100	70
Posture A	120	120+	90	70
Posture B	120	120+	90	70

Posture A assumes a Nike-X system plus damage-limiting measures costing $12.2 billion. Posture B is for a $21.7 billion Nike-X program.

In other words, the Defense Secretary was saying that efforts to raise a stout shield would increase the level of attack and wash out the value of ballistic defense. Commenting on the table, Mr. McNamara concluded: "In all probability, all we would accomplish would be to increase greatly both their defense expenditures and ours without any gain in real security to either side—and that is the nub of the argument."

6. A U.S. decision to go for Nike-X would appear to many a foreign nation as the building up of the ramparts of Fortress America. A nation such as Japan or India, looking at the deployment of this ballistic system, might well conclude that it would be left out in the cold if a real crisis developed. They would feel that the U.S. self-interest buttressed by a sense of security, well-founded or not, would prevail, and allies would be left to shift for themselves.

Despite these complexities, there is no denying that Soviet initiative in deploying ABM sites around certain of its cities might force the U.S. hand. Members of Congress viewed with alarm this Soviet development, which they promptly interpreted as invalidating the power of our strategic retaliation. Mr. McNamara's answer to the charge that Soviet ABM measures rob our retaliatory punch of a real deterring impact is that under no conditions will he abandon a capability for "assured destruction" of Soviet targets. U.S. missile systems are in a cyclic state of being improved and replaced by more sophisticated weapons. This upgrading of the U.S. strategic striking power embodies improvements in propellants, missile design, guidance, and maneuverability of the final stage. These nonnuclear developments give the missile designer latitude for complicating the defender's problem. The heavier payloads permit use of multiple warheads (MIRV) which may be shot down like buckshot on a single target or guided individually to separate cities. In the latter case a single "space bus" is programmed to eject warheads along different trajectories. This highly sophisticated strategic offensive system is currently being developed by the United States.

Increasing missile payloads has a very great advantage in the development of penetration aids. These include inert and electronic material and devices that are intended to confuse the intelligence-gathering radar so vital to ballistic interception. For example, the payload may include "dummy" warheads, which present a discrimination problem to the defender; he must decide on the basis of radar data which of the objects are nuclear warheads and which are decoys. Even when discrimination is successful and an interceptory missile streaks up to kill the true warhead, the attacker may thwart this "kill" by "hardening" the warhead. The hardening technique consists of a variety of warhead modifications that reduce the explosive's vulnerability to blast, heat, and radiation.

Penetration aids and hardened warheads may well be the Achilles' heel of ballistic missile defense. Whereas it takes five years or more to deploy a Nike-X system, novel penetration aids and hardening techniques may be developed in a much shorter time. This may catch the defender off-guard if he is prepared to intercept much less sophisticated warheads. Here the defender's woes are magnified by his inability to learn quickly enough or reliably enough the nature of the devices that will be used.

The pendulum of military advantage has swung far to the side of the offense, so far in fact, that one may justifiably ask why the Soviets elected to deploy a defensive system. It is not the first time that they have started on such a path; two previous beginnings were terminated and, at this stage, no one can foresee how far the limited Soviet ABM deployment will go. My own hunch is that the Soviet decision to deploy an ABM system is fundamentally based on the Kremlin's awareness that it was futile to attempt to outdo the U.S.A. in the area of strategic offense. No matter how they tried they could not hope to overcome the problem of delivering enough warheads on U.S. strike-back sites to avoid unacceptably high damage to the homeland. Kremlin planners, strongly influenced by the thinking of the Red Army, had once before given higher priority to air defense than to the long-range air force. Given the Soviet sensitivity to defense (Napoleon and Hitler are names not soon forgotten in Russia) and uneasiness about a U.S. first strike (not entirely without reason), strategists could develop a paranoiac longing for a nuclear shield. To top it off, the Soviet Union has its own weapons culture, different from ours, capable of promoting new weapons systems.

A closed society such as the Soviet Union may actually fool itself into thinking an ABM system is effective, when in fact it is not. If Soviet planners and leaders, as well as leaders in other countries, come to believe that they have a near-perfect system, they may take undue risks in international crises. This is the most frightening aspect of the entire ABM issue—not that it will be an effective defense, but that someone may think it is. In which case the appearance of defense becomes as important as perfect performance.

Conceivably, the Soviets could be building missile defenses as insurance against less-than-massive nuclear attack—that is, along the lines which Defense Secretary McNamara gave as the reason for deploying a "thin" Nike-X system. After all, if the United States spends $5 billion on insurance against Chinese miscalculation, is not the Soviet Union justified in doing the same? The Soviet Union has thousands of miles of contiguous territory with Red China and has good reason to be concerned about nuclear misadventure. There is also the unhappy thought that the Kremlin may be banking on their ABM system as insurance against a U.S. "miscalculation." What's sauce for the goose is sauce for the gander. But suppose that the Soviets have in mind at some time making aggressive moves, possibly peripheral to their borders in the Near East, where they would have reason to fear that the United States would invoke its nuclear power—and not on a retaliatory basis. They might feel that the United States would be tempted to resort to a limited nuclear strike—not an ecliptic blitz but a nuclear jab designed to indicate that the United States meant business. While hoping to keep their aggression below this provocative limit, the Soviets could look to their ABM system as protection against this nuclear "convincer."

We shall discuss briefly the Nike-X system as it applies to a massive, determined first strike. The defense system for continental U.S.A. is fourfold in concept. It embodies electronic ears for detection of missile attack, computer brains for identifying warheads and predicting their course, rocket muscles for interception, and a nuclear punch for making the kill. The United States has to dispose its electronic sensors or radars to achieve the earliest possible warning of an impending attack. Over-the-horizon radar, developed recently, may provide as much as 25 minutes of advance warning; this long-distance radar perceives the attacking rockets as they zoom up into space during the initial phase of their trajectory. Such warning, if it could be interpreted quickly enough, might serve as the basis for a national "go-to-shelter" command, provided, of course, that shelters exist to which metropolitan populations may scurry in time. Even tentative early warning of a strategic attack would serve to alert the U.S. strategic forces, sending strategic bombers into the air and letting the missile men get ready for action.

Radar perception of a strategic missile attack is an extraordinarily complex task involving the use of four different systems, which are designed to deal with the problems of detection, identification, and tracking of hostile missiles. They are linked to the defense of a given area, where Spartan interceptors bear the burden of stopping the attack, and to "point defense," where Sprint missiles are deployed to defend a point target like a city or a missile base. Spartan missiles are designed to intercept warheads out to ranges of 400 miles, whereas Sprint interceptors are limited to lower altitudes. The Spartan-Sprint combination is the one-two punch of the defensive force. If Spartan fails to kill off the invader 100 or more miles from the target area, the Sprint missiles form a last-ditch defense. Spartan missiles form the real kill-power of a thin or area defense while Sprint interceptors are required for a thick defensive shield.

The four defense radars include:

Multi-function Array Radar (MAR). This is a highly sophisticated radar system designed to meet a broad range of functions, especially those required for dealing with a massive attack. Powerful radars search space for oncoming ICBM's, acquire data on the trajectory of a specific hostile object, discriminate between the *real thing* and decoys or dummy warheads, and direct interceptor missiles up to kill off the warhead. A scaled-down version of MAR, called TACMAR (for Tactical MAR), made up of less powerful radars, is designed for dealing with less sophisticated attacks.

Perimeter Acquisition Radar (PAR). Spartan missiles require information on the intercept point of a hostile missile with enough time to let them be fired and soar several hundred miles out in space to make the kill. This means that radars like PAR are required to detect and track ICBM's as they arc down from their Polar zeniths, 700 miles or more above the Arctic.

Missile Site Radar (MSR). Each area or point target to be defended would require a local radar control to guide the intercept course of Sprint missiles. In the event that one Sprint missile goes wide of its mark at high altitude, or fails to kill its warhead target, or is deceived by a decoy, then back-up Sprints must make a second or third stab at the oncoming warhead. The Sentinel system concentrates on the PAR and MSR radars.

A thick defense costing $20 billion at a minimum, and possibly twice that amount before it was complete, would require

a $13 billion investment in radar installations. One can under-
stand how U.S. electronics companies would have great self-
interest in promoting a thick Nike-X defense. Spartan-Sprint-
missile costs for a thick defense would total about $5 billion, of
which electronics concerns would receive very considerable
amounts because of the guidance systems and control devices
needed for the missiles. An additional $2 billion would be
required for the nuclear warheads for Spartan and Sprint.

Spartan warheads are in the megaton range, but because the
numbers of these long-range interceptors would be far smaller
than those for the short-range Sprint missiles, the principal
nuclear cost would be for thousands of Sprint warheads. The
Spartan missile is an outgrowth of the Nike-Zeus missile development. It is a three-stage, solid-fuel rocket about 50 feet in
length and three feet in diameter. The Spartan warhead can
be maneuvered to its target based on commands received from
MSR computers. With a slant range of 400 miles, Spartan missile sites can provide continental coverage against a light and
unsophisticated attack, with batteries protecting the following
cities:

Albany, N.Y.	Los Angeles
Atlanta	Miami
Baltimore	Minneapolis
Boston	New Orleans
Buffalo	New York
Charleston, S.C.	Philadelphia
Chicago	Pittsburgh
Cleveland	Portland, Oregon
Denver	St. Louis
Detroit	San Francisco
El Paso	Seattle
Honolulu	Washington, D.C.
Houston	

Defense against a heavy nuclear attack would involve going
far beyond the presently authorized $5 billion Sentinel system.
It would involve deploying missiles sites to protect:

Allentown, Pa.	Kansas City, Mo.	San Antonio, Tex.
Bridgeport, Conn.	Louisville, Ky.	San Bernardino, Cal.
Cincinnati, O.	Memphis, Tenn.	San Diego, Cal.
Columbus, O.	Milwaukee, Wis.	San Jose, Cal.
Dallas, Tex.	New Haven, Conn.	Springfield, Mass.
Dayton, O.	Norfolk, Va.	Tacoma, Wash.
Flint, Mich.	Paterson, N.J.	Toledo, O.
Indianapolis, Ind.	Providence, R.I.	Trenton, N.J.
	Rochester, N.Y.	

The Defense Department has not disclosed the basis on which the above cities qualify for missile protection. Certainly, if the thick Nike-X system is authorized there will be anguished debate over the matter of which cities should be protected. It will be noted that a score of states are not represented by cities in the above lists.

Should a full-scale ABM program be approved, not only the above 50 cities but also strategic military installations and perhaps key national facilities will be ringed with Sprint missile batteries. For example, if the Strategic Air Command deploys ABM defenses to protect its 100 control centers for 1,000 Minutemen, it will have to site Nike bases around the following:

Ellsworth AFB, S. Dak.	(150 Minutemen)
Grand Forks AFB, N. Dak.	(150 ")
Malmstrom AFB, Mont.	(200 ")
Minot AFB, N. Dak.	(150 ")
Warren AFB, Wyo.	(200 ")
Whiteman AFB, Mo.	(150 ")

There are many ways in which a Nike-X defense might function without regard to the nature of the targets to be defended, whether they be cities, Minuteman sites, Nike-X radar centers, or vital military-industrial facilities. Parenthetically, one should note that in a missile attack on the U.S., atomic and missile production facilities would be very low-class targets since in a nuclear war one worries about firepower on tap, not that which might be available months later.

Assuming that radar intelligence correctly grasps the trajectory of the incoming warhead, and computers faithfully

analyze the downward course and project the point at which
a Spartan interception may be made, the job remaining is to
launch the solid-fueled rocket, guide it to the intercept point
and make the kill. By virtue of its megaton warhead, Spartan
does not have to hit the hostile warhead; it is sufficient if the
nuclear explosive goes off within several miles of the attacking
warhead. To understand why this is true and to appreciate how
enemy countermeasures may rob Spartan of some of its lethal
punch, we need to study the physical effects of a nuclear
weapon exploded in the vacuum conditions of earth-space.

At ground level or at altitudes of several miles where there
is still palpable atmosphere, a nuclear explosion produces a
characteristic ball of fire, a surge of heat, and a subsequent
blast wave that travels through the atmosphere and smashes
stationary objects with pile-driver force. Development of the
ball of fire and the roll-out of the damaging air-blast is not
instantaneous but takes from a few seconds to over a minute,
depending on the power of the bomb and the altitude of
detonation. Accompanying the explosion is a fearful concussive
"bang." In other words, except for the high temperature of the
nuclear explosion and a prompt emission of penetrating radiation, which is confined to a distance of two to three miles from
the center of the explosion, the megaton detonation strongly
resembles the vast pile of TNT implicit in the "mega" of
megaton.

When a megaton weapon is exploded in the absence of an
atmosphere high above the earth, its effects are markedly different from those we have just described. All of the fantastic
energy of the explosion pours out in a fraction of one millionth
of a second. Very little light or ordinary heat is emitted and
there is no sound. It is a quick, silent flicker of X rays, and it
is this radiation that must make the "kill" in space. The lack of
sound is explained by the fact that—like the high-school physics
experiment featuring a bell "ringing" inside an evacuated bell
jar—in space there is no air to transmit any noise.

Spartan's killing effect depends upon the burst of radiation,
which is instantaneously flashed out. The example of a hot

poker illustrates the nature of Spartan's lethal radiation. If an iron poker is heated in a fire, it soon glows a cherry red, then yellow and finally "white hot." If by using a superhot furnace we raise the poker's temperature still more, it begins to emit ultraviolet light. Inside a detonating nuclear weapon the temperature exceeds that of the sun's fiery core, and the radiation is emitted in the form of X rays.

Roughly four fifths of the energy of a one-megaton weapon escapes as X rays. Just as visible light has different colors ranging from blue to red, X rays are varicolored, but instead of speaking about hues we talk in terms of "hard" and "soft" X rays. For example, "soft" X rays are used in the treatment of certain skin ailments; they are quickly absorbed in the outer layers of the skin. More penetrating X rays are produced in dental X-ray machines; they have the power to go through the patient's jaw and produce images of teeth. The X rays emitted by a Spartan warhead are quite soft, usually not energetic enough to flash through a sheet of aluminum.

Although the "kill data" on Spartan warheads are highly classified, it is rather easy to calculate the X-ray effects. The burst of X ray flashes out in all directions, outward into the darkness of space and downward toward earth. The latter need not concern us here, although rather gaudy auroral and illumination effects are produced when X rays interact with the thin atmosphere 50 miles above sea level. These downward-sent X rays are quickly absorbed by the atmosphere and do not get close to earth. But since there is no air to stop them in space, the Spartan X rays diminish in intensity according to a rule whereby a doubling of the distance reduces the number of X rays four-fold. Thus if one mile away from an exploding warhead the intensity of X rays is an arbitrary 100, then at two miles it will be 25 and at four miles it will be 6.25, and so on. The question is: At what distance will the X rays be intense enough to produce destructive impact on a hostile warhead? We need first to analyze how such an object may be damaged by X rays. A patient in a dentist's chair does not feel the "impact" of X rays when a dental film is taken. But the sensitive photographic emulsion does sense an effect—the absorption of X rays serves to produce a blackening result when the film is developed. In the case of a Spartan kill the X rays are absorbed in the outer skin and mantle of the ICBM warhead. If the explosion is a mile or two away, the absorption converts the solid material into an ionized gas or plasma. Physicists call this the fourth state of matter. An ICBM warhead struck by an X-ray burst would have its bombward side seared; a plasma sheath or ion envelope would form instantaneously. The result: intense heat and hydrodynamic shock.

Calculations show that a megaton explosion would impose serious-to-lethal X-ray impacts on a warhead out to a distance of four miles. The lethal effect would depend on how the hostile warhead was constructed and whether or not the enemy had hardened his warhead to withstand heat and shock. It is no secret that nuclear warheads can be designed to withstand very heavy shocks; it is more difficult to protect against ion-heat, but all ICBM's are heat-shielded to cope with the thermal effects of reentry. Degradation of the heat shield by ripping off part of the surface would put a chink in the thermal armor, rendering the warhead vulnerable to burn-up in the reentry zone.

No weapons expert would overlook the possibility of devising countermeasures to rob the X rays of their killing sting. Here we come to the "cops and robbers" aspect of ballistic missile defense as played in the Stygian gloom of earth space. The United States has contracted with many companies to develop means of fending off or otherwise counteracting the lethality of X-ray kill. For example, one technique involves equipping an ICBM warhead with inflatable X-ray "bumpers"; the latter consist of metallic foil which is pressure-expanded to form a protective balloonish quilt around the warhead. Incident X rays get absorbed in this foil and are thus insulated from direct impact on the warhead itself. There are literally scores of techniques for outwitting the defender, but none give really close-in protection—that is, down to a fraction of a mile.

It should be added that in addition to the X rays emitted by a Spartan warhead there is also a burst of penetrating nuclear radiation that is not so easily absorbed as the X rays. However, these nuclear "bullets" do not have the lethal range of X rays and constitute an effect that is important closer in toward the detonation point. A great deal of publicity has been given to X rays, but this may be part of a "fad"; my own calculations show that the neutron-kill cannot be disregarded and may come back into vogue, especially when weapons experts gain confidence in X-ray countermeasures.

The Sentinel defense will provide an area defense for the United States against the threat of a light attack that did not focus too great a thrust at any single target system. The thin system would involve about 14 radar sites and Spartan batteries; each would cover an elliptical area or "footprint" enclosing about 200,000 square miles. It is a kind of lightweight umbrella, so to speak, designed for a sprinkle but not for a downpour. An attacking foe, knowing its potential, would presumably not oblige by staging an attack that conformed to the defense capability, but would rather attack it at a few points with concentrated fire, thus overwhelming the thin defenses. The concentration of U.S. population in a few metropolitan areas is such that this kind of attack could be very serious.

Speaking to the point of Chinese attack with ballistic missiles, Sen. Joseph Clark of Pennsylvania asked in midsummer of 1967: "But how dumb do we think the Chinese are? What if the Chinese, instead of international missiles, use long-range submarines not as yet in existence to fire medium-range ballistic missiles under an ABM defense? Or simply fire very 'dirty' nuclear weapons in the atmosphere off the coast of California and allow the prevailing westerlies to cover the United States with deadly radiation, or even smuggle nuclear bombs into Chinatown in a suitcase?"

Defense officials play down the effects of such an unconventional mode of attack as "totally unlikely" and "extremely unlikely," yet the whole case for a thin Nike-X defense is based on a "highly improbable" miscalculation. In the vocabulary of the Pentagon the subtle difference between the characteristics amounts to $5 billion.

The whole point here is that the more defense is positioned to meet a set challenge, the less likely an enemy is to play into your hand. Defense planners often become victims of their own preconceptions and predilections and stubbornly persist along a fixed trajectory of planning. This is all the more dangerous because of the all-or-none nature of a nuclear attack and the impossibility of carrying out operational tests of any system which truly simulate the "real thing." The situation is parallel to that of a metropolitan fire department that develops a capability to fight small fires but cannot cope with a conflagration.

Recognizing that an area defense can at best cope with a limited number of attacking warheads, defense experts look upon Spartan as the first line of defense, which must be backed up with a lower tier of interception. Sprint is the U.S. Army's choice as the back-up interceptor designed to kill off enemy warheads which evade Spartan. In contrast to Spartan's potent nuclear warhead, Sprint has a nuclear explosive in the kiloton range.

The large number of Sprint interceptors is made mandatory by the multiplicity of target sites to be defended and the confusing attack problem presented by decoys in the atmosphere. Sprint missiles are designed to be popped out of an underground silo by means of a gas-driven piston. The two-stage, 27-foot-long missile is then ignited and given very high acceleration so as to reach high altitude in time to intercept incoming objects. As Lt. Gen. Austin W. Betts, chief of U.S. Army Research and Development, puts it: "The Sprint can travel 1 mile in the time it takes your heart to beat twice." Tacmar, short for "tactical multifunction array radar," provides Sprint with radar-beam steering necessary to keep it on collision course with its target.

Once launched, Sprint must be guided to its intercept point by surface-based equipment which must be capable of discriminating between true and false warheads. This discrimination problem is not so critical for Spartan because its kill radius in space is so extended that it envelops the probable volume in which deployed decoys might diverge at high altitude. Sprint's effective ceiling of about 100,000 feet above the earth's surface means that it must make its kill in a zone bounded by a lower altitude of around 50,000 feet. Hostile weapons exploded at an altitude of, say, 50,000 feet may not inflict critical blast over-pressures on surface targets, although this depends on the mega-tonnage assumed for enemy warheads, but the heat effect from such middle-altitude bursts could produce serious damage to exposed people and to vulnerable buildings. Indeed, hostile war-heads might be armed to trigger automatically in response to a Sprint detonation so as to produce some, though not maximal, damage on surface targets. Thus in backing up Spartan, Sprint faces a tremendous challenge—it must make its kill high enough in the atmosphere so that the hostile warhead is destroyed or explodes harmlessly.

As the real warhead and its decoys descend into the atmos-phere, a measure of discrimination is made possible by the fact that the heavy true warhead sinks faster in the air than the lighter decoys. On the other hand, the attacker may elect to use multiple warheads scattered over an area that forces the defender to commit Sprints to each object. Or warheads may be given terminal boost to skew them over a ballistic trajectory and thus confound the missile-site radar. An attacker might also explode a high-yield nuclear weapon high above the target zone so as to interfere with radar acquisition of data on missiles which would be phased in to take advantage of the ionospheric disturbances. Many ways are open to an attacker to outwit the Spartan-Sprint defenses, and the defender could never be sure what options the offense might exercise. A defender could never feel confident that the Spartan-Sprint complex, even in its most elegant configuration, would stand up to the weight of a heavy attack. Not even the most wild-eyed advocate of Nike-X claims that it would provide perfect protection, but the lack of per-fection is critical to the whole ballistic missile issue.

What is the allowable leakage of hostile missiles through

Nike-X? This is a question that Nike-X enthusiasts avoid discussing. Oddly enough, one such proponent backed his way·into such a discussion in the summer of 1967. Representative Craig Hosmer, chairman of the House G.O.P. Conference Committee on Nuclear Affairs, submitted a report to his fellow Republicans in which he postulated an attack on the U.S.A. with just 18 high-yield nuclear weapons. According to Mr. Hosmer, a senior member of the Joint Committee on Atomic Energy, the following damage was inflicted:

> . . . almost the entire states of Massachusetts, Rhode Island, and New Jersey burst into flames. So did New York City, Hartford, Philadelphia, Baltimore, and Washington, D.C. Essentially the entire East Coast from Portland, Maine, to Norfolk, Virginia, up to 150 miles inland, became one raging, all-consuming fire storm.
>
> At the same moment a 170-mile-wide 22,500 square-mile circle of flame erupted across southern portions of Louisiana, Mississippi and Alabama from New Orleans and Baton Rouge through Biloxi to Mobile, destroying all within it. Detroit, Toledo, Cleveland and half of Ohio met a single fate, as did portions of Wisconsin, Illinois and Indiana from Milwaukee through Chicago, on to Gary and South Bend.

Mr. Hosmer allocated three of his 18 weapons to the Pacific Coast—targeting Portland-Seattle, San Francisco and Southern California and incinerating nine million Southern Californians. He also dropped one bomb in the Pacific to inundate Alaska, and eight weapons were allocated to western states containing U.S. ICBM complexes. This bombing pattern produced fire storms in 34 of 50 U.S. states, and Mr. Hosmer's final tally read: "Three of every five Americans were dead and the nation's military-industrial back was broken."

Ironically, the California congressman urged deployment of Nike-X to reinforce the U.S. deterrent. His attack scenario dramatizes the nature of nuclear war and the strict requirement for perfection in missile defense. While the public and the Congress may "buy" Nike-X as a stout shield, many experts view ballistic missile defense as a complement to deterrence.

This aspect of Nike-X involves not only point defense of continental strategic sites but also damage limitation and psychological factors such as the impact of the defense measures on the attitudes of an aggressor and of allies.

It is tempting to think that the pendulum of technology can be swung back from supremacy of offense to a resurgence of defense. Many laymen have been seduced by technology to the point where they believe that weapons experts can develop any conceivable system, provided they get enough money. However, the technological innovations open to the offense, as well as military options for varying an attack, continue to confer upon offense a marked margin of superiority. In the case of the United States the high vulnerability of metropolitan target areas and the exorbitant social, political, and economic costs involved in reducing this nakedness to attack plagues Nike-X. Since the latter cannot be perfect and even a small leakage rate can have serious consequences, the United States cannot depend on the Nike-X shield alone. It must be linked to a backup system of civil defense capable of absorbing the impact of the warheads which slip through the defenses. Defense Secretary McNamara made this point repeatedly in his annual appearances before various congressional committees, but then, wearying of any public support for civil defense, he gave up asking for funds to build shelters. Instead, the Defense Department continued with its "fallout only" shelter program of identifying and marking such metropolitan building spaces as appear to provide a reasonable degree of protection from fallout radiation. The shelters are also stocked with emergency supplies of food and water. High-yield nuclear weapons penetrating the Spartan-Sprint defense or those killed at too low an altitude would impose high levels of blast damage on most metropolitan structures. Existing fallout shelters would provide occupants with protection from the primary heat flash but not from violent secondary fires. The shelters would afford only a measure of security from blast damage. The problem of revamping American cities to be fairly blast-resistant is one which city planners never had in mind when metropolitan areas were designed. In any event, the transformation or hardening of a huge city to provide good shelter space for millions of Americans is an incredibly difficult undertaking. Dr. John E. Ullmann, chairman of Hofstra University's Department of Management, Marketing, and Business Statistics, estimates that blast-resistant shelters for 120 million Americans would cost from $254 to $302 billion.

It is not the cost that deters politicians from underwriting a shelter system—it is the fact that the public has indicated a strong distaste for becoming embodied as part of the nuclear deterrent system. But if it should come to pass that the United States would try to harden its cities, the weapons culture would see a complete envelopment of the civilian sector in a Fortress America. In the process of erecting a nuclear shield over the nation, the United States might draw back from its global commitments. The very fact that the United States has begun building its Sentinel system has already set our allies wondering how much they can depend on U.S. aid in a future crisis.

Japan, for example, is much closer to Red China and much more vulnerable to nuclear attack than the United States. If the U.S.A. pretends to erect its Nike-X defenses against Peking's miscalculations at some time in the future, why should not Japan seek similar ballistic defenses even sooner? After all, in making a case for Nike-X as a thin shield against Red Chinese missiles, the U.S. Defense Department has assumed that deterrents will not deter Red China from lashing out at the United States. Why should Japan not make the same assumption, especially since it wields no atomic sword? One would expect Japan to press for U.S. aid in an oriental version of Nike-X.

By 1970, when the Nike-X hardware begins to take substantive shape, there is the likelihood that strong pressure will develop for the U.S. resumption of atmospheric nuclear testing in order to prove out the ballistic missile defense system. Military men are notoriously hardheaded about proof-testing weapons systems; they are disinclined to believe in scientific experiments as "paper proof." What they will believe is actual destruction of a ballistically propelled ICBM warhead by Spartan in space and by Sprint in the lower atmosphere. Since the United States is bound by the Nuclear Test Ban Treaty of 1963 not to conduct nuclear tests in the atmosphere, Nike-X operational tests will pose a real dilemma for the U.S. State Department. If the Soviets conduct such tests first, it will save face for the United States.

The irony of such operational tests is that they can never really simulate an actual attack situation. Soviet missile technology and warhead configurations cannot be known with any assurance. The U.S. experts who test a U.S. ICBM imitation of a Soviet warhead must make a number of assumptions about Soviet designs—*i.e.*, warhead multiplicity, maneuverability, penetration aids, and weapon hardening and fusing. Indeed, if the testers are to simulate an actual attack, they may have to explode a number of weapons in a single test in order to approach the nuclear tumult which a concerted attack on a target city might involve.

Up to now we have focused attention on interception of ICBM's relatively close to continental U.S. targets. Few will dispute the fact that it is hazardous to wait until the warheads are so close to their targets—and are accompanied by so many countermeasures—before interception is attempted. As defensive missile technology advances and more proficient radars are developed, we may expect that interception will be aimed at points higher on the ballistic arc of the incoming missiles.

The U.S. Navy has proposed a system which would strike at enemy missiles even before they leave their home territory. This sea-based antiballistic missile intercept system, known as SABMIS, is designed to launch interceptory missiles from undersea or surface ships close to the Soviet Union or to other foreign powers. By detecting ICBM's as they streak upward from their launch sites, SABMIS would intercept somewhere along the upward trajectory, thus neutralizing the technical advantages of decoys and countermeasures unique to ICBM's as they near their targets. The U.S. Army, recalling how the Navy had robbed the Air Force of part of the nuclear strategic mission through development of Polaris as a rival of Minuteman, could not have viewed SABMIS as anything but a competitor to Nike-X. But the Navy did not manage to bring SABMIS to more than a study phase in 1967 and thus it did not really challenge the Army's defense project.

Had the SABMIS concept been developed sooner, it might have been a weapons system that could have been specific to a Pacific-based defense against Chinese missiles. But considering the politics of the Nike-X decision, this might have been a real liability for the U.S. Navy. If, as it appears most probable, the U.S. ballistic defense was really a response to Soviet threats, then the SABMIS system might gain favor in the future, pending appropriate technological development. Attractive as the SABMIS concept for early interception may seem, it has serious strategic defects. For example, the necessity for prompt action once enemy missiles are launched reduces decision time to a minimum. And it raises the puzzling issue of what kind of information would be necessary for a SABMIS fire-order. Would not the Soviet strategists regard SABMIS as a highly provocative development tantamount to a Polaris-Poseidon system geared to a first-strike capability?

The whole ballistic-missile defense problem is shot through with uncertainties that tend to complicate the already intricate machinery of the deterrent apparatus. Perhaps the most unsettling of these is the provocative nature of Nike-X. What must the Soviet planners think when they see the United States begin a $5 billion deployment of a system that may mushroom into a 10-fold greater national investment? The Soviets are not unaware of the deplorable, ghetto-like condition of major U.S. cities. When the United States bypasses the central problem of metropolitan repair and rehabilitation to spend billions on Nike-X, then Soviet experts may honestly believe that a new phase of the arms race has begun. Conceivably—and military strategists must plan for the worst—the Americans are preparing to make a first strike at the Soviet Union, or to take aggressive action elsewhere.

Another complication that Nike-X introduces into nuclear strategy is that last-minute interception precludes any rational decision-making in the waging of a nuclear war. There was a time when Pentagon strategists talked of "graduated nuclear response" along the lines of making the punishment fit the crime—*i.e.*, waiting it out in a "nuclear exchange" before responding with the full weight of retaliatory fire. But if one depends upon Nike-X to protect cities and missile bases, then there is a double uncertainty. In the instance of a U.S. President watching the electronic display of attack data on the screen we described in the previous chapter, he could assume a hit for every incoming missile when there was no missile defense. But with dependence on Nike-X, the President would have to wait for news about the success of interception; in effect, Nike-X would delay or even confuse the nature of the "crime" and thus rule against moderating the "punishment." Even more serious would be the fact that uncertainty about the survival of Minuteman bases would predispose a massive spasm response. The attacked nation, fearing for the safety of its return fire, would be prone to salvo its retaliation and make of nuclear war a convulsive catastrophe.

Defense Secretary McNamara, in announcing the U.S. decision to build a "thin" nuclear shield, made a most persuasive case against expanding this to a "thick" one. But once started, Nike-X will probably grow like Topsy.

The political coupling of the Sentinel system to communities is illustrated by an item that appeared in the Great Falls, Mont., *Tribune* on October 14, 1967, less than a month after the Nike-X decision:

> (Senator Mike) Mansfield said the construction north of Great Falls will involve the location of a Perimeter Acquisition Radar (PAR) with protective Sprint and Spartan missiles in the immediate vicinity.
>
> "When completed, this installation will probably have a contingent of up to 600 people permanently stationed or employed," he said. About half of the 600 will be civilians he added.
>
> "At this time only one PAR is planned, although if this system is expanded later, I feel confident Montana will receive another location," the senator said.

The intimate merger of political forces with the military-industrial complex bodes ill for those who seek to apply controls to the arms race. No sooner was the Nike-X decision announced than Mr. McNamara was forced to disclose Soviet work on an orbital weapons system which he dubbed FOBS— for fractional orbital bombardment system. Simultaneously, congressional forces headed by Sen. Henry Jackson began to beat the drums for matching the Soviet system.

Actually the Soviet delivery system was one that American experts had debated in the early 1960's. They had rejected it as being of poor military value. As developed by Soviet experts, FOBS consisted of throwing a final missile stage into a 100-mile-high orbit for three quarters of a trip around the earth. Then at an appropriate point in orbit, the nuclear payload was ejected by applying a retrothrust so that the weapon package descended to earth along a short ballistic trajectory. By following a low orbit and by approaching the United States from a southerly direction—as opposed to ICBM's, which would arc over the North Pole at an altitude of over 700 miles—the partially-orbited warheads would escape the U.S. ballistic-missile early warning system. Then, with some three minutes of warning, they would impact on U.S. targets.

The Soviet orbital-eject system has inherent drawbacks that severely undercut its military worth. First, because of the higher speed that has to be imparted to an orbital vehicle, the military payload is less than a third that carried by an ICBM. Second, the deorbiting of the nuclear warhead capsule makes for less accuracy than that attainable with an ICBM. The combination of these two deficiencies makes the weapon system poorly adapted for striking at point, or hard, targets like Minuteman sites. Allowable targets are cities and bomber bases. The latter is questionable since the alert time given by over-the-horizon radar—about an hour for the 18,000-mile journey through space —would allow the bombers to be airborne by the time of bombardment. Finally, the orbital weapon requires a very large booster for launch, and rockets in this category do not lend themselves to being deployed in underground silos. In order to be effective, hundreds of the rockets would have to blast off simultaneously or within a very short time span.

Adding up all of these factors, the FOBS type of attack is a sheer terror weapon, which has to come out of the blue. Since it is a soft-based, vulnerable system very similar to bombers on the ground, it cannot be used in time of international crisis as a believable force. One cannot threaten an opponent with a weapons system that is so vulnerable that it can be used only as a first strike. In a true crisis, the existence of such a perilous first-strike force would represent a great temptation to one's opponent. Furthermore, since this kind of first strike cannot eliminate the retaliatory fire of the attacked nation, the FOBS would be a suicidal weapons system.

Nuclear weapons circulated in orbit for more than one pass around the planet represent a very poor military investment. For one thing, the technical problem of summoning the nuclear capsules to target is much more difficult than in the case of a fractional orbit where the launch site and the target lie in the same line of flight. As a weapons carrier orbits, the earth turns underneath it, and the target shifts out of its shadow path. This means that, except for coincidental occasions when the satellite and target do line up, the nuclear capsule would have to be given a diverting thrust from its plane in order to hit the target. Such a procedure requires additional on-board thrust and guidance systems that further reduce the military payload. For another, the circulation in orbit of hundreds of heavy satellites would be a dead giveaway of enemy intention and a loss of strategic surprise.

Nonetheless, the temper of the Congress is such that it is easily excited by displays of enemy hardware and it is prone to panic itself into demanding counterweapons. There is an irony here in that careful defense analyses are brushed aside and politics prevails. Such was the case in the U.S. decision to deploy Nike-X, and no doubt the example will be repeated in other domains of weaponry. Meanwhile, the nuclear abyss deepens and its brink becomes ever more treacherous. More nations possess more nuclear weapons and the defense systems themselves become less stable. The possibility of accident or miscalculation looms ever larger as nations come to rely on hair-trigger attack-and-response weapons systems.

VIII

WEAPONS AND SOCIETY

"Priorities are reflected in the things we spend money on. Far from being a dry accounting of bookkeepers, a nation's budget is full of moral implications; it tells what a society cares about and what it does not care about; it tells what its values are."

—SENATOR J. W. FULBRIGHT
August 8, 1967

Any accountant going over the postwar books of the United States would find some rather discouraging facts. Over seven tenths of federal expenditures have been for national security. In the vital area of federally funded research and development, almost nine tenths of this work was directed to defense-atomic-space activities. Less than one tenth of one percent of these funds went to support research in problems of urban development. Naturally, a nation must look to its security, but the material developed in previous chapters suggests that the United States overreacted to foreign threats. Furthermore, in view of the recent decision to build up ballistic defenses, it appears that this country is stepping up the tempo of the arms race.

Robert L. Heilbroner, in his *Limits of American Capitalism*, states: "No attempt to speak of the long-run prospects for American capitalism can overlook the central fact that it is now a semimilitarized economy and that it will probably become even more so during the next decade." Gradually the U.S. involvement with defense industry has proceeded to the point where weapons-making begins to dominate our society. This protracted dedication of American effort to devising and manufacturing new arms has created a techno-military establishment that threatens to make greater inroads upon our economy. A central problem for democracy is the control of this military-industrial complex that has grown in influence as its political connections have ramified.

No nation can devote so much of its ingenuity, manpower, and resources to the works of war without at the same time being deeply changed in the process. Many of the changes are subtle, slow to surface, and hard to trace as to origin. There is a certain aseptic and detached quality to our techno-militarization which insulates people from its impact. The Long Island housewife who assembles tiny electronic components for a bomb mechanism does not associate herself with the weapons that may bring death to some victim. She lives in her own microcosm and, if queried about her occupation, may shrug off the questioner with the reply, "A job is a job." The scholarly professor who probes the chemical secrets of certain compounds may fail to associate his research with destructive defoliants. The senator who champions a $40 billion Nike-X defense will reject the charge that he is his own lobbyist, asserting that his only concern is with national security. The industrialist who mass-produces napalm may brush aside any qualms he may have with the contention that he simply fulfills orders given to him by his Government.

This is a deteriorating situation that contributes to allowing the arms race to run out of control, for if all are compliant and feel no responsibility, then our democracy is in jeopardy. A new order of discourse is called for—linking the American people to major national decisions in which their security is intimately involved. It needs to be a spirited dialogue, marked by the sharpest questioning of techno-military issues. Those who criticize or seek to examine the wisdom of national decisions need not have the answers; it is sufficient if they phrase the questions properly and publicly. Any operations analyst knows that half the problem is finding the right questions to ask.

Here are some of the key questions that need expression:

1. How does the nation arrive at a rational determination of the strategic forces adequate for a policy of nuclear deterrence?
2. Given the decision on a "thin" ballistic-missile defense, how does a democracy prevent automatic escalation to a "thick" defense system?
3. What constitutes an effective mechanism for objectively evaluating whether or not a "megaton gap" poses a real threat to U.S. security?
4. What should be done about future defense contracting with firms fully committed to having the U.S. Government as a single customer?
5. How should the nation's scientific and technical resources, so preponderantly oriented to atomic-space-defense, be converted to a larger share of peaceful missions?
6. What can the United States do to arrest the momentum of the runaway arms race and start on the road to arms controls?
7. How does a democracy go about applying restraints to the military-industrial-political complex, which fuels the arms race?

This list of questions does not end here; it is merely a beginning, but it may serve to suggest the dimensions of the debate needed if democracy is not to be tyrannized by defense technology.

There has been so much recent publicity about the peacetime benefits of federal technology, especially with regard to civilian space programs like Project Apollo, that this "technological fallout" or spinoff needs to be put in perspective. It is true that certain wartime developments like radar and jet aircraft development did feed through to the civilian economy. But as atomic-space-defense technology has extrapolated to such requirements as the ICBM, lunar rockets, and space weapons, it has gotten farther and farther from the civilian marketplace.

There is a deeply held conviction among many people that technology advances in lock step with war—and that this is the only feasible avenue for technological innovation. But the farm tractor came long before the armored tank and the Wright brothers enjoyed no military subsidy.

When the Supersonic Transport (SST) reached the development stage, the aircraft companies found that they could not borrow military technology to take shortcuts and save money on the new plane. In the case of the work undertaken for manned lunar flight, a program costing some $30 billion, much of the effort went to huge boosters, enormous tanks, pumps, and "freak out" engineering with little relevance to the civilian economy. While the National Aeronautics and Space Administration concentrated on getting men to the moon, metropolitan surface travel and city-to-city air travel clogged the available traffic lanes. The safety of air passengers was jeopardized as NASA spent less than one percent of its funds on aeronautics.

One of the underlying reasons for the massive NASA space activity, it must be recalled, was the image of military proficiency that this technology projected. A number of air-power enthusiasts were quick to seize upon the notion that the control of space would grant a nation supremacy in military power. Even the moon's surface was not too remote a rendezvous for some military men—Gen. James M. Gavin, for example, testified before a Senate committee investigating the U.S. space potential: "If I, as a soldier, were asked by my superiors in this country, is the moon of any significance to us, if the Soviets, for example, are occupying it, I would say absolutely, yes. We have got to get out there. We have got to get out there first, and if they are out there, we have got to have some understanding of who is going to occupy the moon."

The success of Project Apollo involved the efforts of about a third of a million aerospace workers, half of whom will be out of jobs in 1968. Presumably the decision on Nike-X will re-employ many of these workers, but the build-up of specialized work forces like that engaged in making the Apollo craft imposes a constraint upon the economy. Companies like Boeing and North American Aviation promoted huge post-Apollo programs, amounting to $6 billion or $7 billion per year. Such activity would help to sustain the upward thrust of the aerospace industry. This very rapidly growing segment of the economy aims at a total of $30 billion in sales for 1970. Even if sales of commercial aircraft increase sharply, this still leaves the bulk of the money to be provided by the Federal Government.

If the U.S. aerospace industry—by all odds, the most rambunctious component of the military-industrial complex—is to fit into the national economy without depending primarily on defense contracts, then the means must be found to convert it to new objectives. This is an especially acute problem for companies like Lockheed, which are so top-heavy in arms sales. The state of California, anticipating conversion problems in the event of defense or space cutbacks, let four study contracts to aerospace companies for analysis of certain problems, such as transportation. The results were widely advertised but added little to California's knowledge of how to solve its transportation problem. The fact is that aerospace industries are quite specialized in their know-how and lack experience in diversifying to invade the civilian market for consumer products on a competitive basis. Much of the aerospace technical talent lies in the field of engineering which is not easily adapted to new endeavors. Furthermore, lack of dollar consciousness in the artificial aerospace business hamstrings companies when they try to penetrate fields already served by experienced corporations. Here the Federal Government, long the exclusive patron of many of the aerospace firms, has a responsibility to help in converting the defense contractors to enter the free play of the marketplace.

The author is no dreamer who thinks that the United States can abandon its commitment to arms overnight. He does not recommend giving up a policy of nuclear deterrence that has been the mainstay of our national security for so many years. It would be foolish in the extreme to believe that peace will break out on this planet in a great wave of international understanding. Therefore, we must be reconciled to large defense budgets for some years to come, but we must also avoid too great extremes in defense, which provoke equal reactions from hostile powers. Since it is the U.S. Congress that controls defense purse strings, it is imperative that this legislative body be equipped with some better and more objective means of analyzing the nation's security needs.

Recently, the Science Policy Research Division of the Legislative Reference Service of the Library of Congress has demonstrated a high quality of objectivity in analyzing certain technical issues, especially for the U.S. Senate. If this activity could be broadened to include a mandate to study defense policy, it might be very useful to the Congress. One of the faults of the committee operations of the Congress is that staff members are often ex-military or federal agency personnel on loan to the committees. Since the committee staff is a vital part of setting up hearings or defining congressional interest in a technical area, a defense-oriented staff in effect becomes an arm of the Pentagon. One does not find pacifists or disarmament-minded men on the staffs of the armed-services committees. Instead there are weapons sub-cultures so lodged that the normal checks and balances of the democratic process are blocked.

If the Congress becomes the obedient handmaiden of the Pentagon, where will our democracy find the means of opposing constant escalation of the defense budget? Or how will it begin to think about and take action on arms controls? Here I believe that scientists have a special responsibility to take the lead in public discussion because many of the issues involve complex technology. Furthermore, over the past two decades many of the nation's scientists have shown that they are capable of stimulating national debate on topics like radioactive fallout, nuclear testing, and arms controls.

Dr. Linus Pauling, for example, demonstrated an ability to pioneer in public discussion of a major issue—namely, that of a nuclear test ban. His famous 1957 petition urging a test ban was signed by 2,875 scientists. Only a dozen scientists working at Atomic Energy Commission facilities, including the Los Alamos weapons laboratory, placed their signatures on the peti-

tion. One may conclude that people working for the AEC felt
that it would be unhealthful for them to associate their names
with Dr. Pauling's cause.

In connection with the Pauling petition, two additional com-
ments are worth making. First, the entire effort was made by a
very few individuals working on their own; no scientific organization like the American Chemical Society aided in circulating
the petition. In general, the professional organizations concerned
with science steer clear of any political action. Second, Dr.
Pauling was vigorously attacked in the press and on Capitol
Hill on the basis that he was aiding the Communist cause and
that he had Communist affiliations. Although pilloried at home,
Dr. Pauling won the Nobel Peace Prize in 1963.

Since Dr. Pauling took his responsibility as a scientist-citizen
to heart in 1957, it has become more difficult for people like
him to act as modern Paul Reveres to alert their fellow citizens
to the dangers of the arms race. For one thing, scientists are
less free than they were a decade ago. More scientists work
for and are implicated in the military-industrial complex and,
in addition, thousands more on campus are intimidated by the
fact that research funds for most colleges and universities come
from the Federal Government. Rightly or wrongly, many scientists feel it is safer to remain aloof from controversy. For
another, the scientist faces a dilemma when he comes to speaking out on a controversial issue. If he has access to classified
data, he runs the risk of violating security when he breaks into
print; if he does not know the secret data, he has to find some
means of generating an authoritative grasp of the subject matter. The nuclear test ban issue was relatively simple compared
to current problems like ballistic-missile defense. On the other
hand, the issues have become more acute and much is at stake—
scientists should be motivated to do the hard work necessary
to understand current defense issues.

Another hurdle facing the dissenting scientist is that he is
often paired off against a weapons scientist, who has the advantage of official position and the backing of the Military Establishment. The scientific community, like any other, has its vari-

ous kinds of characters—left wing and rightist, hawks and doves, emotional and cold-blooded—so it is not surprising that some scientists in the weapons business should be as militant as the most swashbuckling general. Nor should it be looked upon as unusual when a man like Dr. Edward Teller takes to the national stage to promote ballistic-missile defense or some new weapons system. Scientists may seem unlike the military, but as sociologists Hans H. Gerth and C. Wright Mills foresaw in 1942: "Precisely because of their specialization and knowledge, the scientist and technician are among the most easily used and coordinated of groups in modern society . . . the very rigor of their training typically makes them the easy dupes of men wise in political ways."

The public may be confused when experts disagree on a national issue, but it is essential that opposing viewpoints be aired; otherwise policy will be determined by a technological elite. It is not proper that Americans should bow their heads before the altar of technology, averting their eyes as did ancient multitudes when high priests sought auguries in animal entrails. As Robert Oppenheimer has remarked: "We do not operate well when the important facts, the essential conditions, which limit and determine our choices are unknown. We do not operate well when they are known, in secrecy and in fear, only to a few men."

The fundamental issue of nuclear superiority as opposed to nuclear parity has never been fully exposed to the public view. In general the news is leaked from the Pentagon or via Capitol Hill that the Soviets have developed or are about to produce a new weapons system. Then there is a clamor for the United States to "catch up" and surpass the Soviets. Most recently this sequence of events was illustrated for ballistic-missile defense. Now an attempt is being made to have the United States "match" the orbital-eject bomb delivery system of the Soviet Union, even though its military value for the Soviets is highly dubious and is even more so for the United States. There is the automatic assumption that any Soviet military development represents a margin of superiority and that it must be offset by a corresponding counterdevelopment. In this manner the arms race escalates and provokes corresponding reactions by the Soviets, which in turn set off new cycles of armament.

If there is ever to be any stability in arming, people must recognize that there is a point in armament beyond which no additional security is purchased. By the same token, an enemy may achieve the same degree of security—that is, nuclear parity by fashioning his strategic deterrent forces to the lethal point. But when either side attempts to multiply its killing power, it invites duplication. In effect, a nation signs its own death certificate in multiple copies.

The concept of nuclear sufficiency—of the military ever having enough of anything—is still so novel that it has not yet gained acceptance in some military and political quarters. Defense Secretary McNamara understood and adopted the principle of nuclear parity as applied to the U.S. missile force, only to be overruled by President Kennedy. The latter, having campaigned on a missile-gap platform, apparently found it politically necessary to commit the nation to more missiles than Mr. McNamara believed to be enough for strategic deterrence. The full consequences of this missile escalation will have to be assessed by historians, but one thing seems clear: If the politics of defense dominates national security, then the world may never disengage from a spiraling arms race. When defense decisions are taken for political reasons—and domestic ones at that—a democracy may become an escalator in the arms race.

On November 6, 1967, the Joint Committee on Atomic Energy began investigating the nation's nuclear defenses in hearings headed up by Sen. Henry M. Jackson. Ostensibly the hearings were designed to explore the nature of the anti-ballistic missile defense problem, but in the course of the investigation it became clear that the committee was concerned with nuclear parity. Senators expressed their alarm over the increasing number of Soviet ICBM's, while the United States did not attempt to add more ICBM's to its own strike force. As I listened to the committee members question witnesses, I could not help but reflect that many of the committee members had served for many years on the Joint Committee; they had heard much testimony in previous years about the catastrophic nature of nuclear war. These men were granted access to data denied the great majority of the Congress. Yet it seemed as though the most elemental arithmetic of the nuclear age had not been absorbed. If these men with access and with so much exposure to the facts about nuclear weapons could not accept the principle of nuclear sufficiency, then how could the other members of Congress be expected to do so?

If a U.S. President authorizes a $5 billion Sentinel system to protect himself from Republican charges of failing to insure the nation's security, then one might just as well junk all the elaborate systems of defense analysis that we possess. If our representative form of government gives disproportionate influence to the military-industrial constituency, we had better seek out checks and balances to offset this menace. If our legislators act as promotional lobbyists for the military-industrial complex, then reforms must be enacted. Needless to say, corrective measures will not be easy because the disease of our weapons culture has metastasized itself into the lymphatic system of our society.

On December 13, 1967, Senator J. W. Fulbright surveyed the impact of the "military-industrial complex" in a Senate speech. "More and more our economy, our Government and our universities are adapting themselves to the requirements of the continuing war—total war, limited war, and cold war." Warning that this adaptation was "making ourselves in a militarized society," Senator Fulbright described the "military-industrial complex" as forming "a giant concentration of socialism in our otherwise free enterprise economy."

Moreover, we have exported our weapons culture. Our Military Establishment has deployed its forces on a global basis. U.S. military forces bulked in groups of more than 3,000 uniformed personnel are to be found in each of 17 foreign countries. We have 132 major installations in foreign countries, some of which have been negotiated at a loss of our prestige. For example, to secure air-base rights in Spain we had to make a deal with Generalissmo Franco. While these foreign military bases are meant to increase our national security, some become liabilities—as in the case of Jupiter missile bases in Turkey.

Not only has the United States stationed its own troops abroad; it has engaged in advising, supervising and training armed forces in 35 foreign nations. This activity includes bringing officers from other countries to the United States for training at our military schools. In 1967 some 12,000 Americans were engaged in military-training operations overseas, not counting the U.S. commitment to Vietnam.

The major U.S. military and foreign-assistance program covering most of the postwar years have involved over $102 billion, as detailed for 54 countries in Appendix IX. In some cases, as for India, Austria, and a few others, the extent of military aid is kept secret. Sen. J. W. Fulbright, chairman of the Senate Foreign Relations Committee, has maintained that much of this foreign aid is dangerous in that it may backfire and encourage conditions that lead to war. Again, there is the action-reaction principle about which Defense Secretary McNamara has warned—the U.S. initiative may be followed by enemy-supported countermoves, and the United States then has to pour in more aid to offset these. This could well have been the case in Vietnam and, if so, the tragedy of our position there was that we boxed ourselves into a situation which our own action magnified into a commitment out of proportion to its strategic significance. Then face-saving, traditionally an Oriental monomania, became critical to the United States.

The U.S. military-industrial complex has profited from contracts for arms that foreign assistance made possible. There is little doubt that the political support for these foreign programs was linked to this domestic tie-in. At one time (1963) the United States was engaged in the sale of armaments to no fewer than 63 foreign governments. As *Business Week* magazine commented: " 'Buy American' is becoming an increasingly prevalent slogan in the world arms market." Considering the diffusion of modern arms across national borders, it is inevitable that

American arms become weapons used against us or nations whose cause we support.

The redemption of our weapons-oriented society is a monumental undertaking; armaments have acquired such momentum that they dictate their own policy. As Konrad Lorenz wrote in *On Aggression*:

> An unprejudiced observer from another planet, looking upon man as he is today, in his hand the atom bomb, the product of his intelligence, in his heart the aggression drive inherited from his anthropoid ancestors, which this same intelligence cannot control, would not prophesy long life for the species.

The separate worlds of Darwin and Einstein are nearing collision. Man, the twig-tip of the fabulous evolutionary tree, is in danger of nuclear blight—a disease of his own making. All too quickly Einstein's ideas have become arsenal items; all too sluggishly do men forget the ways of war.

America is now a land of incredible violence—in many forms and in many places——

A thousand sleek missiles, deadly warheads pretargeted at Soviet cities, stud our western prairies, once solely a source of life-giving grain.

Sunny California slopes, once orange-blossomed and fruitful, now sprout cavernous plants where engineers design orbital weapons.

Boston's Route 128 is festooned with mushrooming research laboratories, a Cold War-financed necklace of industrial innovation.

In Maryland's richest farmland, a few miles west of Frederick, biologists at the highly secret Fort Detrick perfect virulent weapons of biological warfare.

Not far away, at the Pennsylvania border, lies the subterranean command post to which the President will be spirited in time of national emergency.

—America, the beautiful; now America, arms-maker and arms merchant to the world.

APPENDICES

Military Prime Contract Awards by State

NET VALUE OF MILITARY PROCUREMENT ACTIONS
FOR SUPPLIES, SERVICES AND CONSTRUCTION[a]
Fiscal Years 1958–1967
Source: Dept. of Defense
(Amounts in Thousands)

State	Rank	1958	1959	1960	1961	1962
TOTAL U. S.		$22,752,260	$23,902,014	$22,462,217	$24,304,677	$27,800,407
NOT DISTRIBUTED BY STATE		1,743,447	1,925,278	2,055,411	2,192,231	2,761,717
STATE TOTALS		21,008,813	21,976,736	20,406,806	22,112,446	25,038,690
Alabama	28	163,220	138,175	103,371	105,564	154,419
Alaska	33	105,931	121,724	78,649	91,797	63,320
Arizona	26	189,314	238,989	168,974	244,837	152,951
Arkansas	43	31,562	16,012	10,891	46,586	84,798
California	1	4,457,666	5,282,659	4,839,252	5,276,760	5,993,244
Colorado	19	205,470	252,476	246,749	465,904	565,279
Connecticut	4	897,283	920,309	838,535	1,018,500	1,213,067
Delaware	41	127,021	62,136	53,352	28,180	47,197
District of Columbia	27	84,573	98,477	95,499	149,551	181,954
Florida	13	308,891	404,663	489,803	492,654	645,478
Georgia	16	323,086	270,821	177,924	300,529	337,478
Hawaii	44	35,821	36,742	48,971	26,916	31,875
Idaho	50	12,050	9,270	46,630	14,131	26,121
Illinois	14	577,329	490,760	385,053	437,250	531,008
Indiana	15	421,046	388,990	310,632	353,202	571,184
Iowa	29	106,199	155,423	147,443	126,819	179,153
Kansas	17	1,169,464	450,204	573,563	538,687	393,507
Kentucky	42	34,422	39,411	32,741	45,778	43,510
Louisiana	22	141,863	151,486	197,157	139,336	244,036
Maine	37	87,237	116,751	32,216	96,977	79,585
Maryland	12	472,275	509,160	515,887	527,591	469,491
Massachusetts	6	734,514	1,150,522	1,070,436	1,072,370	1,310,055
Michigan	11	531,791	782,914	600,947	590,480	677,786
Minnesota	21	155,891	238,400	192,984	188,652	297,306
Mississippi	31	42,589	86,724	46,946	69,395	100,220
Missouri	9	498,744	571,505	336,668	337,500	545,553
Montana	45	35,184	27,712	27,058	94,538	31,264
Nebraska	39	47,025	62,589	71,034	51,123	53,172
Nevada	51	10,533	10,828	8,965	8,850	8,246
New Hampshire	35	33,634	41,313	72,272	104,589	58,926
New Jersey	7	884,589	918,916	1,274,664	949,737	1,063,096
New Mexico	36	77,397	72,743	77,707	63,540	60,729
New York	2	2,424,043	2,408,734	2,377,522	2,642,803	2,668,744
North Carolina	20	329,537	321,272	172,899	237,196	268,990
North Dakota	40	19,558	17,416	8,683	12,980	99,627
Ohio	5	1,007,230	1,030,556	907,068	1,004,245	1,129,017
Oklahoma	30	173,880	134,562	146,519	123,433	135,825
Oregon	46	27,917	31,486	23,963	27,626	46,129
Pennsylvania	8	700,262	684,331	671,314	804,389	952,058
Rhode Island	38	24,174	27,478	26,081	25,292	57,966
South Carolina	34	57,654	38,323	31,314	40,804	65,212
South Dakota	47	13,099	12,315	43,591	27,626	112,682
Tennessee	25	80,489	106,096	109,396	144,069	183,794
Texas	3	1,446,482	1,304,740	1,138,026	1,138,471	1,006,253
Utah	23	76,391	174,550	176,394	349,611	298,596
Vermont	49	17,895	13,645	18,746	16,176	16,421
Virginia	18	220,947	292,576	422,164	505,158	446,183
Washington	10	1,202,354	961,238	715,087	646,359	921,115
West Virginia	32	15,997	89,154	36,098	61,884	133,782
Wisconsin	24	161,190	168,221	167,214	221,749	258,735
Wyoming	48	6,100	41,239	41,754	24,252	22,551

1963	1964	1965	1966	1967	10-Yr. Total	
$28,107,882	$27,470,379	$26,631,132	$35,713,061	$41,817,093	$280,961,122	Percentage State to U.S.A.
2,874,642	3,053,272	3,363,052	3,999,758	4,435,430	28,404,238	(State Total)
25,233,240	24,417,107	23,268,080	31,713,303	37,381,663	252,568,248	
194,990	190,681	165,176	281,549	297,049	1,794,194	0.7
103,476	101,545	74,175	71,666	85,648	897,931	0.4
285,751	173,825	176,857	248,228	249,559	2,129,285	0.8
39,114	29,731	39,284	95,701	127,180	520,859	0.2
5,835,670	5,100,650	5,153,639	5,813,078	6,688,851	54,441,469	21.5
444,196	389,511	249,151	255,893	210,409	3,285,038	1.3
1,048,449	1,126,054	1,180,111	2,051,560	1,935,895	12,229,763	4.9
67,035	30,424	38,239	37,445	51,672	542,701	0.2
238,120	222,947	247,576	328,111	357,666	2,004,474	0.8
583,237	782,591	633,332	766,955	799,022	5,906,626	2.3
423,290	520,169	662,417	799,362	1,148,354	4,973,430	2.0
45,206	52,112	72,213	64,170	65,445	479,471	0.2
8,634	7,804	11,724	20,004	14,772	171,140	0.1
486,067	429,201	421,899	919,779	1,063,776	5,742,699	2.3
486,759	537,940	604,925	1,068,259	898,247	5,641,184	2.2
130,406	103,392	133,951	247,619	279,328	1,609,733	0.6
331,687	289,045	229,051	312,629	398,899	4,686,736	1.9
55,725	40,476	42,749	70,057	124,294	529,163	0.2
195,341	181,427	255,834	302,906	656,031	2,465,417	1.0
58,409	31,531	68,771	51,340	56,558	679,375	0.3
606,365	547,936	584,333	842,527	869,808	5,945,373	2.4
1,060,165	1,032,062	1,178,729	1,335,952	1,422,272	11,367,077	4.5
633,047	591,290	532,897	918,426	1,033,706	6,893,284	2.7
273,757	217,941	259,500	497,994	650,584	2,973,009	1.2
186,039	155,911	152,188	162,305	114,800	1,117,117	0.4
686,111	1,349,071	1,060,781	1,112,665	2,277,616	8,776,214	3.5
79,349	16,422	69,375	13,779	78,452	473,133	0.2
33,559	33,921	42,708	80,478	103,522	579,131	0.2
13,143	6,361	19,142	32,028	29,315	147,411	0.1
51,174	64,857	52,400	109,591	162,551	751,307	0.3
1,251,608	917,561	820,309	1,090,122	1,234,768	10,405,370	4.1
61,642	71,486	84,137	86,230	80,472	736,855	0.3
2,500,146	2,496,438	2,229,473	2,819,153	3,261,750	25,828,806	10.2
258,987	273,516	288,408	449,331	447,608	3,047,744	1.2
64,855	192,025	48,997	83,113	16,729	563,983	0.2
1,345,686	1,028,946	863,113	1,588,955	1,602,593	11,507,409	7.3
111,204	122,489	119,803	158,492	157,350	1,383,566	0.5
41,777	29,104	39,624	89,983	99,319	456,928	0.2
887,452	883,065	988,811	1,665,087	1,649,142	9,885,911	3.9
46,970	38,173	86,323	131,722	198,030	662,209	0.3
57,747	51,621	81,580	176,424	180,777	781,456	0.3
80,630	23,308	21,062	23,315	9,486	367,114	0.1
183,478	193,564	197,283	502,168	538,225	2,238,570	0.9
1,203,123	1,294,431	1,446,769	2,291,454	3,546,978	15,816,727	6.7
408,127	340,040	191,173	169,681	178,850	2,363,413	0.9
12,258	14,012	32,202	81,066	100,157	322,578	0.1
484,989	690,852	469,097	425,487	665,240	4,622,693	1.8
1,041,581	1,085,696	545,607	444,368	606,114	8,169,519	3.2
162,201	87,327	90,312	149,300	140,324	966,379	0.4
219,427	177,217	203,003	364,684	383,602	2,325,042	0.9
125,081	49,408	7,867	11,112	32,868	362,232	0.1

Prime Military Contracts Awards 1960-1967 to U.S. Companies

For firms totaling more than $1 billion in this 7-year period.

(Amounts in millions of dollars)

Fiscal Year	1961	1962	1963	1964	1965	1966	1967	7-yr. Total	Percent of Total Sales
1. Lockheed Aircraft	1,175	1,419	1,517	1,455	1,715	1,531	1,807	10,619	88%
2. General Dynamics	1,460	1,197	1,033	987	1,179	1,136	1,832	8,824	67
3. McDonnell Douglas	527	779	863	1,360	1,026	1,001	2,125	7,681	75
4. Boeing Co.	920	1,133	1,356	1,365	583	914	912	7,183	54
5. General Electric	875	976	1,021	893	824	1,187	1,290	7,066	19
6. No. American-Rockwell	1,197	1,032	1,062	1,019	746	520	689	6,265	57
7. United Aircraft	625	663	530	625	632	1,139	1,097	5,311	57
8. American Tel. & Tel.	551	468	579	636	588	672	673	4,167	9
9. Martin-Marietta	692	803	767	476	316	338	290	3,682	62
10. Sperry-Rand	408	466	446	374	318	427	484	2,923	35
11. General Motors	282	449	444	256	254	508	625	2,818	2
12. Grumman Aircraft	238	304	390	396	353	323	488	2,492	67
13. General Tire	290	366	425	364	302	327	273	2,347	37
14. Raytheon	305	407	295	253	293	368	403	2,324	55
15. AVCO	251	323	253	279	234	506	449	2,295	75
16. Hughes	331	234	312	289	278	337	419	2,200	u
17. Westinghouse Electric	308	246	323	237	261	349	453	2,177	13
18. Ford (Philco)	200	269	228	211	312	440	404	2,064	3
19. RCA	392	340	329	234	214	242	268	2,019	16

20.	Bendix	269	286	290	257	235	282	296	1,915	42
21.	Textron	66	117	151	216	196	555	497	1,798	36
22.	Ling-Temco-Vought	47	133	206	247	265	311	535	1,744	70
23.	Internat. Tel. & Tel.	202	244	266	256	207	220	255	1,650	19
24.	I.B.M.	330	155	203	332	186	182	195	1,583	7
25.	Raymond International*	46	61	84	196	71	548	462	1,568	u
26.	Newport News Shipbuilding	290	185	221	400	185	51	188	1,520	90+
27.	Northrop	156	152	223	165	256	276	306	1,434	61
28.	Thiokol	210	178	239	254	136	111	173	1,301	96
29.	Std. Oil of N.J.	168	180	155	161	164	214	235	1,277	2
30.	Kaiser Industries	-	87	49	152	219	441	306	1,255	45
31.	Honeywell	86	127	170	107	82	251	306	1,129	24
32.	General Tel.	61	116	162	229	232	196	138	1,124	25
33.	Collins Radio	94	150	144	129	141	245	202	1,105	65
34.	Chrysler	158	181	186	170	81	150	165	1,091	4
35.	Litton	-	88	198	210	190	219	180	1,085	25
36.	Pan. Am. World Air.	127	147	155	164	158	170	115	1,046	44
37.	F.M.C.	88	160	199	141	124	163	170	1,045	21
38.	Hercules	117	182	183	137	101	120	195	1,035	31

u—unavailable.

* Includes Morrison-Knudsen, Brown & Root, and J. A. Jones Construction Co.

Source: Dept. of Defense, Directorate for Statistical Services.

Defense Contract Awards and Payrolls—1966

Source: Statistical Abstract of U.S.A. 1967.

(Amounts given in millions of dollars)

State	Defense Contract Awards	Annual Payroll Military	Annual Payroll Civilian
Alabama	$ 282	$ 144	$ 233
Alaska	72	163	51
Arizona	248	107	46
Arkansas	96	55	20
California	5,813	1,067	1,195
Colorado	256	183	128
Connecticut	2,052	20	28
Delaware	37	41	9
District of Columbia	328	192	166
Florida	767	375	191
Georgia	799	421	240
Hawaii	64	208	153
Idaho	20	26	3
Illinois	920	250	217
Indiana	1,068	48	95
Iowa	248	9	4
Kansas	313	118	33
Kentucky	70	191	90
Louisiana	303	168	46
Maine	51	64	10
Maryland	843	257	304
Massachusetts	1,336	166	186
Michigan	918	106	80
Minnesota	498	27	15
Mississippi	162	116	47
Missouri	1,113	147	141
Montana	14	55	8
Nebraska	80	92	30
Nevada	32	36	19
New Hampshire	110	35	61

State	Defense Contract Awards	Annual Payroll	
		Military	Civilian
New Jersey	1,090	212	182
New Mexico	86	117	80
New York	2,819	197	320
North Carolina	449	266	74
North Dakota	83	70	10
Ohio	1,589	120	329
Oklahoma	158	167	191
Oregon	90	23	20
Pennsylvania	1,665	81	521
Rhode Island	132	40	65
South Carolina	176	250	117
South Dakota	23	37	9
Tennessee	502	93	45
Texas	2,292	934	444
Utah	170	27	169
Vermont	81	2	...
Virginia	426	453	575
Washington	444	194	175
West Virginia	149	3	1
Wisconsin	365	20	15
Wyoming	11	25	4
U.S. Total	$35,713	$8,257	$7,211

Estimated Defense Expenditures 1967*

Industry	Defense Purchases

MANUFACTURING

1.	Aircraft and parts	$ 9,656
2.	Electronics, communication	4,258
3.	Ordnance	4,200
4.	Petroleum products	1,306
5.	Transportation equipment	906
6.	Food products	877
7.	Motor vehicles	868
8.	Chemical products	670
9.	Electrical industrial equipment	563
10.	Scientific instruments & controls	523
11.	Apparel	488
12.	Office, computer equipment	458
13.	Fabrics	370
14.	Drugs, cleaning & toilet preparations	368
15.	Optical & photographic equipment	296
16.	Structural: metal products	260
17.	Engines & turbines	250
18.	Electronic components	236
19.	Metalworking machinery & equipment	227
20.	Construction, mining equipment	215
	All other manufacturing	2,270
		$29,265

SERVICES

1.	Transportation & warehousing	$ 2,371
2.	Wholesale & retail trade	812
3.	Medical, educational & nonprofits	540
4.	Business services	534
5.	Electric, gas, water & sewage	362
6.	Research & development	350
7.	Communications	306
	All other services	348
		$ 5,643

SPECIAL INDUSTRIES

Government industry	$17,120
IMPORTS	$ 2,019
CONSTRUCTION (and others)	$ 325
Grand Total	$54,373

* Data derived from *Monthly Labor Review* (Dept. of Labor, Bureau of Labor Statistics, p. 15, Sept. 1967). Dollar values are given in producers' prices, 1958 dollars.

Top 100 U.S. Defense Contractors for Fiscal Year 1967

Rank	Companies	Millions of Dollars	Rank	Companies	Millions of Dollars
	U.S. Total	$39,219	50.	Sanders Associates	124
	Total, 100 Companies	25,219	51.	TRW Inc.	121
1.	McDonnell Douglas	2,125	52.	Asiatic Petroleum	117
2.	General Dynamics	1,832	53.	Signal Oil & Gas	117
3.	Lockheed Aircraft	1,807	54.	Harvey Aluminum	117
4.	General Electric	1,290	55.	Pan American World	115
5.	United Aircraft	1,097	56.	Mobil Oil	109
6.	Boeing	912	57.	Eastman Kodak	109
7.	North American Aviation	689	58.	Mason and Hanger-Silas	108
8.	American Tel. & Tel.	673	59.	Pacific Arch. & Eng.	107
9.	General Motors	625	60.	Lear-Siegler	101
10.	Ling-Temco-Vought	535	61.	Magnavox	98
11.	Textron	497	62.	Mass. Inst. Technology	95
12.	Grumman Aircraft	488	63.	A.M.F.	94
13.	Sperry Rand	484	64.	Texas Instruments	94
14.	Raymond International	462	65.	Fairchild Hiller	94
15.	Westinghouse Electric	453	66.	Curtiss-Wright	91
16.	AVCO	449	67.	Teledyne	88
17.	Hughes Aircraft	420	68.	Dillingham Overseas	88
18.	Ford (Philco)	404	69.	Chamberlain Corp.	74
19.	Raytheon	403	70.	Flying Tiger Line	73
20.	Honeywell, Inc.	314	71.	Intl. Harvester	73
21.	Northrop Corp.	306	72.	Federal Cartridge	72
22.	Kaiser Industries	306	73.	Johns Hopkins Univ.	71
23.	Bendix	296	74.	Aerospace Corp.	71
24.	Martin Marietta	290	75.	Dow Chemical	67
25.	Ryan Aeronautical	290	76.	Continental Airlines	66
26.	General Tire & Rubber	273	77.	White Motor	65
27.	RCA	268	78.	Condec Corp.	63
28.	Intl. Tel. & Tel.	255	79.	Western Union	62
29.	Ogden Corp.	237	80.	Emerson Electric	62
30.	Standard Oil, N.J.	235	81.	Firestone Tire & Rubber	61
31.	Uniroyal	217	82.	Bethlehem Steel	60
32.	Collins Radio	202	83.	Airlift Intl.	59
33.	Hercules, Inc.	195	84.	Hughes Tool Co.	59
34.	International Bus. Mach.	195	85.	Cessna Aircraft	57
35.	Newport News	188	86.	Atlantic Research	57
36.	Litton Industries	180	87.	Svedrup & Parcel	57
37.	du Pont de Nemours	180	88.	American Mfg. of Texas	55
38.	Thiokol Chemical Corp.	173	89.	J. P. Stevens & Co.	53
39.	F.M.C.	170	90.	Vinnell Corp.	53
40.	Chrysler	165	91.	Westinghouse Air Brake	52
41.	Goodyear Tire & Rubber	155	92.	System Development Corp.	50
42.	Olin Mathieson Chemical	154	93.	Northwest Airlines	50
43.	Standard Oil, Cal.	153	94.	Gulf Oil	50
44.	Day & Zimmerman	142	95.	Smith Investment Co.	49
45.	General Tel. & Electronics	139	96.	Motorola	48
46.	Morrison-Knudsen	136	97.	Cities Service	48
47.	Norris Industries	127	98.	Tumpane Co.	47
48.	General Precision Equip.	124	99.	Union Carbide	47
49.	Texaco, Inc.	124	100.	Maxson Electronics	46

Top 100 Space Contractors (National Aeronautics and Space Administration) for Fiscal Year 1967

Rank	Companies	Thousands of Dollars
	Total Awards to Business	$3,864,133
1.	North American Aviation, Inc.	983,814
2.	Grumman Aircraft Engineering Corp.	481,137
3.	Boeing Co.	273,514
4.	McDonnell Douglas Corp.	243,913
5.	International Business Machines Corp.	186,355
6.	General Electric Co.	179,261
7.	Bendix Corp.	120,028
8.	Aerojet-General Corp.	95,691
9.	Chrysler Corp.	76,602
10.	General Motors Corp.	65,222
11.	General Dynamics Corp.	60,990
12.	Radio Corp. of America	57,512
13.	TRW Inc.	52,551
14.	LTV Aerospace Corp.	46,326
15.	Lockheed Aircraft Corp.	42,036
16.	United Aircraft Corp.	39,989
17.	Sperry Rand Corp.	38,666
18.	Philco-Ford Corp.	32,059
19.	Trans World Airlines, Inc.	25,091
20.	General Precision, Inc.	24,987
21.	Honeywell, Inc.	22,647
22.	Hughes Aircraft Co.	19,850
23.	Brown Engineering Co., Inc.	16,713
24.	Martin Marietta Corp.	12,828
25.	Union Carbide Corp.	12,648
26.	Federal Electric Corp.	12,305
27.	Computer Sciences Corp.	11,796
28.	Air Products & Chemicals, Inc.	11,788
29.	Thiokol Chemical Corp.	11,455
30.	Mason-Rust	11,213
31.	Catalytic Construction Co.	11,051
32.	Westinghouse Electric Corp.	10,388
33.	Brown & Root Co./Northrop Corp. (Joint Venture)	10,000
34.	Fairchild Hiller Corp.	9,794
35.	Bellcom, Inc.	9,318
36.	Garrett Corp.	9,293
37.	Bechtel Corp.	9,198
38.	Vitro Corp. of America	8,988
39.	Bell Aerospace Corp.	8,877
40.	Northrop Corp.	8,815
41.	Hayes International Corp.	7,289
42.	Control Data Corp.	7,111
43.	Graham Engineering Co., Inc.	7,109
44.	Scientific Data Systems	7,080
45.	Spaco, Inc.	6,785

Rank	Companies	Thousands of Dollars
46.	Ball Brothers Research Corp.	$ 6,648
47.	Dow Chemical Co.	6,471
48.	ILC Industries, Inc.	6,336
49.	Documentation, Inc.	5,880
50.	Warrior Constructors, Inc./Notkin, Inc./National Constructors, Inc.	5,776
51.	Sanders Associates, Inc.	5,626
52.	Zia Co.	5,096
53.	Space-General Corp.	5,007
54.	Management Services, Inc.	4,745
55.	Basic Construction Co.	4,737
56.	Allis-Chalmers Manufacturing Co.	4,731
57.	Southern Bell Telephone Co.	4,432
58.	American Telephone & Telegraph Co.	4,397
59.	American Science & Engineering, Inc.	4,175
60.	Aero Spacelines, Inc.	3,631
61.	Gillmore-Olson Co.	3,602
62.	Perkin-Elmer Corp.	3,546
63.	Western Union Telegraph Co.	3,472
64.	Computer Application, Inc.	3,461
65.	Wolf Research & Development Corp.	3,360
66.	Computing & Software, Inc.	3,337
67.	Electronic Associates, Inc.	3,312
68.	Pacific Crane & Rigging Co.	3,234
69.	Lawrence, J. H. Co.	3,226
70.	Ampex Corp.	3,176
71.	Avco Corp.	3,049
72.	Electro Optical Systems, Inc.	2,896
73.	Air Reduction Co.	2,754
74.	Communications Satellite Corp.	2,745
75.	International Telephone & Telegraph Corp.	2,651
76.	Melpar, Inc.	2,640
77.	Radiation, Inc.	2,506
78.	Texas Instruments, Inc.	2,440
79.	Consolidated Electrodynamics Corp.	2,405
80.	Systems Engineering Laboratory, Inc.	2,360
81.	GCA Corp.	2,342
82.	New Orleans Public Service, Inc.	2,312
83.	Western Electric Co.	2,282
84.	Motorola, Inc.	2,219
85.	Dynalectron Corp.	2,162
86.	Keltec Industries, Inc.	2,098
87.	Virginia Electric Power Co.	2,053
88.	Kaiser Industries Corp.	2,032
89.	Goodyear Aerospace Corp.	1,997
90.	Greenhut Construction, Inc.	1,960
91.	Electro-Mechanical Research, Inc.	1,945
92.	Kollsman Instrument Corp.	1,939
93.	Minnesota Mining & Manufacturing Co.	1,935
94.	Sylvania Electric Products, Inc.	1,880

		Thousands of Dollars
Rank	Companies	
95.	Pearce DeMoss King, Inc.	$ 1,858
96.	Hazeltine Corp.	1,807
97.	Cleveland Electric Illuminating Co.	1,790
98.	ITT World Communication, Inc.	1,764
99.	Marquardt Corp.	1,758
100.	Western Union International, Inc.	1,742
	Other	286,315

APPENDIX VI

Total Federal Obligations to Federal Contract Research Centers Administered by Universities and Colleges, 1966

[Dollar amounts in thousands]

Location and name	Total Federal obligations 1966	Sponsoring agency	Administered by
Total	$931,402		
Alaska: Naval Arctic Research Laboratory	1,411	DOD	University of Alaska.
Arizona: Kitt Peak National Observatory	5,791	NSF	Association of Universities for Research in Astronomy, Inc.
California:			
Jet Propulsion Laboratory	230,091	NASA	California Institute of Technology.
Stanford Linear Accelerator Laboratory	50,969	AEC	Stanford University.
Navy Biological Laboratory	1,766	DOD	University of California.
Lawrence Radiation Laboratory	169,870	AEC	University of California.
Colorado: National Center for Atmospheric Research.	11,791	NSF	University Corporation for Atmospheric Research.
District of Columbia:			
Center for Research in Social Sciences	1,808	DOD	American University.
Human Resources Research Office	2,752	DOD	George Washington University.
Illinois: Argonne National Laboratory	87,255	AEC	University of Chicago.
Iowa: Ames Laboratory	9,089	AEC	Iowa State University.
Maryland: Applied Physics Laboratory	52,491	DOD	Johns Hopkins University.
Massachusetts:			
Apollo Guidance Project	16,019	NASA	Massachusetts Institute of Technology.
Cambridge Electron Accelerator	{ 6,130 / 3,517 }	AEC	{ Harvard University. / Massachusetts Institute of Technology.
Lincoln Laboratory	64,060	DOD	Massachusetts Institute of Technology.
New Jersey:			
Princeton Stellerator	6,556	AEC	Princeton University.
Princeton-Penn. Proton Accelerator	8,825	AEC	Princeton University.
	1,801		University of Pennsylvania.
New Mexico: Los Alamos Scientific Laboratory	103,311	AEC	University of California.
New York:			
Brookhaven National Laboratory	64,407	AEC	Associated Universities, Inc.
Hudson Laboratory	4,673	DOD	Columbia University.
Pennsylvania: Ordnance Research Laboratory	9,597	DOD	Pennsylvania State University.
Tennessee: Oak Ridge Associated Universities	6,168	AEC	Oak Ridge Associated Universities.
Washington: Applied Physics Laboratory	5,145	DOD	University of Washington.
West Virginia: National Radio Astronomy Observatory	4,719	NSF	Associated Universities, Inc.
Wisconsin: Army Mathematics Center	1,390	DOD	University of Wisconsin.

Source: Adapted from NSF-67-14.

*Obligations by the Department of Defense for Research and Development
at 100 Universities and Colleges Receiving the Largest Amounts, 1964*
(Dollar Amounts in Thousands)

Institution Name	State	Rank	DOD	Army	Navy	Air Force	Def. Agency
Mass. Inst. of Technology	Mass.	1	46,819	3,965	18,807	21,928	2,119
University of Michigan	Mich.	2	14,736	5,413	1,284	4,966	3,073
Stanford University	Cal.	3	12,815	1,824	5,214	4,573	1,204
Columbia University	N.Y.	4	9,194	1,489	4,459	3,184	36
University of Illinois	Ill.	5	7,612	2,524	1,704	1,343	2,041
U. of Cal. Los Angeles	Cal.	6	6,871	397	5,221	1,106	147
U. of Cal. Berkeley	Cal.	7	5,424	439	3,140	1,592	253
Univ. of Pennsylvania	Pa.	8	5,304	1,473	673	961	2,197
University of Texas	Tex.	9	5,281	571	3,502	1,208	0
Ohio State University	Ohio	10	5,256	466	253	4,185	0
University of Chicago	Ill.	11	4,615	774	1,702	1,374	765
Harvard University	Mass.	12	4,539	705	1,425	1,010	1,399
Carnegie Inst. Technology	Pa.	13	4,519	130	334	340	3,668
Cornell University	N.Y.	14	4,358	510	680	452	2,570
California Inst. of Tech.	Cal.	15	4,232	348	1,673	2,211	0
New York University	N.Y.	16	4,019	1,750	1,239	1,030	0
Illinois Inst. of Tech.	Ill.	17	3,852	2,069	352	1,431	0
University of Denver	Colo.	18	3,773	488	81	3,204	0
Johns Hopkins University	Md.	19	3,732	1,098	757	1,867	0
Princeton University	N.J.	20	3,709	561	1,863	1,285	0
Northwestern University	Ill.	21	3,461	332	843	722	1,564
Polytechnic Inst. Brooklyn	N.Y.	22	3,254	113	1,411	1,730	0
University of Maryland	Md.	23	3,089	1,001	210	1,324	514
Duke University	N.C.	24	2,946	2,341	169	436	0
Brown University	R.I.	25	2,746	325	647	389	1,385
University of Colorado	Colo.	26	2,709	2,163	152	394	0
University of Dayton	Ohio	27	2,643	0	0	2,643	0
U. of Cal. San Diego	Cal.	28	2,455	0	29	2,426	0
University of Miami	Fla.	29	2,174	467	1,605	102	0
New Mexico State Univ.	N.M.	30	2,157	1,546	343	268	0
University of Pittsburgh	Pa.	31	2,080	886	340	680	100
Syracuse University	N.Y.	32	2,046	337	382	1,327	0
University of Washington	Wash.	33	1,986	199	1,381	406	0
Purdue University	Ind.	34	1,981	477	10	694	800
Yale University	Conn.	35	1,813	274	530	1,009	0
Northeastern University	Mass.	36	1,685	98	12	1,575	0
Univ. of Southern California	Cal.	37	1,617	121	462	1,034	0
George Washington Univ.	D.C.	38	1,526	395	926	205	0
Univ. of N.C. at Chapel Hill	N.C.	39	1,441	211	74	605	551
Pennsylvania State Univ.	Pa.	40	1,214	381	89	744	0
Texas A. & M. University	Tex.	41	1,204	233	808	163	0
University of New Mexico	N.M.	42	1,199	0	150	1,049	0
University of Oklahoma	Okla.	43	1,193	533	36	624	0
U. of Wis. Madison	Wisc.	44	1,102	358	278	466	0
University of Iowa	Iowa	45	1,077	0	947	55	75
U. of Minn. Mnpls.-St. Paul	Minn.	46	1,076	0	764	312	0
Indiana University	Ind.	47	1,075	153	342	580	0
University of Virginia	Va.	48	1,030	295	643	92	0
Tufts University	Mass.	49	1,021	303	88	630	0

Institution Name	State	Rank	DOD	Army	Navy	Air Force	Def. Agency
University of Utah	Utah	50	1,020	333	69	618	0
Wentworth Institute	Mass.	51	979	0	0	979	0
Univ. of Minn. All Campuses	Minn.	52	967	0	0	967	0
University of Florida	Fla.	53	958	352	143	308	0
Okla. St. U. Agric. & App. Sci.	Okla.	54	924	119	111	694	0
Oregon State University	Oreg.	55	887	46	453	388	0
University of Rochester	N.Y.	56	877	314	152	411	0
Univ. of Rhode Island	R.I.	57	857	1	751	105	0
Texas Western College	Tex.	58	846	781	0	65	0
Stevens Institute of Tech.	N.J.	59	839	247	350	242	0
American University	D.C.	60	834	780	54	0	0
Lowell Technological Inst.	Mass.	61	748	79	0	669	0
University of Arizona	Ariz.	62	725	213	199	172	27
Western Reserve Univ.	Ohio	63	720	417	126	177	0
Utah State University	Utah	64	713	100	0	613	0
Georgia Institute of Tech.	Ga.	65	710	419	214	77	0
Catholic Univ. of America	D.C.	66	679	110	228	155	186
Boston College	Mass.	67	661	25	0	636	0
Georgetown University	D.C.	68	658	550	33	75	0
University of Cincinnati	Ohio	69	648	134	0	474	40
University of Hawaii	Hawaii	70	612	103	253	256	0
Florida State University	Fla.	71	607	81	134	392	0
Case Inst. of Technology	Ohio	72	594	71	197	326	0
N. Mex. Inst. Mining & Tech.	N.M.	73	554	0	540	14	0
Washington University	Mo.	74	552	235	160	157	0
Arizona State University	Ariz.	75	532	65	54	413	0
University of Puerto Rico	P.R.	76	531	502	29	0	0
University of Delaware	Del.	77	502	198	109	195	0
Rensselaer Poly. Institute	N.Y.	78	500	149	212	139	0
University of Missouri	Mo.	79	494	369	76	49	0
University of Connecticut	Conn.	80	469	340	0	129	0
Colorado State University	Colo.	81	446	297	95	54	0
Michigan State University	Mich.	82	428	145	71	89	0
Iowa St. U. of Sci. & Tech.	Iowa	83	424	213	0	151	0
Brandeis University	Mass.	84	422	253	30	139	0
University of Alaska	Alaska	85	402	80	74	248	0
Medical Col. of Virginia	Va.	86	386	157	45	0	184
Boston University	Mass.	87	383	150	32	201	0
Rutgers—The State Univ.	N.J.	88	379	158	89	132	0
St. Univ. N.Y. All Inst.	N.Y.	89	370	0	0	370	0
Tulane Univ. of Louisiana	La.	90	369	248	30	75	0
Ohio University	Ohio	91	368	0	15	353	0
Dartmouth College	N.H.	92	364	173	76	115	0
Yeshiva University	N.Y.	93	364	115	10	239	0
St. Louis University	Mo.	94	361	114	15	232	0
Univ. of N.C. St. at Raleigh	N.C.	95	344	113	67	164	0
U. of Cal. San Francisco	Cal.	96	343	297	46	0	0
University of Georgia	Ga.	97	327	0	13	134	0
University of Louisville	Ky.	98	325	315	10	0	0
U. of Cal. Riverside	Cal.	99	319	62	0	257	0
Emmanuel College	Mass.	100	312	0	0	312	0

Source: National Science Foundation Report 67-14 (July 1967).

Appendix VIII

Total Federal Obligations (1966) by Various Federal Agencies by State

(Amounts shown in thousands of dollars)

Source: NSF-67-14

State	Total (all agencies)	Atomic Energy Commission	Department of Defense	Dept. of Health Educ. & Welfare	National Aeronautics & Space Administration	National Science Foundation
Alabama	$ 34,694	$ 75	$ 635	$ 26,316	$ 1,812	$ 1,482
Alaska	7,424	55	708	2,874	946	1,770
Arizona	29,586	560	860	16,377	2,533	7,490
Arkansas	19,372	261	86	14,227	255	808
California	346,407	14,224	47,557	200,684	21,731	54,576
Colorado	45,773	1,055	7,200	24,761	3,126	6,625
Connecticut	52,115	3,819	1,946	35,535	1,194	8,177
Delaware	5,339	45	336	3,214	180	724
Dist. Columbia	58,156	104	5,827	47,609	1,418	3,097
Florida	67,839	1,811	3,895	42,152	3,645	13,116
Georgia	47,073	696	1,667	33,991	1,576	3,995
Hawaii	18,700	527	914	11,014	2,478	2,533
Idaho	5,993	26	53	3,744	71	644
Illinois	176,849	10,437	25,029	107,902	6,193	22,179
Indiana	72,708	2,921	4,752	44,453	2,020	14,411
Iowa	37,370	479	1,239	24,637	2,650	4,349
Kansas	32,761	646	348	24,002	589	4,405
Kentucky	43,668	118	499	35,480	653	1,454
Louisiana	47,055	332	986	31,015	684	10,078
Maine	7,407	74	11	4,997	169	713
Maryland	62,946	2,729	7,162	42,899	2,782	5,296
Massachusetts	187,823	5,961	47,973	98,005	11,362	22,332

State						
Michigan	128,789	4,335	22,646	76,715	5,723	13,738
Minnesota	57,186	2,219	2,595	39,674	3,014	5,708
Mississippi	23,077	50	296	16,474	480	1,127
Missouri	73,424	578	3,076	57,282	1,405	6,595
Montana	9,183	92	21	6,017	387	795
Nebraska	24,545	179	160	20,551	104	1,119
Nevada	4,586	52	36	2,314	169	701
New Hampshire	11,831	85	764	6,442	1,191	2,300
New Jersey	54,589	1,381	5,234	29,254	4,292	12,640
New Mexico	17,689	150	2,957	7,612	2,473	2,938
New York	311,114	15,526	39,593	204,504	8,324	37,161
North Carolina	85,455	1,692	5,779	56,486	1,110	13,697
North Dakota	7,337	23	47	4,558	96	922
Ohio	117,198	2,072	11,271	82,674	5,565	10,388
Oklahoma	28,929	227	727	20,277	1,147	2,890
Oregon	40,029	898	1,399	28,056	282	6,521
Pennsylvania	163,235	3,705	18,276	113,696	5,396	16,589
Rhode Island	24,810	675	5,575	12,437	632	4,660
South Carolina	17,031	128	254	11,661	262	1,209
South Dakota	8,562	9	11	4,888	85	1,341
Tennessee	52,211	1,984	913	40,126	1,005	3,833
Texas	116,912	2,916	8,404	78,507	9,455	10,315
Utah	27,360	1,213	2,276	18,500	568	2,792
Vermont	7,742	—	147	5,439	246	935
Virginia	37,469	878	2,024	25,644	1,881	3,263
Washington	53,950	3,118	2,160	35,830	793	8,547
West Virginia	16,005	184	65	12,069	294	902
Wisconsin	66,184	3,210	1,711	47,136	1,456	8,120
Wyoming	4,611	77	—	1,998	209	829
Totals	$3,017,509	$96,873	$298,356	$1,955,459	$126,156	$374,484

*Major U.S. Military and Foreign Assistance Programs**

* Data from Statistical Abstract of U.S. 1967 and Congr. Rec. pp. S14297-99 (1967).

Area	Nation	Military Aid (1950-1967)	Foreign Aid (1946-1966)	Total
		(in millions)		
FAR EAST				
	Australia	$ 126	$ 37	$ 163
	Cambodia	87	256	343
	China, Republic of ..	2,492	2,150	4,642
	Indochina	710	*	710
	Indonesia	64	708	772
	Japan	898	2,587	3,485
	Korea	2,524	4,037	6,561
	Malaysia	24	35	59
	Philippines	378	1,151	1,529
	Thailand	667	384	1,051
	Vietnam	1,512	2,831	4,343
	Other	251	1,323	1,574
	Totals	$ 9,733	$15,499	$ 25,233
NEAR EAST				
	Greece	$ 1,489	$ 1,656	$ 3,145
	India	*	5,901	5,901
	Iran	1,037	687	1,724
	Iraq	47	47	94
	Israel	28	908	936
	Jordan	68	525	593
	Lebanon	30	86	116
	Pakistan	#	2,804	2,804
	Saudi Arabia	242	12	254
	Turkey	2,703	1,888	4,591
	United Arab Republic	—	1,106	1,106
	Other	23	1,191	1,214
	Totals	$ 5,667	$16,811	$ 22,478
EUROPE				
	Austria	#	$ 1,089	$ 1,089
	Belgium	$ 1,248	680	1,928
	Denmark	618	263	881
	France	4,233	4,042	8,275
	Germany	901	2,849	3,750
	Italy	2,290	2,793	5,083
	Luxembourg	8	—	8
	Netherlands	1,219	828	2,047
	Norway	897	236	1,133
	Portugal	323	162	485
	Spain	573	910	1,483
	United Kingdom	1,034	6,450	7,484
	Yugoslavia	696	2,009	2,705
	Other	209	1,193	1,402
	Totals	$14,249	$23,504	$ 37,753

Area	Nation	Military Aid (1950-1967)	Foreign Aid (1946-1966)	Total
		(in millions)		
AFRICA				
	Congo	$ 22	$ 277	$ 299
	Liberia	7	184	191
	Libya	32	208	240
	Morocco	41	497	533
	Other	12	1,459	1,471
	Totals	$ 114	$ 2,627	$ 2,740
LATIN AMERICA				
	Argentina	$ 71	$ 377	$ 448
	Bolivia	19	374	393
	Brazil	271	1,892	2,163
	Chile	96	822	918
	Colombia	83	474	557
	Cuba	11	41	52
	Dominican Republic..	19	224	243
	Ecuador	38	144	182
	Guatemala	12	165	177
	Mexico	7	457	464
	Nicaragua	10	78	88
	Paraguay	7	71	78
	Peru	107	282	389
	Uruguay	39	64	103
	Venezuela	97	189	286
	Other	38	597	635
	Totals	$ 925	$ 6,251	$ 7,176
WORLDWIDE (Other)		$ 4,684	$ 2,595	$ 7,279
GRAND TOTAL		$35,372	$67,287	$102,659

* Not available, listed under other. # Classified.

Federal Expenditures for National Defense and Research & Development 1940–1968

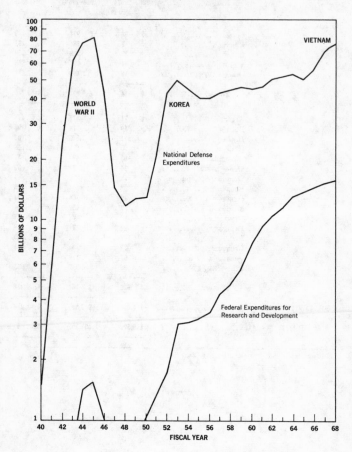

Growth of Nuclear Explosive Power TNT Equivalent of World's Stockpile

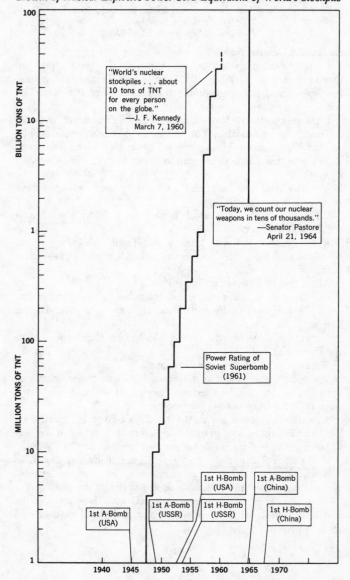

Remarks by Secretary of Defense Robert S. McNamara Before
United Press International Editors and Publishers
San Francisco, California
Monday, September 18, 1967

Ladies and Gentlemen:

I want to discuss with you this afternoon the gravest problem that an American Secretary of Defense must face: the planning, preparation and policy governing the possibility of thermonuclear war.

It is a prospect most of mankind would prefer not to contemplate.

That is understandable. For technology has now circumscribed us all with a conceivable horizon of horror that could dwarf any catastrophe that has befallen man in his more than a million years on earth.

Man has lived now for more than twenty years in what we have come to call the Atomic Age.

What we sometimes overlook is that every future age of man will be an atomic age.

If, then, man is to have a future at all, it will have to be a future overshadowed with the permanent possibility of thermonuclear holocaust.

About that fact, we are no longer free.

Our freedom in this question consists rather in facing the matter rationally and realistically and discussing actions to minimize the danger.

No sane citizen; no sane political leader; no sane nation wants thermonuclear war.

But merely not wanting it is not enough.

We must understand the difference between actions which increase its risk, those which reduce it, and those which, while costly, have little influence one way or another.

Now this whole subject matter tends to be psychologically unpleasant. But there is an even greater difficulty standing in the way of constructive and profitable debate over the issues.

And that is that nuclear strategy is exceptionally complex in its technical aspects. Unless these complexities are well understood, rational discussion and decision making are simply not possible.

What I want to do this afternoon is deal with these complexities and clarify them with as much precision and detail as time and security permit.

One must begin with precise definitions.

The cornerstone of our strategic policy continues to be to deter deliberate nuclear attack upon the United States, or its allies, by maintaining a highly reliable ability to inflict an unacceptable degree of damage upon any single aggressor, or combination of aggressors, at any time during the course of a strategic nuclear exchange—even after our absorbing a surprise first strike.

This can be defined as our "assured destruction capability."

Now it is imperative to understand that assured destruction is the very essence of the whole deterrence concept.

We must possess an actual assured destruction capability. And that actual assured destruction capability must also be credible. Conceivably, our assured destruction capability could be actual, without being credible—in which case, it might fail to deter an aggressor.

The point is that a potential aggressor must himself believe that our assured destruction capability is in fact actual, and that our will to use it in retaliation to an attack is in fact unwaivering.

The conclusion, then, is clear: if the United States is to deter a nuclear attack on itself or on our allies, it must possess an actual, and a credible assured destruction capability.

When calculating the force we require, we must be "conservative" in all our estimates of both a potential aggressor's capabilities, and his intentions. Security depends upon taking a "worst plausible case"—and having the ability to cope with that eventuality.

In that eventuality, we must be able to absorb the total weight of nuclear attack on our country—on our strike-back forces; on our command and control apparatus; on our industrial capacity; on our cities; and on our population—and still, be fully capable of destroying the aggressor to the point that his society is simply no longer viable in any meaningful twentieth-century sense.

That is what deterrence to nuclear aggression means. It means the certainty of suicide to the aggressor—not merely to his military forces, but to his society as a whole.

Now let us consider another term: "first-strike capability." This, in itself, is an ambiguous term, since it could mean simply the ability of one nation to attack another nation with nuclear forces first. But as it is normally used, it connotes much more: the substantial elimination of the attacked nation's retaliatory second-strike forces.

This is the sense in which "first-strike capability" should be understood.

Now, clearly, such a first-strike capability is an important strategic concept. The United States cannot—and will not—ever permit itself to get into the position in which another nation, or combination of nations, would possess such a first-strike capability, which could be effectively used against it.

To get into such a position vis-a-vis any other nation or nations would not only constitute an intolerable threat to our security, but it would obviously remove our ability to deter nuclear aggression—both against ourselves and against our allies.

Now, we are not in that position today—and there is no foreseeable danger of our ever getting into that position.

Our strategic offensive forces are immense: 1000 Minutemen missile launchers, carefully protected below ground, 41 Polaris submarines, carrying 656 missile launchers—with the majority of these hidden beneath the seas at all times; and about 600 long-range bombers, approximately forty percent of which are kept always in a high state of alert.

Our alert forces alone carry more than 2200 weapons, averaging more than one megaton each. A mere 400 one-megaton weapons, if delivered on the Soviet Union, would be sufficient to destroy over one-third of her population, and one-half of her industry.

And all of these flexible and highly reliable forces are equipped with devices that insure their penetration of Soviet defenses.

Now what about the Soviet Union?

Does it today possess a powerful nuclear arsenal?

The answer is that it does.

Does it possess a first-strike capability against the United States?

The answer is that it does not.

Can the Soviet Union, in the foreseeable future, acquire such a first-strike capability against the United States?

The answer is that it cannot.

It cannot because we are determined to remain fully alert, and we will never permit our own assured destruction capability to be at a point where a Soviet first-strike capability is even remotely feasible.

Is the Soviet Union seriously attempting to acquire a first-strike capability against the United States?

Although this is a question we cannot answer with absolute

certainty, we believe the answer is no. In any event, the question itself is—in a sense—irrelevant. It is irrelevant since the United States will so continue to maintain—and where necessary strengthen —our retaliatory forces, that whatever the Soviet Union's intentions or actions, we will continue to have an assured destruction capability vis-a-vis their society in which we are completely confident.

But there is another question that is most relevant.

And that is, do we—the United States—possess a first-strike capability against the Soviet Union?

The answer is that we do not.

And we do not, not because we have neglected our nuclear strength. On the contrary, we have increased it to the point that we possess a clear superiority over the Soviet Union.

We do not possess first-strike capability against the Soviet Union for precisely the same reason that they do not possess it against us.

And that is that we have both built up our "second-strike capability"[a] to the point that a first-strike capability on either side has become unattainable.

There is, of course, no way in which the United States could have prevented the Soviet Union from acquiring its present second-strike capability—short of a massive pre-emptive strike on the Soviet Union in the 1950s.

The blunt fact is, then, that neither the Soviet Union nor the United States can attack the other without being destroyed in retaliation; nor can either of us attain a first-strike capability in the foreseeable future.

The further fact is that both the Soviet Union and the United States presently possess an actual and credible second-strike capability against one another—and it is precisely this mutual capability that provides us both with the strongest possible motive to avoid a nuclear war.

The more frequent question that arises in this connection is whether or not the United States possesses nuclear superiority over the Soviet Union.

The answer is that we do.

[a] A "second-strike capability" is the capability to absorb a surprise nuclear attack, and survive with sufficient power to inflict unacceptable damage on the aggressor.

But the answer is—like everything else in this matter—technically complex.

The complexity arises in part out of what measurement of superiority is most meaningful and realistic.

Many commentators on the matter tend to define nuclear superiority in terms of gross megatonnage, or in terms of the number of missile launchers available.

Now, by both these two standards of measurement, the United States does have a substantial superiority over the Soviet Union in the weapons targeted against each other.

But it is precisely these two standards of measurement that are themselves misleading.

For the most meaningful and realistic measurement of nuclear capability is neither gross megatonnage, nor the number of available missile launchers; but rather the number of separate warheads that are capable of being *delivered* with accuracy on individual high-priority targets with sufficient power to destroy them.

Gross megatonnage in itself is an inadequate indicator of assured destruction capability, since it is unrelated to survivability, accuracy, or penetrability, and poorly related to effective elimination of multiple high-priority targets. There is manifestly no advantage in over-destroying one target, at the expense of leaving undamaged other targets of equal importance.

Further, the number of missile launchers available is also an inadequate indicator of assured destruction capability, since the fact is that many of our launchers will carry multiple warheads.

But by using the realistic measurement of the number of warheads available, capable of being reliably delivered with accuracy and effectiveness on the appropriate targets in the United States or Soviet Union, I can tell you that the United States currently possesses a superiority over the Soviet Union of at least three or four to one.

Furthermore, we will maintain a superiority—by these same realistic criteria—over the Soviet Union for as far ahead in the future as we can realistically plan.

I want, however, to make one point patently clear: our current numerical superiority over the Soviet Union in reliable, accurate, and effective warheads is both greater than we had originally planned, and is in fact more than we require.

Moreover, in the larger equation of security, our "superiority" is of limited significance—since even with our current superiority, or indeed with any numerical superiority realistically attainable, the blunt, inescapable fact remains that the Soviet Union could still—with its present forces—effectively destroy the United States, even after absorbing the full weight of an American first strike.

I have noted that our present superiority is greater than we had planned. Let me explain to you how this came about, for I think it is a significant illustration of the intrinsic dynamics of the nuclear arms race.

In 1961, when I became Secretary of Defense, the Soviet Union possessed a very small operational arsenal of intercontinental missiles. However, they did possess the technological and industrial capacity to enlarge that arsenal very substantially over the succeeding several years.

Now, we had no evidence that the Soviets did in fact plan to fully use that capability.

But as I have pointed out, a strategic planner must be "conservative" in his calculations; that is, he must prepare for the worst plausible case and not be content to hope and prepare merely for the most probable.

Since we could not be certain of Soviet intentions—since we could not be sure that they would not undertake a massive build-up —we had to insure against such an eventuality by undertaking ourselves a major build-up of the Minuteman and Polaris forces.

Thus, in the course of hedging against what was then only a theoretically possible Soviet build-up, we took decisions which have resulted in our current superiority in numbers of warheads and deliverable megatons.

But the blunt fact remains that if we had had more accurate information about planned Soviet strategic forces, we simply would not have needed to build as large a nuclear arsenal as we have today.

Now let me be absolutely clear. I am not saying that our decision in 1961 was unjustified. I am simply saying that it was necessitated by a lack of accurate information.

Furthermore, that decision in itself—as justified as it was—in the end, could not possibly have left unaffected the Soviet Union's future nuclear plans.

What is essential to understand here is that the Soviet Union and the United States mutually influence one another's strategic plans.

Whatever be their intentions, whatever be our intentions, actions —or even realistically potential actions—on either side relating to the build-up of nuclear forces, be they either offensive or defensive weapons, necessarily trigger reactions on the other side.

It is precisely this action-reaction phenomenon that fuels an arms race.

Now, in strategic nuclear weaponry, the arms race involves a particular irony. Unlike any other era in military history, today a substantial numerical superiority of weapons does not effectively translate into political control, or diplomatic leverage.

While thermonuclear power is almost inconceivably awesome, and represents virtually unlimited potential destructiveness, it has proven to be a limited diplomatic instrument. Its uniqueness lies in the fact that it is at one and the same time, an all powerful weapon—and a very inadequate weapon.

The fact that the Soviet Union and the United States can mutually destroy one another—regardless of who strikes first— narrows the range of Soviet aggression which our nuclear forces can effectively deter.

Even with our nuclear monopoly in the early postwar period, we were unable to deter the Soviet pressures against Berlin, or their support of aggression in Korea.

Today, our nuclear superiority does not deter all forms of Soviet support of communist insurgency in Southeast Asia.

What all of this has meant is that we, and our allies as well, require substantial non-nuclear forces in order to cope with levels of aggression that massive strategic forces do not in fact deter.

This has been a difficult lesson both for us and for our allies to accept, since there is a strong psychological tendency to regard superior nuclear forces as a simple and unfailing solution to security, and an assurance of victory under any set of circumstances.

What is important to understand is that our nuclear strategic forces play a vital and absolutely necessary role in our security and that of our allies, but it is an intrinsically limited role.

Thus, we and our allies must maintain substantial conventional forces, fully capable of dealing with a wide spectrum of lesser forms of political and military aggression—a level of aggression against which the use of strategic nuclear forces would not be to our advantage, and thus a level of aggression which these strategic nuclear forces by themselves cannot effectively deter. One cannot fashion a credible deterrent out of an incredible action. Therefore security for the United States and its allies can only arise from the possession of a whole range of graduated deterrents, each of them fully credible in its own context.

Now I have pointed out that in strategic nuclear matters, the Soviet Union and the United States mutually influence one another's plans.

In recent years the Soviets have substantially increased their offensive forces. We have, of course, been watching and evaluating this very carefully.

Clearly, the Soviet build-up is in part a reaction to our own build-up since the beginning of this decade.

Soviet strategic planners undoubtedly reasoned that if our build-up were to continue at its accelerated pace, we might conceivably reach, in time, a credible first-strike capability against the Soviet Union.

That was not in fact our intention. Our intention was to assure that they—with their theoretical capacity to reach such a first-strike capability—would not in fact outdistance us.

But they could not read our intentions with any greater accuracy than we could read theirs. And thus the result has been that we have both built up our forces to a point that far exceeds credible second-strike capability against the forces we each started with.

In doing so, neither of us has reached a first-strike capability. And the realities of the situation being what they are—whatever we believe their intentions to be, and whatever they believe our intentions to be—each of us can deny the other a first-strike capability in the foreseeable future.

Now, how can we be so confident that this is the case?

How can we be so certain that the Soviets cannot gradually outdistance us—either by some dramatic technological break-through, or simply through our imperceptibly lagging behind, for whatever reason: reluctance to spend the requisite funds; distraction with military problems elsewhere; faulty intelligence; or simple negligence and naivete?

All of these reasons—and others—have been suggested by some commentators in this country, who fear that we are in fact falling behind to a dangerous degree.

The answer to all of this is simple and straightforward.

We are not going to permit the Soviets to outdistance us, because to do so would be to jeopardize our very viability as a nation.

No President, no Secretary of Defense, no Congress of the United States—of whatever political party, and of whatever political persuasion—is going to permit this nation to take that risk.

We do not want a nuclear arms race with the Soviet Union— primarily because the action-reaction phenomenon makes it foolish and futile. But if the only way to prevent the Soviet Union from obtaining first-strike capability over us is to engage in such a race, the United States possesses in ample abundance the resources, the technology, and the will to run faster in that race for whatever distance is required.

But what we would much prefer to do is to come to a realistic and reasonably riskless agreement with the Soviet Union, which would effectively prevent such an arms race. We both have strategic nuclear arsenals greatly in excess of a credible assured destruction capability. These arsenals have reached that point of excess in each case for precisely the same reason: we each have reacted to the other's build-up with very conservative calculations. We have, that is, each built a greater arsenal than either of us needed for a second-strike capability, simply because we each wanted to be able to cope with the "worst plausible case."

But since we now each possess a deterrent in excess of our individual needs, both of our nations would benefit from a properly safe-guarded agreement first to limit, and later to reduce, both our offensive and defensive strategic nuclear forces.

We may, or we may not, be able to achieve such an agreement. We hope we can. And we believe such an agreement is fully feasible, since it is clearly in both our nations' interests.

But reach the formal agreement or not, we can be sure that neither the Soviets nor we are going to risk the other obtaining a first-strike capability.

On the contrary, we can be sure that we are both going to maintain a maximum effort to preserve an assured destruction capability.

It would not be sensible for either side to launch a maximum effort to achieve a first-strike capability. It would not be sensible because the intelligence-gathering capability of each side being what it is, and the realities of lead-time from technological breakthrough to operational readiness being what they are, neither of us would be able to acquire a first-strike capability in secret.

Now, let me take a specific case in point.

The Soviets are now deploying an anti-ballistic missile system. If we react to this deployment intelligently, we have no reason for alarm.

The system does not impose any threat to our ability to penetrate and inflict massive and unacceptable damage on the Soviet Union. In other words, it does not presently affect in any significant manner our assured destruction capability.

It does not impose such a threat because we have already taken the steps necessary to assure that our land-based Minuteman missiles, our nuclear submarine-launched new Poseidon missiles, and our strategic bomber forces have the requisite penetration aids —and in the sum, constitute a force of such magnitude, that they guarantee us a force strong enough to survive a Soviet attack and penetrate the Soviet ABM deployment.

Now let me come to the issue that has received so much attention recently: the question of whether or not we should deploy an ABM system against the Soviet nuclear threat.

To begin with, this is not in any sense a new issue. We have had both the technical possibility and the strategic desirability of an American ABM deployment under constant review since the late 1950s.

While we have substantially improved our technology in the field, it is important to understand that none of the systems at the present or foreseeable state of the art would provide an impenetrable shield over the United States. Were such a shield possible, we would certainly want it—and we would certainly build it.

And at this point, let me dispose of an objection that is totally irrelevant to this issue.

It has been alleged that we are opposed to deploying a large-scale ABM system because it would carry the heavy price tag of $40 billion.

Let me make it very clear that the $40 billion is not the issue.

If we could build and deploy a genuinely impenetrable shield over the United States, we would be willing to spend not $40 billion, but any reasonable multiple of that amount that was necessary.

The money in itself is not the problem: the penetrability of the proposed shield is the problem.

There is clearly no point, however, in spending $40 billion if it is not going to buy us a significant improvement in our security. If it is not, then we should use the substantial resources it represents on something that will.

Every ABM system that is now feasible involves firing defensive missiles at incoming offensive warheads in an effort to destroy them.

But what many commentators on this issue overlook is that any such system can rather obviously be defeated by an enemy simply sending more offensive warheads, or dummy warheads, than there are defensive missiles capable of disposing of them.

And this is the whole crux of the nuclear action-reaction phenomenon.

Were we to deploy a heavy ABM system throughout the United States, the Soviets would clearly be strongly motivated to so increase their offensive capability as to cancel out our defensive advantage.

It is futile for each of us to spend $4 billion, $40 billion, or $400 billion—and at the end of all the spending, and at the end of all the deployment, and at the end of all the effort, to be relatively at the same point of balance on the security scale that we are now.

In point of fact, we have already initiated offensive weapons programs costing several billions in order to offset the small present Soviet ABM deployment, and the possibly more extensive future Soviet ABM deployments.

That is money well spent; and it is necessary.

But we should bear in mind that it is money spent because of the action-reaction phenomenon.

If we in turn opt for heavy ABM deployment—at whatever price —we can be certain that the Soviets will react to offset the advantage we would hope to gain.

It is precisely because of this certainty of a corresponding Soviet reaction that the four prominent scientists—men who have served with distinction as the Science Advisors to Presidents Eisenhower, Kennedy, and Johnson, and the three outstanding men who have served as Directors of Research and Engineering to three Secretaries of Defense—have unanimously recommended against the deployment of an ABM system designed to protect our population against a Soviet attack.

These men are Doctors Killian, Kistiakowsky, Wiesner, Hornig, York, Brown, and Foster.

The plain fact of the matter is that we are now facing a situation analogous to the one we faced in 1961: we are uncertain of the Soviets' intentions.

At that time we were concerned about their potential offensive capabilities; now we are concerned about their potential defensive capabilities.

But the dynamics of the concern are the same.

We must continue to be cautious and conservative in our estimates—leaving no room in our calculations for unnecessary risk. And at the same time, we must measure our own response in such a manner that it does not trigger a senseless spiral upward of nuclear arms.

Now, as I have emphasized, we have already taken the necessary steps to guarantee that our offensive strategic weapons will be able to penetrate future, more advanced, Soviet defenses.

Keeping in mind the careful clockwork of lead-time, we will be forced to continue that effort over the next few years if the evidence is that the Soviets intend to turn what is now a light and modest ABM deployment into a massive one.

Should they elect to do so, we have both the lead-time and the technology available to so increase both the quality and quantity of our offensive strategic forces—with particular attention to highly reliable penetration aids—that their expensive defensive efforts will give them no edge in the nuclear balance whatever.

But we would prefer not to have to do that. For it is a profitless waste of resources, provided we and the Soviets can come to a realistic strategic arms-limitation agreement.

As you know, we have proposed U.S.-Soviet talks on this matter. Should these talks fail, we are fully prepared to take the appropriate measures that such a failure would make necessary.

The point for us to keep in mind is that should the talks fail—and the Soviets decide to expand their present modest ABM deployment into a massive one—our response must be realistic. There is no point whatever in our responding by going to a massive ABM deployment to protect our population, when such a system would be ineffective against a sophisticated Soviet offense.

Instead, realism dictates that if the Soviets elect to deploy a heavy ABM system, we must further expand our sophisticated offensive forces, and thus preserve our overwhelming assured destruction capability.

But the intractable fact is that should the talks fail, both the Soviets and ourselves would be forced to continue on a foolish and feckless course.

It would be foolish and feckless because—in the end—it would provide neither the Soviets, nor us, with any greater relative nuclear capability.

The time has come for us both to realize that, and to act reasonably. It is clearly in our own mutual interest to do so.

Having said that, it is important to distinguish between an ABM system designed to protect against a Soviet attack on our cities, and ABM systems which have other objectives.

One of the other uses of an ABM system which we should seriously consider is the greater protection of our strategic offensive forces.

Another is in relation to the emerging nuclear capability of Communist China.

There is evidence that the Chinese are devoting very substantial resources to the development of both nuclear warheads, and missile delivery systems. As I stated last January, indications are that they will have medium-range ballistic missiles within a year or so, an initial intercontinental ballistic missile capability in the early 1970s, and a modest force in the mid-70s.

Up to now, the lead-time factor has allowed us to postpone a decision on whether or not a light ABM deployment might be advantageous as a countermeasure to Communist China's nuclear development.

But the time will shortly be right for us to initiate production if we desire such a system.

China at the moment is caught up in internal strife, but it seems likely that her basic motivation in developing a strategic nuclear capability is an attempt to provide a basis for threatening her neighbors, and to clothe herself with the dubious prestige that the world pays to nuclear weaponry.

We deplore her development of these weapons, just as we deplore it in other countries. We oppose nuclear proliferation because we believe that in the end it only increases the risk of a common and cataclysmic holocaust.

President Johnson has made it clear that the United States will oppose any efforts of China to employ nuclear blackmail against her neighbors.

We possess now, and will continue to possess for as far ahead as we can foresee, an overwhelming first-strike capability with respect to China. And despite the shrill and raucous propaganda directed at her own people that "the atomic bomb is a paper tiger," there is ample evidence that China well appreciates the destructive power of nuclear weapons.

China has been cautious to avoid any action that might end in a nuclear clash with the United States—however wild her words—and understandably so. We have the power not only to destroy completely her entire nuclear offensive forces, but to devastate her society as well.

Is there any possibility, then, that by the mid-1970s China might become so incautious as to attempt a nuclear attack on the United States or our allies?

It would be insane and suicidal for her to do so, but one can conceive conditions under which China might miscalculate. We wish to reduce such possibilities to a minimum.

And since, as I have noted, our strategic planning must always be conservative, and take into consideration even the possible irrational behavior of potential adversaries, there are marginal grounds for concluding that a light deployment of U.S. ABMs against this possibility is prudent.

The system would be relatively inexpensive—preliminary estimates place the cost at about $5 billion—and would have a much higher degree of reliability against a Chinese attack, than the much more massive and complicated system that some have recommended against a possible Soviet attack.

Moreover, such an ABM deployment designed against a possible Chinese attack would have a number of other advantages. It would provide an additional indication to Asians that we intend to deter China from nuclear blackmail, and thus would contribute toward our goal of discouraging nuclear weapon proliferation among the present non-nuclear countries.

Further, the Chinese-oriented ABM deployment would enable us to add—as a concurrent benefit—a further defense of our Minuteman sites against Soviet attack, which means that at modest cost we would in fact be adding even greater effectiveness to our offensive missile force and avoiding a much more costly expansion of that force.

Finally, such a reasonably reliable ABM system would add protection of our population against the improbable but possible accidental launch of an intercontinental missile by any one of the nuclear powers.

After a detailed review of all these considerations, we have decided to go forward with this Chinese-oriented ABM deployment, and we will begin actual production of such a system at the end of this year.

In reaching this decision, I want to emphasize that it contains two possible dangers—and we should guard carefully against each.

The first danger is that we may psychologically lapse into the old over-simplification about the adequacy of nuclear power. The simple truth is that nuclear weapons can serve to deter only a narrow range of threats. This ABM deployment will strengthen our defensive posture—and will enhance the effectiveness of our land-based ICBM offensive forces. But the independent nations of Asia must realize that these benefits are no substitute for their maintaining, and where necessary strengthening, their own conventional forces in order to deal with the more likely threats to the security of the region.

The second danger is also psychological. There is a kind of mad momentum intrinsic to the development of all new nuclear weaponry. If a weapon system works—and works well—there is strong pressure from many directions to procure and deploy the weapon out of all proportion to the prudent level required.

The danger in deploying this relatively light and reliable Chinese-oriented ABM system is going to be that pressures will develop to expand it into a heavy Soviet-oriented ABM system.

We must resist that temptation firmly—not because we can for a moment afford to relax our vigilance against a possible Soviet first-strike—but precisely because our greatest deterrent against such a strike is not a massive, costly, but highly penetrable ABM shield, but rather a fully credible offensive assured destruction capability.

The so-called heavy ABM shield—at the present state of technology—would in effect be no adequate shield at all against a Soviet attack, but rather a strong inducement for the Soviets to vastly increase their own offensive forces. That, as I have pointed out, would make it necessary for us to respond in turn—and so the arms race would rush hopelessly on to no sensible purpose on either side.

Let me emphasize—and I cannot do so too strongly—that our decision to go ahead with a *limited* ABM deployment in no way indicates that we feel an agreement with the Soviet Union on the limitation of strategic nuclear offensive and defensive forces is any the less urgent or desirable.

The road leading from the stone axe to the ICBM—though it may have been more than a million years in the building—seems to have run in a single direction.

If one is inclined to be cynical, one might conclude that man's history seems to be characterized not so much by consistent periods of peace, occasionally punctuated by warfare; but rather by persistent outbreaks of warfare, wearily put aside from time to time by periods of exhaustion and recovery—that parade under the name of peace.

I do not view man's history with that degree of cynicism, but I do believe that man's wisdom in avoiding war is often surpassed by his folly in promoting it.

However foolish unlimited war may have been in the past, it is now no longer merely foolish, but suicidal as well.

It is said that nothing can prevent a man from suicide, if he is sufficiently determined to commit it.

The question is what is our determination in an era when unlimited war will mean the death of hundreds of millions—and the possible genetic impairment of a million generations to follow?

Man is clearly a compound of folly and wisdom—and history is clearly a consequence of the admixture of those two contradictory traits.

History has placed our particular lives in an era when the consequences of human folly are waxing more and more catastrophic in the matters of war and peace.

In the end, the root of man's security does not lie in his weaponry.

In the end, the root of man's security lies in his mind.

What the world requires in its 22nd Year of the Atomic Age is not a new race towards armament.

What the world requires in its 22nd Year of the Atomic Age is a new race towards reasonableness.

We had better all run that race.

Not merely we the administrators. But we the people.

Glossary

Ablation shield	Thermal protective coating designed to combat heat of reentry as ballistic missiles penetrate the earth's atmosphere.
ABM	Anti-ballistic missile.
AEC	Atomic Energy Commission.
ANP	Aircraft, nuclear propulsion.
Apollo	Name given to the U.S. lunar project.
"Barrier"	Micropored separation unit in gaseous diffusion plants.
BMEWS	Ballistic missile early warning system.
Bravo	Code-name for U.S. nuclear test of March 1, 1954.
Chain reaction	Nuclear process whereby fission of uranium or plutonium is sustained either on a controlled basis, as in a nuclear reactor, or in an uncontrolled manner, as in an A-bomb explosion.
Deuterium	Technical name for heavy hydrogen found in heavy water.
Diffusion plant	Uranium separation plant of the type built at Oak Ridge, Tenn.
DOD	Department of Defense, U.S.A.
Fission	The splitting of a heavy atom such as uranium.
Fissionable material	Nuclear material such as uranium-235 or plutonium which sustains a chain reaction.
First-strike	An initial strategic attack involving the use of nuclear weapons.
FOBS	Fractional orbital bombardment system.
Fusion	Synthesis of hydrogen to form helium, as in a thermonuclear reaction.
Gamma rays	Penetrating radiation emitted in a nuclear explosion or from radioactive fallout.

"Hard" base	A missile site, such as Minuteman, built in the form of a concrete silo.
H-bomb	A nuclear weapon deriving part of its energy from fusion of light elements.
"Hex"	Uranium hexafluoride.
"Hot" line	A reliable system of prompt communication linking Moscow and Washington.
ICBM	Intercontinental ballistic missile.
IRBM	Intermediate range ballistic missile.
K-25	Code symbol for the Oak Ridge uranium separation plant.
Kiloton	The equivalent explosiveness of 1,000 tons of TNT.
MAR	Missile acquisition radar.
Megaton	One million tons of TNT equivalent.
Mev	Million electron volts (of energy).
Mike	Code name for U.S. first test of an H-bomb.
Minuteman	A 3-stage solid-fueled ICBM.
MIRV	Multiple, independently targetable reentry vehicle.
MSR	Missile site radar.
Neptunium	Element number 93 produced from uranium in nuclear reactors.
Neutron	Fundamental particle released in nuclear processes such as fission and fusion.
Nike-X	U.S. ballistic missile defense system.
NSF	National Science Foundation.
"Nuke"	Nuclear slang for the inner core of a nuclear weapon.
PAR	Perimeter acquisition radar.
Pershing	U.S. Army ballistic missile equipped with a nuclear warhead and having a range of 400-500 miles.
Polaris	U.S. Navy 2-stage ballistic missile.
Poseidon	U.S. Navy ballistic missile designed to replace Polaris.
Power breeder	Nuclear reactor designed to produce power and breed nuclear fuel.
Reactor	A nuclear assembly in which a chain reaction is sustained for producing power and/or plutonium.
SABMIS	Sea-based antiballistic missile intercept system.
Samos	Code name given to U.S. secret orbital reconnaissance system.
Second strike	Nuclear strategic response to an enemy first-strike.
Sentinel system	Name given to U.S. "thin" ballistic missile defense.

Skybolt	Missile designed to be launched from bombers for attacking strategic targets.
SLBM	Submarine-launched ballistic missile like the U.S. Polaris.
"Soft" base	Missile installation which is vulnerable to enemy attack.
Spartan	Long range U.S. missile interceptor used in Nike-X system.
Sprint	Short range U.S. missile designed to intercept ICBM's in the atmosphere.
Sputnik	Soviet satellite.
Strontium-90	Species of radioactive fallout.
SST	Supersonic transport.
TFX	U.S. multiple-use fighter-bomber. Also known as F-111.
Tritium	Form of hydrogen used in H-bombs, produced by nuclear bombardment of lithium.
U-2	U.S. high-altitude reconnaissance aircraft.
U-235	Fissionable form of uranium.
U-238	Heavy isotope of uranium.
X rays	Penetrating radiation, especially as emitted by a space explosion of a nuclear weapon.
X-ray kill	Use of X rays from a thermonuclear explosion to intercept an ICBM warhead.
Yellow cake	Name given to uranium concentrates.

Index